By the end of 1780 the war for American independence appeared to be approaching a stalemate. After five years of war, Washington's armies remained in the field. Once France, and then Spain, joined the war, Lord Sandwich as First Lord of the Admiralty was faced with a constant struggle to balance the forces needed at home and overseas, while facing constant hostile pressure from the opposition.

However, events were conspiring to bring about a showdown in North America, which would take place in the waters off Chesapeake Bay. This book describes how, step by step, the crisis was reached. After France had accepted the need for a major effort to support the Americans, the Comte de Grasse arrived in the West Indies in April 1781 with a large fleet, intending to arrive off the North American coast in July. Once he had opted to sail to Virginia, Washington began to move south. Meanwhile Lord Cornwallis, the British commander in the Carolinas, had chosen without authority to march to Virginia, where he arrived in May to link up with a force that had been sent to establish a naval base in the Chesapeake.

De Grasse reached Chesapeake Bay with his whole fleet at the end of August, outnumbering the British fleet under Graves which arrived on 5 September. The battle that followed was indecisive, though the French had the best of it. Cornwallis was now besieged at Yorktown by Washington; a force intended to relieve him arrived too late and on 19 October he capitulated at Yorktown. The war for American independence was decisively lost; all that remained was a bitter debate as to who was to blame.

Quintin Barry is a retired solicitor and employment judge. He has also held a variety of offices in both public and private sectors including the NHS and local radio. Following a lifelong interest in history, he is the author of a number of books on military and naval history. These include an acclaimed two volume history of the Franco-Prussian war of 1870-1871, a history of the Austro Prussian War of 1866, and the first modern history of the Russo Turkish war of 1877-1878. He has made a particular study of the life and career of Helmuth von Moltke. He has also written a biography of the 17th Earl of Derby. Among his recent books are: *The War in the North Sea 1914-1918, Far Distant Ships: The Blockade of Brest 1793-1815*, and a study of the naval operations of the Spanish-American War of 1898.

Crisis at the Chesapeake

The Royal Navy and the Struggle for America 1775-1783

Quintin Barry

Helion & Company Limited

To My Parents

Helion & Company Limited
Unit 8 Amherst Business Centre
Budbrooke Road
Warwick
CV34 5WE
England
Tel. 01926 499619
Email: info@helion.co.uk
Website: www.helion.co.uk
Twitter: @helionbooks
Visit our blog at http://blog.helion.co.uk/

Published by Helion & Company 2021
Designed and typeset by Mach 3 Solutions Ltd (www.mach3solutions.co.uk)
Cover designed by Paul Hewitt, Battlefield Design (www.battlefield-design.co.uk)

ISBN 978-1-913336-53-0

British Library Cataloguing-in-Publication Data.
A catalogue record for this book is available from the British Library.

For details of other military history titles published by Helion & Company Limited, contact
the above address, or visit our website: http://www.helion.co.uk

We always welcome receiving book proposals from prospective authors.

Contents

List of Plates

List of Maps

Acknowledgements

As has been the case with several of my previous books of naval history, I have drawn heavily on a number of the published volumes of the Navy Records Society. They constitute an invaluable resource, casting a vivid light on the personality and motivations of many of the key figures involved. The naval side of the American War of Independence has of course been extensively covered by historians, and I am indebted also to many of those who have written on the subject.

I should also like to acknowledge the help I have received in the writing and publication of this book, particularly from my publisher Duncan Rogers, who as always has been supportive and helpful; from Andrew Bamford, who has been a most thoughtful and careful editor; and from George Anderson, who drew the maps. I should like also to thank Tim Readman, who read the book in draft and made a number of useful suggestions.

Introduction

The outbreak of the rebellion in the American colonies was not at first perceived as being a war. It was seen as a provincial insurrection that must be put down by the British government, and something that did not concern any other nation. That said, its suppression soon began to present some remarkably difficult logistical problems, for which the government was completely unprepared. This applied in particular to the British Admiralty.

For Britain, the Seven Years War had ended in a comprehensive victory, and her international position had never been stronger. Across the Atlantic, Canada was firmly a British possession after France's defeat. However, all was not well in North America. After the end of the Seven Years War there had been a steady deterioration in the effectiveness of British government there, and in New England in particular the situation was rapidly getting worse. In London, the British Cabinet was reluctant to face the truth. Popular feeling in America against Britain was mounting, and there was an increasing likelihood that this would be translated into military action. One incident led to another: the Stamp Act crisis of 1765, customs disputes, the burning of the Admiralty schooner *Gaspée* in 1772, the Boston Tea Party and the passing of the Coercive Acts led the colonies step by step towards military insurrection. By 1774 it was clear that the situation had reached crisis point; Lieutenant General Thomas Gage, who returned to America as both Governor of Massachusetts and commander-in-chief of the troops in North America, warned that only a great army could put down the incipient rebellion. For the British Admiralty, the problems which the Royal Navy would face were largely novel and peculiarly difficult.

The Royal Navy had been shaped in the course of two centuries of European war, against the Spanish, the Dutch, and the French in particular. Its reputation had been made in a long series of battles at sea, largely in home waters, in most of which it had been successful. Fundamentally, the task now facing the navy at the start of the American Revolution was defensive. Its duty was to ensure the safe arrival in North America of supplies and reinforcements; it was responsible for intercepting small enemy vessels intent on the smuggling of arms and munitions to the rebels; and it was required to act in support of the army.

For these responsibilities, the huge fleet of ships of the line which the Navy possessed was almost entirely irrelevant. It was generally the case that any criticism of the Admiralty focused on the number of ships of the line that were in commission at any time, but so far as North America was concerned this was never the problem. What were required there were frigates, sloops and schooners, and there were never enough of them. It has been calculated that in spite of constant requests from commanding officers on the North American station, less than 60 percent of the Royal Navy's vessels in American waters after 1763 were sloops and schooners, and it was these that were particularly needed to catch smugglers.[1] Many of the smaller vessels operated by the Navy were purchased locally by officers on the spot. These were particularly useful as tenders to be sent into shallow waters in search of smugglers. The Navy Board was billed for the cost of purchasing these.[2] In addition, the American Board of Customs itself operated a number of revenue cutters, which were particularly active in endeavouring to enforce the new laws aimed at increasing revenue for the customs service; these cutters were responsible for more than half of the seizures condemned by Vice Admiralty courts in America between 1767 and 1775.[3]

Between 1764, the year after the Treaty of Paris ended the Seven Years War, and 1774, when the gathering pace of the American Revolution had become entirely clear, the annual average number of Royal Naval ships on the North American station was 37, and the average number of guns carried by this force was 679, or approximately 19 guns per ship. It has been pointed out that this was a far greater number of ships than had been found necessary during previous periods of peace, and this was in spite of the fact that, with the ejection of the French from Canada, the potential threat from foreign nations was accordingly much reduced.[4] Although substantial, this force had to cover an enormously long coastline, from Quebec down to Pensacola, and, for the duties required of it, the North American Station never had sufficient ships in hand. The navy was being used in support of the efforts to enforce the revenue and trade laws enacted by Parliament, and they were also required to reduce smuggling in the direct trade to Europe and the West Indies. This soon began to discourage the naval officers employed on the station, not least because of the limited opportunity to profit from seizures of smuggling vessels. As the years went by, and the operations of the navy were frequently found by those attempting to execute the Admiralty's instructions to be ineffective, the morale of those involved declined further.

The cost of maintaining a substantial number of ships 3,000 miles from home was considerable; for reasons of economy the Admiralty never provided sufficient

1   Julian Gwyn, 'The Royal Navy in North America 1712-1776' in J.R. Black and P. Woodfine (eds), *The British Navy and the Use of Naval Power in the Eighteenth Century* (Leicester: Leicester University Press 1988), p.141.
2   Gwyn, 'The Royal Navy in North America 1712-1776', p.143.
3   Neil R. Stout, *The Royal Navy in America, 1760-1775. A Study of Enforcement of British Colonial Policy in the Era of the American Revolution* (Annapolis, Maryland: Naval institute Press, 1973), p.31.
4   Gwyn, 'The Royal Navy in North America 1712-1776', p.141.

ships to undertake the tasks required, which had steadily grown in complexity and difficulty as the insurrection gathered momentum: 'The Royal Navy proved time and again to be worthy of the respect of all the navies of the world when it went into battle. It inspired less awe in coves and courts and customs houses'.[5]

The need to reduce government spending led to a mistaken decision on the part of the Admiralty. Daniel Baugh has pointed out that, in previous wars, the common practice of the Admiralty was to order new frigates and sloops from commercial yards immediately on the outbreak of war, but that in respect of the hostilities in North America this was not done, which contributed to the severe shortage:

> It is an interesting fact that at the very moment (late 1774) when this administration and its Parliamentary majority were laying down a hard line that risked open rebellion and war in America, they were also approving reductions in the naval budget. The number of shipwrights employed in dockyards actually dropped in 1775 and did not recover its 1774 level until 1778. The government asked estimates for a navy of only 18,000 seamen for 1775, 21,000 for 1776, and 45,000 for 1777.[6]

The effect of this reduction in government spending is shown by the statistics of shipbuilding during the relevant period. Between 1771 and 1775 a total of 24 ships of 50 guns and under was launched in British yards, for a total tonnage of 15,462. In each of the two years which followed, 18 and 17 such ships respectively were launched to a total tonnage of 13,243, and the number continued to rise in subsequent years.[7]

Thus, it will be seen that the role of the navy in suppressing rebellion, difficult enough in theory, became almost impossible in practice. In this book I have endeavoured to trace the course of the naval war in North America which, in its early years, was a war against a relatively weak, ill-equipped but ingenious enemy which had time and space on its side. In 1778, with the outbreak of war against France, the situation became entirely different. It was a development which had been foreseen but in respect of which measures were not taken soon enough, and which brought with it the prospect of fleet actions on both sides of the Atlantic,

Thereafter the Admiralty was constantly engaged in the task of balancing the needs of the navy in North America and the West Indies with the need to defend the British Isles. David Syrett has emphatically argued that the priority accorded by Sandwich and the British Cabinet to home defence was a fatal error, similar to

---

5   Stout, *Royal Navy in America*, p.164.
6   Daniel Baugh, 'Why did Britain lose command of the sea during the war for America?' in Black and Woodfine (eds), *The British Navy and the Use of Naval Power*, p.155
7   R.J.B. Knight, 'The Royal Navy's Recovery after the Early Phase of the American Revolutionary War' in George J. Andreopoulos and Harold F. Selesky (eds), *The Aftermath of Defeat* (New Haven, Connecticut: Yale University Press, 1994), p.15.

the decision made in 1756 to detach ships from the Channel Fleet which resulted in the loss of Minorca. In another example of the need to make a strategic choice, he distinguished the willingness to detach Nelson's squadron from St Vincent's fleet, a decision which led to the victory of the Nile. He concluded that St Vincent and Spencer, the then First Lord of the Admiralty, 'were a lot tougher and had more nerve than Keppel and Sandwich'. As Syrett pointed out, 'the problem comes down to how much of a risk one is prepared to run with the security of the British Isles in the face of a threatened invasion'.[8] In 1778, the King, like Churchill in 1940, was prepared to take such a risk; but the members of his Cabinet were not, and in the face of the huge invasion fleet which the French and Spanish assembled it is possible to say that they were wrong only with the benefit of hindsight.

During the War of American Independence, the influence of the Royal Navy was always going to be crucial. One American historian has remarked that it 'fought the great prototypical eighteenth century war. British naval power was put to every test it was designed to meet and several more besides'.[9] There was in the end no way in which the Americans could have ultimately been denied their independence; but the war that was fought to achieve it was substantially a naval war, and it was at sea that it would be decided. George Washington, in particular, knew that this was so, as he wrote to Rochambeau and Ternay on 15 July, 1780: 'In any operations, and under all circumstances, a decisive naval superiority is to be considered as a fundamental principle, and the basis upon which every hope of success must ultimately depend'.[10]

8   David Syrett, 'Home Waters or America? The Dilemma of British Naval Strategy in 1778', *The Mariner's Mirror* (November 1991), p.376.

9   John A. Tilley, *The British Navy and the American Revolution* (Colombia, South Carolina: University of South Carolina Press, 1987), p.xiv.

10 Dudley W. Knox, *The Naval Genius of George Washington* (Boston, Massachusetts: Houghton Mifflin, 1932), p.64.

1

The American War

As the American crisis deepened, and in particular after it had become apparent that to subdue the rebellion it would be necessary to use force, the British government, the press, the people and their King massively underestimated the scale of the task. As a result, the strategy to be adopted was hopelessly flawed and inconsistent, and the resources committed to the war against the American colonists were completely inadequate. Nowhere was this more evident than in the response of the British Admiralty and the resources which it immediately made available.

The commander-in-chief of the North American station from 1771 to 1774, the crucial years that led to the outbreak of war, was Rear Admiral John Montagu. He made clear to the Admiralty his belief that firm action was called for, writing to Lord Sandwich, the First Lord, in March 1773 that 'without some measures are taken to check these people it must in a little time be attended with fatal consequences'. It was a message he sent more than once, very conscious of the important role that the navy must play; he added, referring to the people of Massachusetts, that 'they are almost ripe for independence, and nothing but the ships prevents them going to greater lengths, as they see no notice taken from home of their behaviour'.[1]

When Montagu's term came to an end, he was succeeded by Vice Admiral Samuel Graves, who arrived to take up his post as commander-in-chief on 30 June 1774. Upon him would devolve the task of maximising the resources at his disposal as the situation in North America steadily deteriorated. His orders were, in particular, strictly to enforce the Boston Port Act, prohibiting the landing, loading or shipping of goods to and from Boston harbour. He was also required to patrol the entire coastline from Florida to the St Lawrence, and to support the civil authorities in quelling insurrection.[2]

---

1   G.R. Barnes and J.H. Owen (eds), *The Private Papers of John, Earl of Sandwich* (London: Navy Records Society, 1932), Vol I, p.49.
2   Donald A. Yerxa, 'Vice Admiral Samuel Graves and the North American Squadron 1774-1776', *The Mariner's Mirror* (1976), p.372.

The appointment of Graves to this post was the personal choice of Sandwich, which he made apparently in spite of the doubts of some of the other members of the Cabinet. Graves, born in 1713, had had an unremarkable career in the navy, becoming a lieutenant in 1739, and receiving his first command, the sloop *Bonetta,* in 1743. Thereafter, he commanded a number of vessels, most notably captaining the *Duke* at the Battle of Quiberon Bay in 1759. He reached the rank of rear admiral in 1762, and that of vice admiral eight years later. He brought, therefore, no great reputation to his demanding new post, but he did enjoy the backing of the First Lord.

It was a hugely difficult assignment. The resources available to him were entirely inadequate effectively to blockade the enormously lengthy coastline of North America. Although such a blockade might have been effective in limiting the scope of the insurgency, the British problem was not merely military, but also political. As it was, the responsibilities which Graves inherited were too great to prevent the passage of arms and supplies, and a large part of his force was required to occupy the port of Boston, and even there the rebels were able to evade his patrols. When Graves arrived, he found that he had only 19 warships at his disposal, and nine of these were employed at Boston, which was seen as the centre of the rebellion. Almost at once, therefore, he began appealing for more ships.

The concentration of a large part of the squadron at Boston, as well as the bulk of the available military forces, was seen as the best way to overawe the population there to such an extent that the rest of the country would submit to the royal authority. It soon became apparent that this was a fundamental mistake:

> But with the beginning of fighting in America, the army in Boston became a strategic liability to the British. The town could not be evacuated owing to a shortage of transports nor could it be defended against a determined attack, for it was dominated by heights that the British did not have the manpower to occupy.[3]

The first request that Graves made for reinforcements was for three schooners and a sloop for Boston harbour, and three or four schooners to strengthen his patrols along the rest of the coast. Sandwich was already reluctant to part with vessels that might be essential in home waters, but after some discussion in Cabinet, he was authorised to send three guard ships to North America. These were ships of the line, and quite unsuited to the purposes for which Graves required additional resources, not least because they were of deeper draught than was suitable for operations in coastal waters. When they arrived, and as winter approached, Graves made the best use of them that he could, stationing them at Boston together with a sloop and several schooners. This arrangement released a number of other ships for patrol

---

3   David Syrett, *The Royal Navy in American Waters 1775-1783* (Aldershot: Scolar Press, 1989), p.2.

duties. This, Graves considered, should enable him to put a stop to the widespread smuggling, but in the event no major seizures of contraband were made. Graves wrote to Philip Stephens, the Secretary of the Admiralty, to say that the efficient interception of smugglers along such a vast coastline was impossible. Nor was he very successful in enforcing the Boston Port Act. Another serious problem which he faced was a chronic shortage of seamen, which he endeavoured to make up by a number of attempts at impressment. This, naturally, did not go down well with the American population, and he was denounced by the Massachusetts Provincial Congress as 'a traitor to his country'.[4] The Admiralty, though, was pleased with the reports of his activity, such as it was.

Another difficulty which the admiral faced was the lack of a good working relationship with Lieutenant General Thomas Gage, the commander of the army in Boston, as well as with a number of his subordinates. One of these, Major John Pitcairn, the commander of a battalion of marines, wrote directly to Sandwich to complain that Graves was withholding 50 marines that should be ashore with his battalion. In his letter he recorded a number of instances of the admiral's conduct, which he found strange. He also offered an opinion as to the right way for the government to proceed: 'I am satisfied that one active campaign, a smart action, and burning two or three of their towns, will set everything to rights. Nothing now, I am afraid, but this will ever convince those foolish bad people that England is in earnest'. This sentiment, when he read Pitcairn's letter, greatly pleased the King, who told Sandwich that 'once these rebels have felt a smart blow, they will submit'. More usefully, he suggested to the First Lord that instead of the three ships of the line that had been sent out, six 50-gun ships would be more useful, and he proposed that these should be fitted out and the necessary crews be recruited. This last was required, he said, 'for that you cannot from any of the ships in commission raise a single man,' which was certainly true.[5]

Meanwhile, British interests had taken a turn for the worse, with the débacle at Lexington and Concord. Graves later claimed that his recommendations had been ignored; he had proposed 'the burning of Charlestown and Roxbury and the seizing of the heights of Roxbury and Bunker Hill'. He was now in an exceedingly belligerent frame of mind; he later wrote, after his return to England, that after Lexington and Concord it had been his opinion that the British forces there should take the offensive by 'burning and laying waste the whole country'.[6] During the summer of 1775 the situation got a lot worse. The pyrrhic victory of Bunker Hill, in the course of which several of Graves' ships had taken part, had not improved the position of the army. The outcome had cost the British such high casualties that there was an awakening realisation that the rebels were going to be harder to over-

---

4   Yerxa, 'Vice Admiral Samuel Graves', p.373.
5   All quotations from Barnes and Owen (eds), *Private Papers of John, Earl of Sandwich*, Vol.I, pp.59-62.
6   Yerxa, 'Vice Admiral Samuel Graves', p.375.

come than had been thought. From day to day, the British forces were continually on the defensive in endeavouring to cope with repeated attacks on British shipping, which the navy was powerless to prevent.

Graves, however, in spite of the belligerence of his statements, was reluctant to carry any of his threats into effect unless he had been expressly ordered to do so. He reported in detail to the Admiralty the growth of rebellious sentiment outwards from Massachusetts, noting that the rebels were 'carrying on war as vigorously as possible'. However, he issued orders on 21 May to his captains that they were not to act offensively except when their ships were in immediate danger or when they received specific orders from a royal governor. Graves had decided for the moment to adopt a basically passive role.[7]

In London, there was a growing understanding of the inadequacy of the naval forces in North America. The King continued to press for reinforcements to be sent. A memorandum written in July 1775 by Rear Admiral Sir Hugh Palliser, the former Comptroller of the Navy who had joined the Board of Admiralty in April, demonstrated clearly that reinforcement was essential. In this paper he calculated in detail the number of ships required 'to be on the coasts of America to annoy the rebellious provinces, to awe those that are refractory, to enforce the Acts for restraining their trade, and to countenance and protect the friends to government'. He concluded that a minimum of 50 ships was required; Graves at this time had less than half that number.[8]

There were increasing rumbles of discontent in Whitehall about the leadership of the British forces in North America, not least concerning their apparent lack of effective cooperation. Sandwich wrote to Graves on 30 July with his 'earnest recommendation' to exert himself to the utmost towards crushing the rebellion, and warning him that if he and the generals did not cooperate, 'the most disagreeable consequences, both public and private' would ensue.[9] Sandwich was becoming aware that Graves' position was now very insecure, and he followed up that letter with another on 25 August spelling out the position more explicitly:

> As I have told you in former letters, you will be liable to universal censure for doing too little, though I should be greatly surprised if you incurred any blame by rather overdoing your part in the other extreme. I think I should not perform the part of a friend, if I endeavoured to conceal from you that the world in general has been full of complaints that the fleet does nothing; and that in particular fresh provisions are wanted in Boston, which the ships have it in their power to procure; they say that you do not consider the rebellious colonies as a people you are actually

7   Yerxa, 'Vice Admiral Samuel Graves', p.375.
8   Barnes and Owen (eds), *Private Papers of John, Earl of Sandwich*, Vol.I, pp.64-65.
9   Barnes and Owen (eds), *Private Papers of John, Earl of Sandwich*, Vol.I, p.66.

at war with; and that though they take every advantage in their power in order to starve the navy and army, you seem to have delicacies about taking possession of whatever is wanted for subsistence or in aid of your operations.[10]

Sandwich added that it was with great difficulty that he had been able to resist the general cry for another commander.

Provoked by the continuing success of the rebels in defying his blockade, and aware that he must be seen to be doing something, Graves decided to adopt a policy of intimidation of the coastal towns of New England, by threatening to burn them if they did not come to heel. He sent Captain Mowat with a force of four ships with orders to destroy and 'chastise' the towns of Cape Ann, Marblehead, Salem, Newburyport, Portsmouth, Ipswich, Saco, Falmouth (now Portland, Maine) and Machias.[11] In only one case was Mowat able to execute this order, due to the weather, lack of ammunition, and the condition of the ships involved. The unlucky victim of this operation was the town of Falmouth, before which Mowat arrived on 17 October. He gave the inhabitants until 9.00 a.m. on the following day to surrender their arms and ammunition and provide four hostages. The town refused to comply, and on the following morning Mowat began his bombardment. The Reverend Jacob Bailey was one of the eyewitnesses who wrote an account of the town's destruction:

> The morning was calm, clear and pleasant … At exactly half an hour after nine the flag was hoisted at the top of the mast and the cannon began to roar with incessant and tremendous fury … The bombardment lasted from half after nine till sunset, during which all the lower end and middle of the town was reduced to a heap of ashes … in a word, about three quarters of the town was consumed.[12]

He estimated that between two and three hundred families were rendered homeless, 'destitute of a hut for themselves' as winter approached.

Washington, when he learned of the town's destruction, was appalled, writing to John Hancock on 24 October to denounce it as 'an outrage exceeding in barbarity and cruelty every hostile act practised among civilised nations'.[13] The practical effect of the operation was to harden the hearts of American patriots, who reacted by embarking on defensive preparations along the coastline. Graves claimed that it

---

10   Barnes and Owen (eds), *Private Papers of John, Earl of Sandwich*, Vol.I, pp.70-72.
11   Syrett, *American Waters*, p.7.
12   Naval Historical Centre, *Naval Documents of the American Revolution* (Washington DC: Department of the Navy, 1964), Vol.II, p.500.
13   Naval Historical Centre, *Naval Documents of the American Revolution*, Vol.II, p.590.

had been a 'severe stroke to the rebels'.[14] In fact, the policy that led to the burning of Falmouth might only have been successful if it had been pursued to its logical conclusion. Graves almost certainly did not have the resources to put every coastal port to the flames, even if he really had the stomach to carry out such an exercise in extreme brutality towards the civil population. Hawks among the British spoke airily of acting in this way as if it was within Graves' power to do so; but it might well have been difficult to carry Parliament along with such a policy.

Although he was not yet to know it, while his forces were destroying Falmouth, Graves' time was up. The King made it known to Sandwich on 8 September that he did not see how, in view of the extensive criticism of the admiral from so many sources, the command could any longer be left 'in such improper hands'.[15]

On 17 September Sandwich bowed to the inevitable, writing to Graves:

> It gives me great concern to be obliged to inform you that I have received his Majesty's commands for your returning home at the close of this year. In a letter I wrote to you not long ago, I mentioned that the world in general expected something essential to be done both by the fleet and army, and General Gage's return to England has made my resistance to your being recalled utterly ineffectual: the torrent has been too strong for me to be able to withstand it.[16]

Sandwich had personally not lost faith in Graves, assuring him that he nevertheless would do him the justice which he deserved, and would declare his opinion that the operational failures were 'more owing to accident than misconduct'. He wrote again on the following day to tell the admiral that his recall 'was known by all the world not to have been moved by me,' but that his best friends believed that he had left Graves in command longer than was in his or the admiral's interest. That he still regarded Graves as competent may be seen from the fact that he subsequently attempted, though unsuccessfully, to get him appointed to command the Mediterranean Fleet. Graves had few other supporters; William Eden, who was close to Lord North, spoke for many when he called him 'a corrupt admiral without any shadow of capacity'. David Syrett, though, judged Graves as 'a man who although not very inspiring, has been much maligned'.[17] Nicholas Rodger, reviewing the criticism of Sandwich over the matter, remarks that 'he has been accused of appointing an incompetent admiral, and refusing to remove him long

---

14 Naval Historical Centre, *Naval Documents of the American Revolution*, Vol.II, p.932.
15 Barnes and Owen (eds), *Private Papers of John, Earl of Sandwich*, Vol.I, pp.72-73.
16 Barnes and Owen (eds), *Private Papers of John, Earl of Sandwich*, Vol.I, pp.73-74.
17 Syrett, *American Waters*, p.1.

after it had become necessary. He has also been accused of offering Graves up as a scapegoat to save his own skin. In short, he was too loyal and not loyal enough'.[18]

Rear Admiral Molineux Shuldham had been chosen by Sandwich to go out to North America as second-in-command. The First Lord had a high opinion of him. When writing to Graves on 30 July to urge him to exert himself to the utmost, he had added: 'you are going to be greatly reinforced, and to have a very able rear admiral to command under you; with his assistance, I think it will show the rebels the weight of an English fleet before the campaign is ended'.[19] Obliged to now find a replacement for Graves, Sandwich decided that Shuldham should go out to take command, formally appointing him on 29 September. Shuldham, delayed for some time by adverse winds, finally reached Boston on 30 December. As his second-in-command, Sandwich's first choice was Rear Admiral John Byron, but he declined the post on the grounds of ill-health, and Commodore Sir Peter Parker was sent in his place.

The build-up of reinforcements for America was already beginning to have a considerable impact upon the navy's resources available in home waters. On 1 January 1776 Palliser wrote to Sandwich reflecting on the situation that might arise if France and Spain chose to intervene while Britain was engaged in North America. He had been considering 'what would be the best plan immediately to adopt upon any sudden alarm from those quarters, whilst we have so many seamen in almost the whole of our frigates employed at such a distance and such a body of our troops in such a situation'.[20] He went on to review in detail a number of steps which should be taken, particularly with regard to the manning of the fleet.

In spite of the reinforcements which had gone or were to go to America, Shuldham was dismayed by what he found there, writing to Sandwich on 13 January:

> Your Lordship will be surprised and concerned to hear how fast the armed vessels of the rebels have multiplied lately; how many of our store ships and victuallers they have taken; and how successfully they have defeated all our force, vigilance, and attention, by their artifice, but more by their being too early in possession of all the harbours, creeks, and rivers, on this coast, most of which they have already fortified.[21]

Shuldham added that he was resigned to the likelihood of malevolent attacks upon his conduct, 'particularly by the friends and dependents of my predecessor'.

The situation in Boston had continued to deteriorate. Shuldham told the Admiralty that it was hopeless, observing that however numerous the ships

---

18   N.A.M. Rodger, *The Insatiable Earl* (New York: W.W. Norton and Co., 1993), p.226.
19   Barnes and Owen (eds), *Private Papers of John, Earl of Sandwich*, Vol.I, pp.66-67.
20   Barnes and Owen (eds), *Private Papers of John, Earl of Sandwich*, Vol.I, p.91.
21   Barnes and Owen (eds), *Private Papers of John, Earl of Sandwich*, Vol.I, p.104.

available or however attentive to their duty were their officers, it had been found impossible to prevent some ordnance and other stores in small vessels falling into the hands of the rebels. In March, with Washington's occupation of Dorchester Heights, the position had got so difficult that it was deemed necessary to evacuate the city, and this was completed by 17 March, the army of almost 9,000 troops being transported to Halifax. It was the intention to employ this force in an attack on New York, but it would be some time before the necessary transports and provisions could be assembled.

In the meantime Shuldham, by the end of April, was in a situation much the same as that of Graves, in that his ships were scattered along the coast from Nova Scotia to Sandy Hook, endeavouring to enforce what was still proving an ineffectual blockade. While he was endeavouring to make the best of his situation, however, events in England were about to present the First Lord with a problem he could have done without, and which would lead to the ending of Shuldham's command.

2

The Growing Threat

It had not been Sandwich's decision to remove Graves, but he was comfortable enough with Shuldham as his successor. The making of such appointments was a crucial part of the responsibilities of the First Lord of the Admiralty, and they were the subject of considerable scrutiny by friends and foes alike. Sandwich was by now, of course, an old hand at this. He had first assumed the post of First Lord in 1748, at the tender age of 30. In 1775 he had been again at the Admiralty for four difficult years, during which time the situation in America had got steadily worse. As a public figure who had originally attained such high office so young, he attracted envious comment from the political world. Bentinck, a former colleague, commented of him: 'Sandwich has ruined himself in the eyes of the public by revealing a limitless ambition to which he has sacrificed everything, with no scruple in his choice of methods'.[1]

Throughout his years at the Admiralty, Sandwich had to endure hostility from many individuals both inside the navy and outside. Among naval officers much of this was generated by his having failed to make appointments which they sought. A First Lord's power of patronage was enormous, but it would have been impossible to satisfy all those with claims of preferment. A modern historian of the American war has pointed up the reasons for the widespread mistrust of Sandwich by asking 'whether it was Sandwich's resistance to private importunity rather than his compliance with it which caused the feeling against him'.[2]

The Royal Navy of the eighteenth century was the product of centuries of organic development. It was too large, too complicated and too hidebound by its traditions to be easily reformed. On the face of it, it would appear to be almost ungovernable. Yet somehow, in spite of this, it succeeded in maintaining its position as the world's dominant naval power, confident always of success – a confidence that was usually justified. The administration of such an unwieldy behemoth was immensely intricate, but was nonetheless carried out by a tiny workforce that, to

1   Quoted Rodger, *The Insatiable Earl*, p.68.
2   Piers Mackesy, *The War for America 1775-1783* (London: Longmans Green, 1964) p 11

twenty-first century eyes, bore an apparently unsustainable load. One historian of the modern Admiralty has written that 'administration is more ubiquitous to a navy than the sea itself, and bureaucratic culture can be more prevalent than seamanship'.[3]

The management of such an organisation was not made any easier by the fact that it was constantly the subject of political debate, which was often rendered particularly acrimonious by the presence as members of Parliament of many of the senior officers of the navy. Admirals were, and perhaps have always been, extremely difficult to manage, as Sandwich observed of their grasp of Admiralty affairs:

> There is no set of men that understand these matters so ill as sea officers; for it scarcely ever happens that, after an action, they do not call in the whole world to hear what complaints they have of each other, and the decision of the world is that all sides are in some degree to blame.[4]

Sandwich was used to pressure. This came from many directions, and not least from King George III, who took a close interest in naval matters, on which he held strong opinions which he frequently expressed. One issue on which he felt particularly strongly was the defence of the sugar islands which, he was to write on 13 September 1779, 'must be defended, even at the risk of an invasion of this island'. Without them, it would be impossible to raise money to continue the war. The King went on:

> We must be ruined if every idea of offensive war is to lie dormant until this island is thought in a situation to defy attack. If there is the smallest spark of resolution in the Country, it must defend itself at home, though not a ship remained for its defence. If ministers will take a firm decided part and risk something to save the Empire, I am ready to be the foremost on the occasion, as my stake is the deepest; but if nothing but measures of caution are pursued, and further sacrifices are made from a want of that boldness which alone can preserve a state when hard pressed, I shall certainly not think myself obliged, after a conduct shall have been held so contrary to my opinion, to screen them from the violence of an enraged nation.[5]

In pressing for aggressive naval action overseas at the expense of concentrating in home waters, the King had put his finger on the key strategic issue which lay at

---

3   C.I. Hamilton, *The Making of the Modern Admiralty* (Cambridge: Cambridge University Press, 2011), p.14.
4   Quoted in Leslie Gardiner, *The British Admiralty* (London: Blackwood, 1968), p.172.
5   Barnes and Owen (eds), *Private Papers of John, Earl of Sandwich*, Vol.III, pp.163-164.

the heart of the decisions made for the deployment of Britain's fleets and armies between 1775 and 1783. He left the Cabinet in no doubt as to the decisions which he believed should be taken. Its members, however, did not always share his views. On the day following his letter the King received a copy of a lengthy memorandum by Sandwich setting out his views as to the future conduct of the naval war, and in particular the crucial importance of home defence. He concluded this with an often-quoted passage in which he explained the problem which the navy faced:

> But it will be asked why, when we have as great if not a greater force than ever we had, the enemy are superior to us. To this it is to be answered that England till this time was never engaged in a sea war with the House of Bourbon thoroughly united, their naval force unbroken, and having no other war or object to draw off their attention and resources. We unfortunately have an additional war upon our hands, which essentially drains our finances and employs a very considerable part of our Army and Navy; we have no one friend or ally to assist us, on the contrary all those who ought to be our allies except Portugal act against us in supplying our enemies with the means of equipping their fleets.[6]

Sandwich had returned to the post of First Lord in 1771 on the retirement of Sir Edward Hawke, and inherited from him a navy that had fallen into so poor a state that it was described as 'a ruined service' by Augustus Hervey.[7]

This was in August 1770; that autumn Thomas Bradshaw, the Secretary of the Treasury, wrote of the mobilisation of the navy which had been ordered:

> The Admiralty have already most miserably *bungled* the business, and they are not only tardy, but every step they mean to take, is already, as well known as it will be, when carried into Execution – from what I have already seen of that office, I not only pity the Country, but the Minister who is to work with such implements.[8]

Much, therefore, needed to be done; it was a task to which Sandwich brought outstanding political and practical skills developed over a lifetime in politics.

As the struggle with the colonists intensified, the demands on the navy had increased, not only in American waters, but also in Europe, where there was a growing need to intercept ships carrying munitions to North America. Efforts were made to check this traffic by diplomatic means, but with limited success; and in the case of supplies of arms from France, the trade was being carried out

---

6   Barnes and Owen (eds), *Private Papers of John, Earl of Sandwich*, Vol.III, p.170.
7   M.R.J. Holmes, *Augustus Hervey* (Bishop Auckland: The Pentland Press, 1996), p.246.
8   Rodger, *The Insatiable Earl*, p.129.

John Montagu, Earl of Sandwich. Engraving by V. Green after Zoffany. (NYPL)

with the active support of the government. The British Cabinet was in little doubt of what was going on; Lord Rochford, the Southern Secretary, was writing in September 1775 to the Chargé d'Affaires at the Paris embassy, Horace St Paul, to express his frustration:

> I cannot defer mentioning to you the general opinion entertained here that the American rebels are constantly assisted by the French nation as well from Europe as from their American islands. I could not avoid taking notice of it last week to Count de Guines, and confirmed it to him afterwards in a note … It is probable that the Count de Vergennes may think it necessary to repeat to you the same assurances the French ambassador here is persuaded he shall have orders to give.[9]

9   Naval Historical Centre, *Naval Documents of the American Revolution*, Vol.II, p.718.

Soon, another dimension was added as the colonists began to fit out warships to attack British trade, requiring the navy to provide escorts for merchant shipping. There was in America a substantial indigenous shipbuilding industry, and a considerable pool of experienced seamen available to man the vessels that menaced British commerce. More and more of the British navy's smaller warships had to be committed to the task of meeting this threat.

The problems which the navy faced were due in considerable part to the short life of wooden warships, and doing something about this involved reforming the relationship between shipbuilding, ship repairing, the size of the fleet and the capacity of the dockyards. Sandwich demonstrated a remarkable understanding of what needed to be done, which led Horace Walpole, one of his severest critics, nonetheless to write:

> The Admiralty, in which he had formerly presided with credit, was the favourite object of Lord Sandwich's ambition; and his passion for maritime affairs, his activity, industry and flowing complaisance endeared him to the profession, re-established the marine, and effaced a great part of his unpopularity. No man in the Administration was so much master of his business, so quick or so shrewd.[10]

As the war in America went on, the threat from France was significantly increasing, and Sandwich was constantly warning his Cabinet colleagues of the need to be prepared for war in Europe. Early in 1778 he wrote to Lord North:

> I cannot avoid pointing out to your Lordship how necessary it seems to me that further exertions should be made in order to keep pace with the French naval equipments. If they have commissioned a ship of 110 guns, surely it is time to commission the *Victory* and every line of battleship that can be got fit for service; they will otherwise have the start of us considerably in their preparations; and if it should appear that with the assistance of Spain that they have more ships in Europe ready for sea than we have, we shall either be obliged to leave our distant possessions defenceless or remain with an inferior force to guard our own coast.[11]

Once war with France had broken out, the problem of reconciling the needs of home defence with those of America and the West Indies would become acute.

Sandwich's grasp of the key strategic issues of the war was not always shared by his Cabinet colleagues. Much of the ongoing struggle between him and Lord George Germain, the Secretary of State for the American Colonies, arose from

---

10   George Martelli, *Jemmy Twitcher* (London: Jonathan Cape, 1962), p.83.
11   Barnes and Owen (eds), *Private Papers of John, Earl of Sandwich*, Vol.I, pp.342-343.

Sandwich's perception that once France had entered the war home defence must take priority. Germain, effectively the minister principally responsible for the prosecution of the war in America, took a diametrically opposing view.

Although as previously quoted the King was constantly pressing for offensive action overseas, he was in general perfectly satisfied with Sandwich's management of the Admiralty. In 1780 pressure from the opposition for Sandwich to be replaced by Admiral Keppel cut no ice with the King, who was to write to North on 3 July that he knew 'no man so fit for his department' and that he could not think it either just or wise to remove him; replacing him, the King thought, with someone who would rekindle controversy would make it even harder to manage the Admiralty effectively.[12]

The slightly curious structure of the British Cabinet meant that it was Sandwich and Germain upon whom actually fell the responsibility for overseeing the naval and military operations against the American colonists, and for leading the Cabinet's debates on the strategy to be followed. From the outset it was evident that the task of suppressing the rebellion called for naval, military and logistical efforts for which there was no precedent. It required the efficient and consistent conduct of a campaign at a remove of 3,000 miles, with all the problems caused by the unavoidable delay in the receipt of reports and the sending of orders. Within the Cabinet the principal responsibility for naval and military operations in America rested formally with the Secretary of State for the Southern Department, who from November 1775 until November 1779 was Lord Weymouth; he was then succeeded by Lord Hillsborough. However, for military operations in America Germain was in practice responsible as the Secretary of State for the American Colonies.

The Admiralty was, therefore, as the war broke out, still nominally subordinate to the Southern Secretary. In practice, though, the authority of the Admiralty had steadily increased to the point where 'only an inexperienced or supine First Lord, which Sandwich was not, would have expected to be under any real control by a Secretary of State'.[13] The relationship between Sandwich and Germain was thus of major significance for the way in which Britain conducted the war.

Germain is a controversial figure. Alan Valentine, in the preface to his critical biography, wrote that 'of no figure in history can it more truthfully be said that his outward career fails to reveal his inner motivations. One is forced to guess at the three-dimensional man behind the public facade'.[14] Unlike Sandwich, whose biography by Professor Rodger is largely sympathetic, Germain does not enjoy the same favour from Valentine, who confessed that he could not bring himself to like his subject. The controversy surrounding Germain had originally begun when, as commander of the British cavalry at the Battle of Minden in 1759 he did not

12   Rodger, *The Insatiable Earl*, pp.252-253.
13   Rodger, *The Insatiable Earl*, p.221.
14   Alan Valentine, *Lord George Germain* (Oxford: Clarendon Press, 1962), p.vi.

Lord George Germain. Mezzotint by James McArdell after Reynolds, dating from 1759 shortly before he was stripped of all military offices. (Anne S.K. Brown Collection)

carry out an order from Prince Ferdinand of Brunswick, the commander-in-chief of the allied army. He was accused of cowardice, and following his court-martial was dismissed from the British army for disobedience. He was not a coward; he later fought a duel with Governor Johnstone, which to most of his contemporaries demonstrated that he was not. However, he did not court popularity, and was cold and arrogant in his public demeanour. Rodger noted that 'he was also a difficult and disloyal colleague, who habitually worked in secret to undermine his fellow ministers. Though never on friendly terms with Sandwich, Germain was not primarily working out personal enmities, but trying to establish himself as the dominant war minister'.[15] Horace Walpole wrote of Germain in his journal for 25 October 1777: 'With Lord Sandwich he had been at variance ever since he received the Seals; he had bullied all the Admiralty. All the ministers had kept aloof from him, and did even at St James'.[16]

For the King, however, Germain had the special merit of sharing his view that the rebellion must be crushed, as firmly and speedily as possible. He also shared the royal opinion that the navy should be employed in taking energetic offensive action in distant waters, rather than being retained in the Channel. It was Germain's view that the loss of the American colonies would have a domino effect, leading to the subsequent loss of Canada, and possibly of Newfoundland and the West Indies as well. This view of the naval priorities, therefore, ensured that there would be a constant source of disagreement between Germain and Sandwich as to strategic decisions.

Their strained relationship accordingly mattered a great deal to the way in which the Cabinet reached its decisions. North, a skilful politician but a weaker man than either of them, was frequently torn between their views. Their conflict was sharpened by disputes over matters of Admiralty patronage. Piers Mackesy has written:

> The two men had little in common. Sandwich was a political jobber, gamester and man of fashion, Germain politically solitary with the stately manners of an old-fashioned country gentleman. To spur the sluggish Admiralty on was a duty in the Secretary of State; and Germain made no effort to conceal his low regard for the navy, its operations and its admirals.[17]

The entry into the war first of France and then Spain would mean that Britain was now fighting a world war. For Germain, this meant a widening of the scope of his ministerial interest. He claimed the right to participate in the formulation of

15 Quoted in Rodger, *The Insatiable Earl*, p.221.
16 Valentine, *Lord George Germain*, p.377.
17 Mackesy, *War for America*, p.54.

strategy for the wider conflict, and this seriously exacerbated his relationship with Sandwich:

> In expanding his influence he was partly justified, since Britain's use of men, ships and resources in any part of the world affected its prosecution of the war in America. But Lord George's insistent participation in European strategy and naval affairs had several unfortunate results.[18]

In addition to annoying Sandwich and other colleagues it was to lead to confusion and delay in the planning and conduct of operations, necessarily distracting Germain to some extent from the situation in America.

---

18   Valentine, *Lord George Germain*, p.327.

3

Lord Howe

Lord North was essentially a man of peace, and it was always his hope that a nego-
tiated settlement might be achieved. He was not alone in this; among his Cabinet
colleagues the Earl of Dartmouth, Secretary of State for the American Colonies
until succeeded by Lord George Germain in November 1775, was firmly among
the doves. Although obliged to go to Parliament to seek approval for coercive measures to be taken against the colonists, North and Dartmouth had been in secret
discussions with Benjamin Franklin, conducted through Lord Hyde. Outside the
Cabinet there were also many who hoped for a peaceful solution. One of these
was Richard, Lord Howe, one of Britain's most distinguished naval commanders
who, with his family, felt close to the American colonies and to Massachusetts in
particular. His elder brother had died fighting at Ticonderoga during the Seven
Years War.

Howe was born in 1726; his mother was believed by many to be an illegitimate
daughter of George I. Whether or not this was so, Howe enjoyed a warm relationship with George III and the royal family; many years later George IV is said to
have recalled that Howe was 'a sort of connection of the family'.[1] Although not one
of Britain's most senior admirals, Howe had had an outstanding career not only in
battle but also as one deeply concerned with the practical aspects of his profession,
and he was much admired in the navy. He was also a very significant figure in the
politics of his time, though personally independent of any party or faction.

Perhaps through Hyde, a near neighbour of his, Howe was encouraged by North
and Dartmouth himself to begin discussions with Franklin, whom he met for the
first time at Christmas 1774. It was already clear that the basic aim of the American
colonists was incompatible with the British government's minimum position, but
Franklin did show interest in the possibility of a peace commission being sent to
America. Howe responded favourably to this, and he began to discuss with the
ministry the possibility that he could go to America to negotiate. Meanwhile, on 2
February 1775 his brother, Major General Sir William Howe, had been appointed

---

1   Ira D. Gruber, *The Howe Brothers and the American Revolution* (New York: Atheneum, 1972), p.47.

Richard, Viscount Howe. Engraved plate from *Hibernian Magazine*, c.1777.
(Anne S.K. Brown Collection)

as second-in-command to Gage in Boston. His appointment was supported by moderate members of the Cabinet, because he was known and respected in America, and favoured reconciliation.

It soon became evident to Howe that the Cabinet, in which a majority favoured war rather than concessions to the rebels, was not disposed to send a peace commission at that time. Instead, therefore, he turned his mind to the possibility that he might be appointed as commander-in-chief of the North American Station with powers to negotiate. In August 1775 his brother was appointed as commander-in-chief of the land forces in North America in succession to Gage. In September Howe had a discussion with Lord George Germain who, though not yet in the Cabinet, was seen as the coming man. He was not in favour of a peace commission, but was certainly interested in the possibility of Howe being sent in command, bearing in mind the general dissatisfaction with the naval leadership in North America. As the year passed, Dartmouth and Hyde, still bent on the project of sending a peace commission, succeeded in persuading North to agree to this and that Howe should be the sole commissioner. The admiral was delighted; but on 7 December an event occurred to change the situation completely.

On this day Admiral Sir Charles Saunders died, leaving vacant the lucrative sinecure of Lieutenant General of the Marines. Acting with remarkable, and as it turned out unfortunate haste, Sandwich immediately persuaded North that it should go to Palliser, who was next day appointed. The first news of the crisis which he had precipitated came to Sandwich that afternoon in the form of a desperate letter from John Robinson, the Secretary to the Treasury:

> We are brought into a situation of great distress by Lord North's acquiescing with your Lordship's recommendation of Sir Hugh Palliser to be Lieutenant-General of Marines and his having kissed hands for it today. Lord Howe had some time ago applied to Lord North for it, which had slipped Lord North's memory, the thing coming so suddenly upon him, and Lord Howe has now told him that he will resign his flag immediately. Lord Howe has left the House this instant after having told Lord North this; and if something is not immediately done you will probably in an hour or two receive a letter for this purpose from Lord Howe.[2]

The first suggestion made that might assuage the outraged admiral was to persuade Admiral Sir John Forbes, who held the Generalcy of Marines, to give it up in exchange for a corresponding pension, so that the post might go to Howe; but after some weeks Forbes refused. A further complication was introduced when Keppel, who was senior to both Palliser and Howe, claimed that he should have had the appointment. In the end, the matter was resolved by giving Howe the North

---

2   Barnes and Owen (eds), *Private Papers of John, Earl of Sandwich*, Vol.II, p.201.

American command together with the peace commission, in which he was to act jointly with his brother; Keppel was promised the command of the Channel Fleet. Even then there was a problem, because Sandwich wished to create a separate command for Shuldham in the St Lawrence, a proposal which Howe refused to entertain. Finally, the question was resolved after crucial meetings with the King, who was able to write to North to tell him that he thought the arrangement without the least objection: 'if there had been any, I should have jumped over it to settle this material affair. Lord Sandwich deserves commendation for being so very complying'.[3]

Part of the deal was that Shuldham should be promoted to vice admiral and given an

Frederick, Lord North. Engraving by Pollard. (NYPL)

Irish peerage. Sandwich wrote shamefacedly to him on 13 February to tell him what was to happen:

> I am going to write to you upon a disagreeable subject; but I flatter myself you are so far convinced of my friendship as to believe me, when I assure you that any resistance I could have made to the measure proposed would have been ineffectual and would have had many unpleasant consequences both to you and myself. In short, in consequence of general opinion, it has been thought proper that Lord Howe should come out to take the command of the fleet in America.[4]

It had not been a very creditable episode.

3   W. Bodham Donne (ed.), *The Correspondence of King George the Third with Lord North from 1768 to 1783 North* (London: J. Murray, 1867), Vol.II, p.11.

4   Barnes and Owen (eds), *Private Papers of John, Earl of Sandwich*, Vol.I, p.119.

Interestingly, Nicholas Rodger suggests that the offer of the North American command was not part of the deal to pacify Howe, but that it was on merit, and that he was to have the Treasurership of the Navy when next it became vacant.[5] Having regard to the correspondence that was exchanged at the time, and especially the fact that Shuldham had only just been sent out by Sandwich in command, the generally accepted view of the matter seems much more probable.

In December grave news had been received of a serious threat to Quebec. A rebel force under Richard Montgomery had advanced from Ticonderoga in September 1775, and after a series of engagements with the heavily outnumbered British forces had taken Montreal on 2 November. A few days later the completely unexpected advance of another rebel force from Maine under Benedict Arnold arrived on the banks of the St Lawrence River opposite Quebec, which was only weakly defended. Its fall seemed inevitable; but a relief column under Maclean arrived just as Arnold's men were scaling the heights of Abraham. Montgomery, in overall command, was now in a quandary. Without the ordnance necessary to mount a regular siege, he felt obliged to attempt a coup de main, which went in on 30 December. The American assault was repulsed with heavy loss; Montgomery was killed, and Arnold seriously wounded. Meanwhile in London news of the crisis in Canada prompted the hasty assembly of a relief expedition, and by May 1776 the leading elements of this had arrived at Quebec to secure the city.

In America an expedition under Clinton and Parker that was organised to assist a rising of loyalists in North Carolina arrived too late to save them from defeat on 27 February; unwisely, Clinton and Parker converted the operation into an attempt to capture Charleston. The British force arrived off Charleston Bar on 1 June. An abortive attempt was made to seize Sullivan's Island in the approaches to the city on 28 June; after three ineffectual weeks Clinton realised that the project was hopeless, and his troops were re-embarked and transported to New York.

There, Sir William Howe had begun his planned campaign to take the city by occupying Staten Island. On 12 July Lord Howe arrived at Sandy Hook, off the entrance to New York harbour. By then the brothers' task as peace commissioners had been made vastly more difficult by the Declaration of Independence on 4 July. En route to America, Howe had prepared a declaration setting out the intentions of the peace commissioners, which he now published. When the members of the Continental Congress read this, and found that the powers of the Howe brothers were limited to the removal of trade restrictions on any colony that was 'at peace with his Majesty,' and to grant pardons to those returning to their allegiance to the Crown, it was apparent to them that the Howes' declaration was irrelevant. An abortive attempt to arrange a meeting with Washington showed Howe that there was nothing for it but to press on with military action. His brother, however,

5   Rodger, *The Insatiable Earl*, pp.256-257.

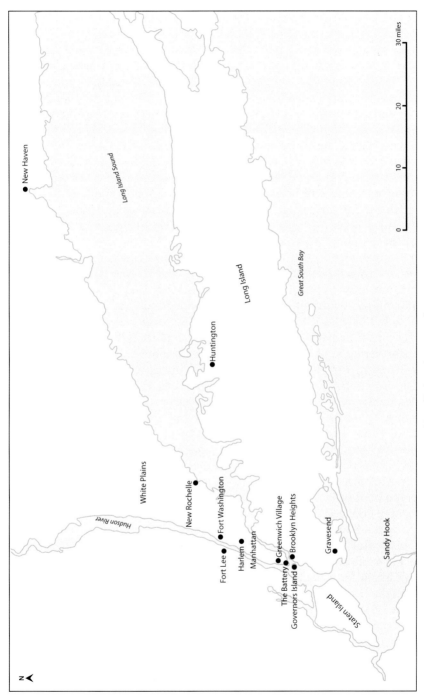

New York and surrounding area.

had decided that he could not take the next step towards the capture of New York, which was to occupy Long Island, until he received reinforcements.

All the same, it was at this point that the British had what has been described as 'the best opportunity of the entire war of inflicting upon the Americans a decisive defeat'.[6] It was not until 22 August that Sir William felt ready to proceed. 6,000 British infantry from Staten Island crossed to Gravesend on Long Island in a skilfully conducted operation, and pushed forward to outflank the American forces at Brooklyn. By the night of 29/30 August Washington was obliged to abandon Brooklyn Heights, and it was possible for the British to plan for the attack on Manhattan. While this was in preparation, Lord Howe sent a message to the Continental Congress in Philadelphia to seek a meeting, and on 11 September he and his brother met with Benjamin Franklin, John Adams and John Rutledge on Staten Island. The discussions got nowhere; the peace commissioners could not discuss independence or treat with the Continental Congress, and the Americans could consider nothing less.

On 15 September the British campaign to take New York commenced; and after a series of engagements Sir William Howe was able to enter the city unopposed, Washington retreating to Harlem. A further long delay ensued before a fresh advance obliged Washington, who was determined to avoid a pitched battle if he could, to fall back to White Plains. After an indecisive engagement there on 28 October, Sir William turned back, and took the important post of Fort Washington at the northern end of Manhattan. In November Fort Lee, on the opposite bank of the Hudson, was also taken, obliging the American forces there to fall back into New Jersey. In December Clinton and Sir Peter Parker took an expedition to Rhode Island, and on 9 December occupied Newport without resistance.

All these operations had required the active and continuous support of the navy, and Lord Howe soon found that his resources did not permit him to maintain an effective blockade while so engaged. During the time that active operations against New York were continuing, 27 out of the total of 70 warships on the North American station were deployed in support of the army, and by November all but 20 were committed in this way. There were no ships blockading the entrances to the Chesapeake and Delaware.[7] In the following months the situation did not materially change; in March 1777 there were only 24 warships on blockade duty and these also had to cover Newport and Halifax. In May there was a convincing demonstration of the ineffectiveness of the navy's blockade when a small American squadron under Captain John Manley escaped from Boston. In June he encountered and captured the frigate *Fox*, 28. However, Manley was in the following month intercepted by a British squadron under Sir George Collier and after a running battle of 39 hours the British captured the *Hancock,* 34, and retook the *Fox.*

6   David Syrett, *Admiral Lord Howe* (Stroud: Spelmount, 2006), p.54.
7   Syrett, *American Waters*, p.58.

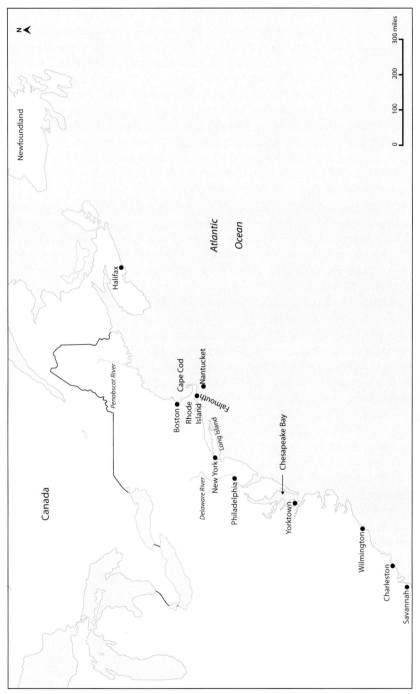

Newfoundland

Canada

Halifax

Atlantic
Ocean

Penobscot River

Boston
Cape Cod
Rhode
Island ● Nantucket
Falmouth
Long Island
New York

Delaware River

Philadelphia

Chesapeake Bay

Yorktown

Wilmington

Charleston
Savannah

N

| 0 | 100 | 200 | 300 miles |

The North American coastline.

With the reconquest of America apparently going rather well, at the end of 1776 a scheme to advance from Canada appeared to offer distinct possibilities. Major General John Burgoyne put forward a proposal to advance southwards in the general direction of Howe's forces in New York and New Jersey, moving by Lake Champlain, with Ticonderoga as its first objective. Burgoyne recognised that Howe, instead of advancing to meet him, might instead move into Pennsylvania, but his scheme was not dependent on a junction of the two armies. His plan was adopted; his orders were simple – to force a way to Albany. However, during the winter, while Burgoyne's plans were being finalised, there came news of a military setback in New Jersey. Washington, striking on Christmas Day 1776, surprised a Hessian brigade at Trenton, which surrendered after a brief engagement in which its commander was killed.

Sir William was not dismayed, though; he was confident that when the substantial reinforcements which he was expecting had arrived, victory over the rebels would be achieved. He had for some months been drawing up his own plans for 1777, based on a call for 15,000 additional troops together with eight or ten ships of the line. He envisaged at this time that offensives would be launched in New England, New Jersey and up the Hudson River. In early 1777 he revised his plans. He now proposed to launch an attack on Philadelphia, both overland and by sea up the River Delaware. After further consideration, he revised his plans again, writing to London that he proposed to leave a garrison at New York and go with the bulk of his army by sea to Philadelphia. It would be a massive operation, calling for the greatest support from the navy. This, Lord Howe was entirely ready to give; throughout the period of his command in North America he had always seen cooperation with the army as the first priority for his extended squadrons.

Lord Howe, too, was calling for significant reinforcements, and the Cabinet, in the teeth of Sandwich's reluctance, duly authorised their despatch. The First Lord wrote to Howe on 3 March to make clear that his own opinion that ships of the line should not be sent remained unchanged, 'but as your Lordship seems to think a further reinforcement of large ships absolutely necessary, we shall send you everything that can be spared with any degree of discretion'.[8] He added that if there seemed any possibility that France would enter the war and send a squadron to North America, he would send also the fireships for which Howe had asked. For the moment, though, he considered French intervention to be unlikely. Howe's forces had been built up steadily; Sandwich pointed out that when the further reinforcements arrived in America, Howe would have 17 ships of the line and at least as many frigates and smaller ships as he had in the previous year.

In one respect at least Lord Howe's conduct of affairs was causing unease in London; he had allowed the inhabitants of coastal towns to continue to use their fishing boats, and Sandwich told him that 'this kind of indulgences are more likely

8   Barnes and Owen (eds), *Private Papers of John, Earl of Sandwich*, Vol.I, p.286.

to protract than hasten the conclusion of this unnatural contest'. The King, he told him, was of like mind. George III continued to be concerned that Howe was inclined to be unduly lenient, and wrote to North to reiterate his opinion: 'To me it has always appeared that there was more cruelty in protracting the war than in taking such acts of vigour which must bring this crisis to the shortest decision'.[9]

The operation to invade Pennsylvania finally got under way on 23 July, when 14,000 troops embarked on 267 transports, and escorted by 22 warships sailed from Sandy Hook. It meant that for the moment at any rate the blockade of the North American coastline had been more or less abandoned. On 30 July the huge convoy arrived off Cape Henlopen at the entrance to Delaware Bay, and the Howe brothers met with Captain Andrew Hamond, the commander of the squadron that had been on blockade duty there. Sir William had left New York with the possibility in his mind of an alternative to pushing up the Delaware, telling Germain that he chose the Delaware as being nearer to New York than the Chesapeake, which he had originally preferred. At the meeting with Hamond the general now changed his mind, and reverted to the Chesapeake as the route to be taken. Hamond recorded his reasons for this:

> As General Washington, by the long passage of the Fleet from New York, had got his army over the Delaware before the fleet arrived, great opposition was expected to be given the Troops at landing at Newcastle or Wilmington the places intended. That the Enemy expecting the fleet to come into the river had made uncommon preparations to annoy the Men of War and Transports with Fire ships, fire rafts, and had besides considerable number of Row galleys, Xebecks, and Floating Battery's, which in the narrow navigation and rapid tides of the river might do great damage among the transports.[10]

The revised destination of the army was Head of Elk in Chesapeake Bay. Light winds delayed the convoy's progress, but on 25 August the army disembarked at the Elk River. After fighting a successful action at Brandywine Creek, the army moved on to occupy Philadelphia on 26 September. In order that it could be sustained there, it was necessary for extensive operations involving the fleet to clear the Delaware River. This involved in particular a bitter struggle for the crucial point of Fort Mifflin. After a campaign which cost the fleet the *Augusta*, a new 64, and the sloop *Merlin*, the fort was finally taken on 15 November.

While Sir William Howe was setting out on his expedition to capture Philadelphia, Burgoyne, who got back to Quebec in early May, was commencing his offensive from Canada. On 6 July he drove the Americans out of Ticonderoga, which was

9   Donne (ed.), *Correspondence of King George*, Vol.II, p.84.
10 Quoted in Syrett, *American Waters*, p.79.

an encouraging start; but thereafter, Burgoyne did not move fast enough, allowing the Americans to build up the strength of their forces barring his path. By the end of August he was in trouble. On 16 August a detachment under Colonel Baum was smashed by 1,500 New Hampshire militia under John Stark. A force of 600 men under Colonel Breymann which Burgoyne sent in answer to Baum's request for reinforcements was driven back with heavy loss. All this time the enemy's strength was increasing. Burgoyne might have avoided disaster if at this point he had accepted that his offensive had failed, and retreated to Ticonderoga. This humiliation he was not prepared to face. Since he had been ordered to force a passage to Albany, he pressed on, and crossed the Hudson, putting the river between himself and his base. Almost at once, the Americans attacked his rear; on 19 September he assaulted the American army under Horatio Gates at Bemis Heights unsuccessfully. He tried again on 21 September and failed again. His situation was becoming desperate; the one hope was that Clinton, advancing from New York, might be able to relieve him. Yet Clinton had a long way to go, and Burgoyne's force was suffering heavily from desertions, while Gates was receiving constant reinforcements. On 1 October Burgoyne launched a final assault which failed disastrously and he fell back to Saratoga. There he awaited the hoped-for relief from Clinton, but he was surrounded now, and on 14 October he began to treat for a capitulation. Three days later this took effect; his troops were granted the honours of war and allowed to return to England on promising to serve no more in America.

This was stunning news, and when it reached Paris in early December it was a contributory factor in the decision of the French government to move towards the recognition of American independence and hence towards the likelihood of war with Britain. The process by which France became involved had at first been gradual, and had begun with purely precautionary steps on the part of the French government to guard against the possibility that the British war against her rebellious American colonists might in some way spread to Europe. Nevertheless, it was apparent to French ministers, and particularly to the Comte de Vergennes, the Foreign Minister, that the situation represented a considerable French opportunity. It was perceived that the loss of her American colonies would result in a serious weakening of British power, and this was put forward by Vergennes as a principal reason for supporting the colonists. That support would take the form of providing money and arms. It led directly to a programme of French naval rearmament, which at first did not lead to any particular response on the part of Britain. Nonetheless, if French support for the Americans was not inevitably to lead to war with Britain, the strong possibility was there from the outset.

The French mobilisation in September 1776 of a squadron intended to protect the shipments of arms to America had produced an increase in the number of British warships stationed at sea as guard ships. This was in part due to the increasing possibility of war between Portugal, Britain's ally, and Spain, but it also marked an increasing escalation in tension between France and Britain. The arrival in Paris of three American commissioners seeking a treaty with France naturally exacerbated the situation, even though their first requests for a formal treaty and naval support were refused; however, further financial support was promised. Meanwhile France's relationship with Britain was gravely affected by the use of French ports by American privateers, prompting vehement protests by the British ambassador. During the first part of 1777 the tension continued to rise, and by August a serious crisis point had been reached, leading Vergennes to believe that Britain was now on the brink of declaring war. By then he had already privately concluded that this must come, but France was by no means ready for it at that time.

4

D'Estaing

By the end of 1777 Sir William Howe had had enough of the criticisms of his performance which were reaching him from London. He was especially put out by a letter which Germain sent him in early August laced with ironic comments that were largely intended to provoke the general into resigning. When Burgoyne's complaints that Howe had not adequately supported him reached his ears, these further rankled. On 21 and 22 October he wrote two letters to Germain denying Burgoyne's charges, and offering his resignation, while seeking to divert attention from his own lack of success. His brother, who had also become disenchanted with the war in America, and who now thought that it was impossible for Britain to win having received the news of Saratoga, also wrote home on 23 November asking to be relieved of his command. In his letter to Sandwich he hinted that his health was failing, while his wife also wrote to Lord North asking that he be allowed to give up the command. Unlike his brother, he was not for the moment challenging the government, though in December he felt obliged to deliver a lengthy defence of his own conduct of affairs.[1]

In London Germain had now got the bit between his teeth, and pressed hard for the removal of Sir William Howe. He suggested that Lord Amherst be sent out in his place, but the latter emphatically declined to accept the command. Germain's pressure for a change in the military command put North on the spot; on 31 January, 1778 the King was obliged to write to him effectively requiring him to choose between his Secretary for the American Colonies and his commander-in-chief there. That brought matters to a head, and on 4 February Germain had the satisfaction of writing to the general to tell him that he could come home.

Although 1777 had begun full of promise, it had in the event proved disastrous, with Saratoga having created the conditions in which France would look increasingly seriously at an alliance with the American colonists, a decision that must necessarily change the war completely. The year had ended with both the

---

1   Barnes and Owen (eds), *Private Papers of John, Earl of Sandwich*, Vol.I, pp.291-292.

Howe brothers having tendered their resignations, producing an upheaval in the command structure, even if they did not take immediate effect.

Important though Saratoga was in influencing French policy, Jonathan Dull has suggested that this has been overstated. Although France would require America, as an ally, to continue to exert pressure on British military resources, he points out that the French Council of State 'had already faced the necessity of eventually abandoning a policy of limited involvement that had been made obsolete by the almost uncontrollable growth of tension with Britain'.[2] Probably, he suggests, it was the work of the French dockyards that had in fact made it possible to commit to the American alliance.

Lord Howe's wish to return home was, however much many Cabinet ministers might feel it now to be just as well, very carefully handled by Sandwich and the King, who went out of their way to give the admiral leave to do so if and when he thought right. In the meantime, the government had to formulate a strategy for 1778. Sandwich wrote a memorandum on 8 December 1777 setting out his views on the naval situation as he saw it, which he sent to North to urge that more efforts should be made at home:

> The mode of carrying on the war in America has been such for the last two years that the fleet has not been employed in the purposes in which it can be most useful towards distressing the enemy, and making them feel their inability of holding out against the mother country. Lord Howe has had this year under his command about 90 ships of all sorts, six of them of the line and ten two deck ships, that is to say ships of fifty and forty four guns; and it was natural to suppose that with such a force properly stationed he could have made it very difficult for the Americans to receive their supplies, carry on their trade, and fit out privateers to annoy the trade of Great Britain.[3]

The reason that that had not happened was because the greater part of the fleet had been engaged in supporting the army. Sandwich accepted that it would never be possible completely to block up every rebel port and put a total stop to privateering; but he believed that very much more could be done, with the aim of so distressing the rebels that it 'would soon make them tired of the war'. To achieve this, the fleet required several bases along the vast American coastline, which must be taken and held by the army, and the ports used by the enemy warships must be destroyed.

---

2   Jonathan Dull, *The French Navy and American Independence* (Princeton New Jersey: Princeton University Press, 1975), p.90.

3   Barnes and Owen (eds), *Private Papers of John, Earl of Sandwich*, Vol.I, pp.327-325.

On 8 March 1778 instructions went to Clinton outlining the strategy to be pursued during the year. It was to be entirely defensive; it was based on a memorandum written by Lord Amherst, which noted that the object of the war had changed, and that its conduct in America had, with the imminent threat from France, become a secondary consideration: 'Our principal object must be distressing France and defending and securing our own possessions against their hostile attempts'.[4] There was also to be a fresh peace commission sent out, although there can have been little expectation that it had much chance of success.

Clinton arrived at Philadelphia on 8 May to relieve Sir William Howe, who departed for Britain on 25 May (after an elaborate leaving party). The new commander-in-chief at once began to make plans for the evacuation of Philadelphia. His first intention was that this should be carried out entirely by sea, sending direct that part of the troops intended for Florida and for the operation planned against St Lucia, and the rest to New York. There were, though, insufficient transports available to carry this out, and instead the army would march overland through New Jersey, while the heavy equipment, and the loyalists who wished to leave at the same time, would go to New York by sea.

The St Lucia expedition was a secret plan adopted by the Cabinet to launch a strike at French possessions in the West Indies while remaining on the defensive in North America. The island of St Lucia would provide an excellent base for operations by the British navy directed in particular against Martinique. The formal announcement in March of the alliance concluded between France and the American colonists was tantamount to a declaration of war, and the British government could now make their plans accordingly, as the King made clear in his letter to North of 13 March:

> The paper delivered to this day by the French ambassador is certainly equivalent to a declaration, and therefore must entirely overturn every plan proposed for strengthening the army under the command of Lieut. Gen. Clinton with an intent of carrying on an active war in North America; what occurs now is to fix what numbers are necessary to defend New York, Rhode Island, Nova Scotia and the Floridas; it is a joke to think of keeping Pennsylvania, for we must from the army now in America form a corps sufficient to attack the French islands, and two or three thousand men ought to be employed with the fleet to destroy the ports and warfs [sic] of the rebels.[5]

Once France had entered the war there were three principal naval theatres with which the British Admiralty must be concerned – home waters, North America,

4   Barnes and Owen (eds), *Private Papers of John, Earl of Sandwich*, Vol.I, p.365.
5   Donne (ed.), *The Correspondence of King George*, Vol.II, p.148.

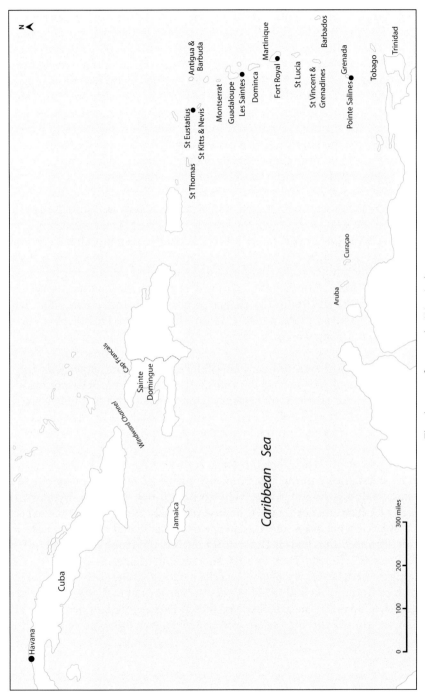

The theatre of war in the West Indies.

and the West Indies. When Spain joined the war in June 1779 in alliance with France, a fourth was added by the commencement of the long-running siege of Gibraltar. The Admiralty had constantly to juggle with the needs of each theatre. The arrival of significant hostile forces off the American coast was a serious threat to the command of the sea that the British had hitherto enjoyed in the war against the colonists. One factor which both sides had to take into account there was the weather. In European waters it was assumed that major fleet actions were generally possible only during the summer, and this was also true of North America. At the same time the hurricane season in the West Indies was so dangerous that fleets operating there would move north to the American coast between July and October before returning to the Caribbean for the winter months.

Managing the navy's finite resources, the Admiralty urgently needed information about French intentions. In general, it had been very well informed. When, therefore, at the start of their war the French sent a fleet across the Atlantic from Toulon under the Comte d'Estaing, it was a necessary response that a fleet under Byron should be detached to match it. D'Estaing did not arrive on the American coast until early July. He had with him 12 ships of the line and five frigates, a much more powerful force than that of Lord Howe. However, the lengthy passage made by d'Estaing deprived him of the chance to trap Howe in Delaware Bay, where he was covering the withdrawal of Clinton's forces from Philadelphia. George Washington commented on this:

> Had a passage of even ordinary length taken place, Lord Howe with the British ships of war and all the transports in the River Delaware must inevitably have fallen; and Sir Henry Clinton must have had better luck than is commonly dispensed to men of his profession under such circumstances, if he and his troops had not shared at least the fate of Burgoyne.[6]

Howe acted swiftly to strengthen the defences of New York, and sent out frigates to watch for d'Estaing's coming. The French commander, who had anchored off the Delaware on 8 July, did not sail for New York until two days later. By now Howe was ready for him, anchoring his squadron off Sandy Hook to meet the expected French attack. In his main line, he had five 64s, one 50 and an armed store ship, with an advanced line two or three miles outside the Hook of one 50 and two smaller vessels. He held back one 64 and several frigates as a reserve. When d'Estaing arrived, he was warned by American pilots that the deeper draught of his heavy ships would make it difficult to pass the bar even at high water. The risk, he decided, was too great; Mahan observed that 'd'Estaing, though personally brave as a lion, was timid in his profession,' and on 22 July, even though a fresh north-east

---

6   Captain A.T. Mahan, *Major Operations of the Navies in the War of American Independence* (London: Sampson Low Marston & Co, 1913) p.63.

wind and a spring tide gave the highest possible water, the French commander backed off and stood away.

D'Estaing's orders had been imprecise; he was generally required to act in support of the American colonists. Thwarted at New York, he turned his attention to Newport, Rhode Island, where he and an American army blockaded the garrison; he then forced his way into the harbour, obliging the captains of four British frigates to scuttle their vessels. Howe had been awaiting the arrival of Byron's fleet, which would have given him the numerical advantage. Unfortunately, living up to his nickname of 'Foul Weather Jack,' Byron had encountered

The Comte d'Estaing. Unsigned engraved plate. (Anne S.K. Brown Collection)

such a severe gale that his ships were widely scattered, arriving in ones and twos. However, Howe, reinforced by two ships of the line from Halifax, and one from the West Indies, as well as the first of Byron's ships to arrive, was prepared to take the initiative, and headed for Newport. D'Estaing came out to meet him; for three days Howe skilfully manoeuvred to make up for the relative weakness of his force, before a fresh gale scattered both fleets. D'Estaing's ships suffered so severely from storm damage that he was obliged to head for Boston to make repairs.

Meanwhile there had been important developments in the West Indies. Both Britain and France, each with important possessions in the Caribbean, saw opportunities arising with the outbreak of war between them. The French were the first to take effective action, launching a surprise attack on the British island of Dominica, adjacent to the French island of Martinique. Rear Admiral Samuel Barrington had been appointed to the command of the Leeward Islands station, and had sailed to take up his post before hostilities commenced. He had been strictly ordered to wait in Barbados until further orders reached him, so that although aware of the loss of Dominica he felt unable to take any immediate action. He had with him only two ships of the line.[7] Reinforcements were, however, on their way. As early as 21 March the Cabinet had agreed that an attack should be launched on the French

---

7   Mahan, *Navies in the War of American Independence*, p.99.

island of St Lucia, and Howe was ordered to detach four ships of the line, three 50s and four frigates and send them south for the purpose, bringing 5,000 troops from the army that was in due course to evacuate Philadelphia. The greatest care was taken to ensure that the secret plan to attack St Lucia should not leak out. The planned move coincided with Howe's recall, the intention being that he should hand over his command to Byron. Since the latter had still not arrived when Howe sailed from New York for home on 11 September, Rear Admiral James Gambier, of whom neither he nor Sandwich had much opinion, took command.

Howe's dislike and disapproval of Gambier was the subject of a complaint from the latter to Sandwich on 22 September:

> On my requesting his advice on some critically circumstanced and important articles in the Admiralty instructions, which being long before meditated might and were to me to admit of a doubt now, and his declining my request and saying he had furnished me with all my instructions et cetera, and had given me my commission, therefore he would give no opinion; and at the same time directed me to announce such to the General, commander-in-chief of the army, and to the Commissioners and other departments, and himself went directly to the general and announced his having relinquished the command would no longer act.[8]

Gambier went on to threaten that if when Byron arrived he insisted on making good the losses in his forces from Gambier's limited resources it would disable him from possibly complying with the intended requisition for St Lucia. Gambier was an irritating and dislikeable man; but if his description of Howe's discourteous treatment of him is accurate, it does put the outgoing commander-in-chief in an unattractive light,

Sandwich found Gambier a wearisome correspondent. He wrote to him on 1 November, observing that he had a volume of Gambier's letters by him which remained unanswered. He did not conceal his impatience with the latter's 'minute and instructive communications,' remarking: 'I am sure you know that I have not time enough on my hands, nor indeed have a turn for entering into the same sort of detail with regard to affairs on this side the Atlantic'.[9]

Gambier was not, however, to hold the chief command for long. On his way back, Howe met Byron at Newport where Foul Weather Jack had finally arrived to take up his command of the North American Station. Howe then finally left on 26 September.

The new plan meant that for the present Britain controlled only two ports within the rebel colonies, at New York and Newport. There were sufficient troops

---

8   Barnes and Owen (eds), *Private Papers of John, Earl of Sandwich*, Vol.II, pp.313-314.
9   Barnes and Owen (eds), *Private Papers of John, Earl of Sandwich*, Vol.II, p.327.

to defend these and still spare the 5,000 troops earmarked for the attack on St Lucia. The convoy bearing these, escorted by the squadron being sent to reinforce Barrington, commanded by Commodore Hotham, finally sailed on 3 November, the day before d'Estaing left Boston for Martinique. In many ways the West Indies now ranked as the most important overseas theatre. It was widely believed that they were crucial to the British economy and commerce, while the French islands represented a target of considerable importance. Their loss would be a damaging blow to France, and the King was even willing, in order to avenge 'the faithless and insolent conduct of France' to come to terms with the colonists if it enabled the conquest of the French islands.[10]

Even before the St Lucia plan was decided on, Sandwich was clear about the transatlantic priorities, suggesting the possible abandonment of operations in America and sending troops and ships to reinforce the West Indies. Hotham, he thought, 'may possibly with those troops be able to take possession of St Lucia, where the fine harbour would be of the utmost use to our fleet, which if we were established there would be a constant watch upon Martinique'.[11] Even Lord Amherst, the newly appointed Commander-in-Chief of the British Army, who was opposed to pulling out of the rebel colonies, accepted that operations there were now a secondary consideration.

Hotham's arrival to join Barrington provided, therefore, a splendid opportunity to strike an important blow against the French, provided that action was taken swiftly. As Hotham and d'Estaing took their fleets southward, neither was aware of the other's proximity until 25 November, when d'Estaing captured one of Hotham's transports. Inexplicably concluding, in the teeth of the advice of his officers, that the convoy was heading for Antigua, he headed for that point.[12] Finding no sign of Hotham there, he anchored at Fort Royal, Martinique on 9 December. Hotham joined Barrington at Barbados on the following day.

Barrington wasted no time. The troops were not disembarked, and the whole force sailed on 12 December and by the following day had anchored in the Grand Cul de Sac, an inlet on the west side of St Lucia. The British troops under Major General Grant quickly seized the shoreline and then Morne Fortuné, the capital, driving the weak garrison into the interior. By 14 December d'Estaing had news of this operation, and sailed at once to St Lucia. Barrington drew up his ships in a defensive line across the bay; d'Estaing attacked him there on 15 December, but two passes along the British line proved ineffectual, and d'Estaing turned instead to military action, landing 7,000 troops north of the Grand Cul de Sac. Three assaults on the British positions followed, without success but with heavy loss, and

---

10 Mackesy, *War for America*, p.184.
11 Barnes and Owen (eds), *Private Papers of John, Earl of Sandwich*, Vol.I, p.359.
12 David Syrett, 'D'Estaing's Decision to Steer for Antigua 28 November 1778', *The Mariner's Mirror* (1975) p.155.

Samuel Barrington. Colour mezzotint by Richard Earlom after Reynolds.
(Anne S.K. Brown Collection)

d'Estaing re-embarked his men, and prepared to attack Barrington's line again. In the meantime, However, Barrington had warped his ships closer in and installed batteries at either end of his line.[13]

The British operations had been extremely successful. On 24 December Barrington reported the position to the Admiralty, adding that he was confident that the island could be held:

---

13   Mahan, *Navies in the War of American Independence*, pp.103-104.

This being the situation of the squadron, and the army being in possession of all the strongholds in the neighbourhood of the bay, such a spirit
of cheerfulness, unanimity and resolution actuates the whole of our little
force both by land and sea (notwithstanding the amazing fatigue they
have undergone) that we are under no apprehensions from any attempts
the enemy may meditate.[14]

Barrington's optimism was justified; confronted by his defensive line, d'Estaing
gave up and withdrew on 29 December, and next day the French governor
capitulated.

   In March, at home, once it was clear that hostilities were about to commence, an
appointment had had to be made to the command of the Channel Fleet. Pursuant
to the arrangements that had been made in early 1776 which had ensured that
Lord Howe would go to North America, this command was to go to Admiral the
Hon Augustus Keppel. Second-in-command was to be Vice Admiral Sir Robert
Harland. Third in command was to be Palliser, an appointment which Sandwich
must have been pleased to make, since he was the colleague upon whom he particularly depended. Perhaps Keppel, though, might have had some lingering resentment
over the affair of the Lieutenant-Generalcy of Marines. When the Channel Fleet put
to sea it encountered the French fleet under the Comte d'Orvilliers off Ushant on 23
July, and after some complex preliminary movements the fleets engaged four days
later. The outcome was inconclusive, and Keppel took the fleet back to Portsmouth.
After a while, rumours began to circulate of misunderstandings between Keppel
and Palliser; these burgeoned until there was a full-blown dispute between them
which culminated in Palliser demanding that Keppel face a court martial. This
was held in January and February 1779, and on 11 February Keppel was acquitted.
Public feeling against Palliser was intense, and a mob attacked his house. He too
faced a court martial; on 5 May he was acquitted, but his career was in ruins.

   Keppel never went to sea again; the command of the Channel Fleet passed to
Admiral Sir Charles Hardy, who in the summer of 1779 had to face an imminent
threat of invasion from a combined Franco-Spanish fleet of 66 ships of the line
under d'Orvilliers. Subsequently, on Hardy's death, the command of the Channel
Fleet passed to Admiral Francis Geary, and later to Vice Admiral George Darby.
The latter enjoyed considerable success, remaining in command until the North
ministry fell in 1782, when he was succeeded by Lord Howe. From the start of the
war with France, and still more when Spain joined in, the task of the Admiralty
in trying to balance the demands made on the navy on both sides of the Atlantic
would prove almost impossibly difficult, until in 1782 the gradual exhaustion of
France and Spain allowed the British navy to regain the dominance at sea that it
had so long enjoyed in the past.

14   D. Bonner-Smith (ed), *The Barrington Papers* (London: Navy Records Society, 1941), Vol.II, p.162.

5

Byron

The capture of St Lucia had given the British navy a valuable anchorage that was extremely well placed to support operations against the French fleet in the West Indies, which Mahan described:

> It was an important acquisition, because at its north west extremity was a good and defensible anchorage, Gros Islet Bay, only thirty miles from Fort Royal in Martinique. In it the British could lie when desirable to close watch the enemy, yet not be worried for the safety of the port when away; for it was but an outpost, not a base of operations, as Fort Royal was.[1]

Notwithstanding his skilful conduct of the operation to capture the island, Barrington was not to remain in command there for very long. On 6 January Vice Admiral Byron arrived with 10 ships of the line; he was senior in rank to Barrington and accordingly assumed effective command of the Leeward Islands station. For some time after this there was no significant activity on the part of either the French or British fleets, although both received reinforcements. Byron's fleet in particular was suffering severely from sickness; Barrington described it as 'a most wretched sickly fleet, without stores, and in the most shattered condition'.[2] It had a lot to do; a large number of American and French cruisers and privateers operated in the Caribbean, soon to be joined by Spanish vessels, and these remained a constant threat to British trade. Barrington, meanwhile, had been promoted to vice admiral.

On 25 May Byron received news of a further substantial French reinforcement which had left Brest for the West Indies. This was a squadron of five ships of the line, three frigates and a convoy of 45 merchantmen, under the command of the highly regarded *Chef d'Escadre* La Motte-Picquet. Byron put to sea from St Lucia in an effort to intercept it, but after cruising for five days to windward of Martinique he

---

1   Mahan, *Navies in the War of American Independence*, pp.104-105.
2   Bonner-Smith (ed), *The Barrington Papers*, Vol.II, p.207.

was obliged to abandon the attempt as another even more important duty was now required of him.

Throughout the spring of 1779 a large convoy of over 200 vessels had been assembling at St Kitts. No convoy had sailed for England since the previous August. In charge of the convoy would be Rear Admiral Thomas Graves, a nephew of Samuel Graves. The convoy carried cargoes of the greatest importance for the British economy, and Byron was required to ensure that it got away safely to England. This meant for the moment giving up his close watch on d'Estaing. Early in June Byron sailed with his entire fleet to St Kitts to cover the convoy, escorting it until it was well out into the Atlantic and out of reach of enemy cruisers. It was, though, risky; there had recently been a decision to send part of the troops in the West Indies to America, seri-

John Byron. Copper engraving from the *Hibernian Magazine* c.1778. (Anne S.K. Brown Collection)

ously reducing the garrisons of the British islands. Barrington, noting that on Germain's order the rest were to follow 'after the Islands are secured' wrote to Sandwich to emphasise the danger:

> Should the General's arrangement take place, be assured, my Lord, the whole Navy of Great Britain cannot protect our Islands, and to convince you of Lord Macartney's opinion on the subject, he assures Admiral Byron that four frigates would take Grenada in its present situation.[3]

Barrington wrote later that 'so strongly was I prepossessed with this idea, that I ever looked forward with dread to the time of the convoy's departure,' since he could see that it would be necessary for the whole fleet to accompany it. He strongly disapproved of the strategy being followed:

3   Bonner-Smith (ed), *The Barrington Papers*, Vol.II, p.290.

The fate of Grenada and St Vincent however seems to have been decided from the moment the hostilities with France commenced. It is true, the operations at St Lucia saved them for a time, but no care was afterward taken for their future security. On the contrary, such was the infatuation which that little success inspired, that, because I had been the fortunate instrument in the hands of Providence of saving them and the other islands, I was given to understand that still further successes were expected from me.

He pointed out that had d'Estaing left the station, and been pursued by Byron as was intended, he would have been left with a pronounced inferiority, and would have had 'the mortification of seeing His Majesty robbed of one island after another, and considered myself fortunate if I could have preserved anyone of them'.[4] His resentment is understandable; but the situation is one more example of the difficulty faced by the Admiralty in meeting all the conflicting demands which it faced.

Barrington's warning was entirely justified. The departure of Byron's fleet to St Kitts gave d'Estaing his chance. Even without waiting for the arrival of La Motte-Picquet's squadron he had a substantial fleet at his disposal and he determined to seize the opportunity. Once he was sure that Byron was out of the way he sent a force of 400 men to attack St Vincent. These landed on 16 June, and the tiny British garrison was soon obliged to capitulate. On 27 June La Motte-Picquet arrived, and three days later d'Estaing sailed with his entire fleet, save for one ship of the line which had been damaged when going aground. He had 24 ships of the line and 12 frigates, and he took with him a convoy of transports carrying 5,500 troops.

His original objective had been Barbados, but encountering adverse winds he made instead for the important island of Grenada. He anchored at St George's Harbour on 2 July. The only British warship there was the small sloop *Lark*. That evening d'Estaing got his troops ashore and next day, after Lord Macartney, the governor, had refused his summons to surrender, the French troops advanced in three columns on the British troops on Hospital Hill. Although the position was a strong one, Macartney had only 150 regulars and 300 militia to defend it, and against the strong French force they stood little chance. On 4 July Macartney accepted terms of capitulation. The French captured not only the *Lark*, but also 30 merchant vessels with their valuable cargoes.

Byron, meanwhile, having seen his convoy safely on its way, had returned to St Lucia on 1 July, to be greeted by the news of the loss of St Vincent. He and Major General Grant at once prepared an operation intended to retake the island. At this point, however, a frigate arrived to report that she had sighted the French fleet at sea, evidently steering for Grenada. Byron sent off a dispatch vessel to warn Macartney, adding that he would come to his support if he learned that Grenada was indeed the French objective.

4   Bonner-Smith (ed), *The Barrington Papers*, Vol.II, pp.331-332.

Byron sailed from St Lucia on 3 July. He had with him 21 ships of the line, one frigate and a convoy of 28 transports carrying troops and equipment. His fleet was organised in the usual three divisions. Barrington led the van, with his flag in the *Prince of Wales*, 74, with Rear Admiral Rowley as his second-in-command in the *Suffolk*, 74; Byron commanded the centre division in the *Princess Royal*, 98, and Rear Admiral Hyde Parker the rear division aboard the *Conqueror*, 74. Byron had sent a frigate to look into Fort Royal, but the enemy frigates there prevented a close reconnaissance. The report which Byron received suggested that there were still 13 French ships of the line there, leading him to suppose that he would encounter only part of d'Estaing's fleet. On 4 July came news that the French were at Grenada, but apparently with only eight ships of the line; on the following day the invasion of the island was confirmed, but with contradictory reports as to the strength of the French fleet.[5]

Approaching Grenada, Byron detached Rowley with three ships of the line to cover the transports. Soon after dawn French flags could be seen flying on the island, and as the British fleet neared St George's Harbour the French fleet could be seen to be getting under way; Barrington noted that it was 'seemingly in great confusion,' apparently due to the lack of wind.[6] Byron decided to seize the opportunity to attack d'Estaing before he could get into line, signalling 'general chase' and ordering Rowley to come up in support. Unaware as he was of d'Estaing's strength, this was a mistake.

Furthermore, the British fleet was at this time itself in some disarray. It was sailing on the port tack, with the wind blowing north east by east, and Mahan is extremely critical of the position in which Byron found himself:

> It was not in order, as is evident from the fact that the ships nearest the enemy, and therefore the first to close, ought to have been in the rear on the then tack. For this condition there is no evident excuse; for a fleet having a convoy necessarily proceeds so slowly that the warships can keep reasonable order for mutual support. Moreover, irregularities that are permissible in case of emergency, or when no enemy can be encountered suddenly, cease to be so when the imminent probability of a meeting exists. The worst results of the day are to be attributed to this fault.[7]

In his later report of the action, Byron justified his impetuous attack by saying that it appeared that the French had no more than 14 or 15 ships of the line, and that his ships were to engage 'and form as they could get up'.[8]

5   Rear Admiral W.M. James, *The British Navy in Adversity* (London: Longmans Green, 1938), p.147.
6   Bonner-Smith (ed), *The Barrington Papers*, Vol.II, p.308.
7   Mahan, *Navies in the War of American Independence*, p.106.
8   James, *British Navy in Adversity*, p.147.

The order for 'general chase' meant that the faster sailing ships drew away from the rest, and the *Sultan*, 74, the *Prince of Wales*, 74 and the *Boyne*, 68, were soon well ahead. These received the fire of the French fleet as they approached, before they could reply, and suffered severely. When they reached the French line they were facing its rear; they wore, and led the British fleet round, standing along the French line to windward of the enemy. The rest of the fleet followed; but three ships, the *Grafton*, 74, *Cornwall*, 74, and *Lion*, 64, had somehow (according to Byron's report of the battle) got to leeward of the French and were seriously damaged. It is not clear how this could have happened; Captain Thomas White, writing in 1830, described their situation:

> While the van was wearing... the sternmost ships were coming up under Rear Admiral Hyde Parker... Among these ships, the *Cornwall* and *Lion*, from being nearer the enemy than those about them (for the rear division had not then formed into line), drew upon themselves almost the whole of the enemy's fire.[9]

This hardly suggests that these ships, and the *Grafton*, were in fact at that time to leeward although, severely crippled, they did then drop back astern of the battle lines and to leeward. Mahan observes that 'no words can show more clearly the disastrous, precipitate disorder in which this attack was conducted'.[10]

It was now all too plain to Byron that he had bitten off more than he could chew. It was also clear to Rowley, as he hastened down the line to join the rest of the fleet, that the battle was not going well. Instead, therefore, of heading for the rear of the fleet to take up a position there, he cut across in the *Suffolk* and made for the van of the French fleet, followed by *Monmouth*, 64. It was a brilliant move, effectively preventing d'Estaing from getting around Byron's fleet to attack the transports, but the two ships did suffer severely in the process. In fact, Rowley's move had uncovered the transports to an attack by d'Estaing's frigates, if the French commander had been minded to order this; but he did not. Byron continued to be determined to keep his van well up with the enemy's leading ships, to prevent them doubling on the head of the British line; but at noon d'Estaing bore up to join some of his ships which had fallen away to leeward. Byron did not follow, and at about 1:00 p.m. firing ceased.

At about 3:00 p.m., d'Estaing's ships tacked together, and made for the *Grafton*, *Lion* and *Cornwall*, which had now been joined by another badly damaged ship, the *Fame*, 74. Captain William Cornwallis, of the *Lion*, reckoned that if he continued on his present course, he would soon be in the midst of the French fleet; with

9   Captain Thomas White, *Naval Researches; or, a candid inquiry into the conduct of Admirals Byron, Graves, Hood, and Rodney* (London: Whittaker Treacher & Arnold, 1830), p.22.
10 Mahan, *Navies in the War of American Independence*, p.108.

only his foremast standing, he put up his helm and stood across the French line, escaping to Jamaica. The other three sustained heavy broadsides as they headed past the French in a northerly direction, but got away, as did the *Monmouth*. D'Estaing's failure to finish off the damaged British ships was roundly criticised by Pierre de Suffren, commanding the *Fantasque*, 64, who wrote: 'Had our admiral's seamanship equalled his courage, we would not have allowed four dismasted ships to escape'.[11]

As it was, d'Estaing was satisfied with what had been achieved, and formed his line to leeward while Byron, realising that the French were firmly in possession of Grenada, sent off his transports with orders to make for Antigua or St Kitts. His fleet laid to for the night. In his report he wrote:

> Although evident from their conduct throughout the whole day that they were resolved to avoid close engagement, yet I would not allow myself to think that with a force so greatly superior, the French Admiral would permit us to carry off the transports unmolested.[12]

The British casualties sustained in this battle were 183 killed and 346 wounded; the French lost 166 killed and 763 wounded. Byron put the best face he could on the outcome, but there was no doubt that it had resulted in a French victory, even though d'Estaing had failed to make the most of the advantage which he had gained. Mahan reckoned that the battle 'viewed as an isolated event, was the most disastrous in results that the British Navy had fought since Beachy Head, in 1690'.[13] Byron took his fleet to St Kitts to refit, arriving on 15 July, but the lack of naval stores there, and throughout the West Indies, meant that it would be a long time before the badly damaged ships could be repaired and made battleworthy. Meanwhile d'Estaing took his fleet back into harbour at Grenada for the time being. Then, on 21 July he sailed for St Kitts and tacked outside the harbour back and forth, to the vexation of the British fleet. This was, however, in no state to come out to do battle, while d'Estaing certainly did not intend to attack.

Barrington, who had been wounded in the Battle of Grenada, asked Byron if he might be granted leave to return home. The two men met on 15 July, and next day Byron wrote to the Admiralty to announce that he had agreed to this:

> Upon consultation with Vice Admiral Barrington yesterday morning it was judged highly expedient in the present very critical situation of affairs, that an officer of rank well acquainted with this station and every step that has lately been taken, should immediately be sent home to lay

---

11   Mahan, *Navies in the War of American Independence*, p.111.
12   James, *British Navy in Adversity*, p.152.
13   Mahan, *Navies in the War of American Independence*, p.110.

before their Lordships the true state of the squadron, as well as to furnish His Majesty's ministers with such information as may be necessary relative to these Islands.[14]

Barrington got back to London in September, and at once had interviews first with Sandwich and then with the King. Although Sandwich noted that Barrington seemed in perfect good humour, and there was no appearance of any disagreement with Byron, it is clear that he did not mince words when commenting on the situation in the West Indies. His report did not go down well with the King, who wrote to Sandwich that Barrington's account of the situation had not edified him:

> I am sorry to add that he has not been cautious in concealing his sentiments on that subject, so that it is now well known that he is of opinion that every one of the possessions in that material part of the world, if attacked by either France or Spain, must inevitably fall. Though I think him a very gallant officer, I cannot say this is a mark of much public virtue, which ought to prevent despondency and to stimulate, when difficulties arise, an increase of alacrity and activity as the sole means of producing a better posture of affairs.[15]

Sandwich was sufficiently troubled by Barrington's candour to write to his brother, Lord Barrington, to find out whether the admiral belonged to any particular political faction, and was no doubt relieved to hear in reply that he had not displayed 'the least disposition to faction of any sort and when he is not pleased it is on a ground of his own'.[16] Sandwich and the rest of the government had many enemies; certainly finding another with a record as distinguished as that of the admiral was something they could do without.

Byron himself was far from well, and on 23 August he too sailed for England, turning over the command to Hyde Parker. The hurricane season had now begun and no further substantial operations would be undertaken until the end of October. For his part d'Estaing received orders to return to France with the ships of the line which he had brought from Toulon the previous year. However, before carrying out these instructions he was heavily pressed by his American allies to do something to support the war effort on the American mainland. A possible target was the city of Savannah, which the British had occupied in December 1778, and which had subsequently been reinforced from Florida.

D'Estaing sailed from Cap Francais with 20 ships of the line, seven frigates, a number of smaller vessels and a convoy of transports carrying 5,000 troops.

14 Bonner-Smith (ed), *The Barrington Papers*, Vol.II, p.xxviii.
15 Bonner-Smith (ed), *The Barrington Papers*, Vol.II, p.xxix.
16 Bonner-Smith (ed), *The Barrington Papers*, Vol.II, p.316.

He arrived off the coast of Georgia on 1 September. His appearance was completely unexpected, and he at once captured the *Experiment*, 50, which was carrying a large sum of money intended for the payment of the British army in Georgia, the 20-gun *Ariel* and two store ships, one of which carried a large quantity of naval stores. On 9 September d'Estaing anchored off the bar of the Savannah River, and next day began to disembark his troops. He summoned Major General Prévost, commanding the defenders of the city, to surrender; Prévost refused, after some abortive negotiations, and settled down to defend the city. On 9 October d'Estaing's troops, now supported by an American army under

Sir Henry Clinton. Sepia stipple-engraving by F. Bartolozzi after Smart. (Anne S.K. Brown Collection)

Benjamin Lincoln, advanced to the assault. In the course of this, d'Estaing was himself severely wounded, and the attack broke down with heavy loss. It had been d'Estaing's plan to assault the city, rather than conduct extended siege operations, as he feared the onset of winter storms. On 26 October he re-embarked his troops, and sailed away, sending squadrons under La Motte-Picquet and de Grasse to take the troops back to the West Indies, and a squadron under Vaudreuil to the Chesapeake. This last, however, was scattered by a heavy gale, and only the flagship reached her destination. With the rest of his fleet d'Estaing returned to France, arriving on 7 December. De Grasse wrote disgustedly of the attempt to take Savannah: 'Good God! It would have to be seen to be believed, and if we only told half we would be taken for exaggerators and biased men. The Navy will feel the effects for a long time'.[17]

The abortive expedition against Savannah did, however, produce one valuable side-effect for the French, when d'Estaing's appearance in Georgia was reported to Sir Henry Clinton in New York. The perceived threat was seen as so serious that Vice Admiral Mariot Arbuthnot, the new commander of the North American

17 Quoted in James, *British Navy in Adversity*, p.162.

station, strongly advised Clinton that he should consider abandoning Rhode Island, in order to concentrate his diminished army at New York. This view prevailed, and the British evacuated their position there, giving up Narragansett Bay, which Admiral Rodney described as 'the best and noblest harbour in America'.[18] It was, as became apparent in the following year, a most unwise decision.

18   Barnes and Owen (eds), *Private Papers of John, Earl of Sandwich*, Vol.III, p.262.

6

Rodney

The selection of admirals for important commands, although somewhat easier since France had entered the war, was still by no means a straightforward matter for the Admiralty. A considerable number of the senior admirals were supporters of the opposition, and at the start of the American rebellion there was a tacit understanding among some of them that they would not accept appointment under the Tory government. Several were strongly opposed to the endeavour to subdue the American colonists; Keppel, in particular, had declined to serve against them. On the other hand, it was, for the King and the members of his government, an important consideration if an admiral shared their determination to suppress the rebellion.

Roger Knight has pointed out that the generally held view, that the principal problem was that the admirals distrusted Sandwich as a civilian who knew as much about the navy as they did, is incorrect. He notes that 'if the admirals did not like Sandwich they liked each other even less'. This was a situation by no means unique to this period, or to the Royal Navy; throughout history admirals (like generals) have been a quarrelsome lot. Serious discord characterised the relationship between many of the leading admirals: 'Richard Howe never got on with Keppel; no one trusted George Rodney; Rodney was suspicious of everyone; Commodore George Johnstone hated Howe'.[1]

In the case of the proposed appointment to the Leeward Islands station in 1779 of perhaps the most distinguished naval commander of the time, the principal considerations were matters of personality rather than politics. The decision was an important one, and could certainly not be taken lightly. Sir George Bridges Rodney was by some way the most famous admiral in the Royal Navy. He had been in the public eye for a considerable time, and his life and character had attracted much attention. He had a well-deserved reputation as a successful and an extremely aggressive commander; however, he had also earned a reputation for greed and dishonesty. Nicholas Rodger, observing that not a few admirals bent the

---

1   Knight, 'The Royal Navy's Recovery', p.17.

rules to their own personal advantage, has described Rodney as unique in the way in which he did so, 'repeatedly and flagrantly misappropriating public money and abusing his powers of patronage'.[2]

Rodney was born in 1718 into a distinguished but impoverished family. He entered the navy at the age of 14, and by 1739 was serving as first lieutenant of the flagship of the Mediterranean fleet. His successful command of a raid to destroy Spanish storehouses at Ventimiglia on the Italian coast in 1742 earned him promotion to post captain at the remarkably early age of 24. Thereafter he enjoyed a brilliant career as the commander of a number of vessels, particularly distinguishing himself at the Second Battle of Cape Finisterre in 1747. He had also succeeded in taking a substantial number of valuable prizes in his various commands, which meant that he had become decidedly affluent, and this allowed him to enjoy his taste for high society.

During the peace he had a stint as governor of Newfoundland, during the course of which he was elected to Parliament as the member for Saltash, a seat in the gift of the Admiralty. In 1753 he married Jenny Compton. It was a happy marriage, but destined to be short. Tragically, his wife died in 1757, leaving Rodney to care for their two surviving children. He was obliged to give up his seat at Saltash, as it was required for another officer at the general election; instead he fought but lost the seat at Camelford. He was still required to go to sea, however, during the years of peace. When war came he managed, by pleading ill health, to avoid sitting on the court martial of Admiral Byng.

Rodney's distinguished career continued during the war, and he became rear admiral in 1759. By now he had returned to Parliament, sitting first for Okehampton and then Penryn. In 1761 he went in command to the Leeward Islands, where he successfully oversaw the capture of Martinique and other islands. He applied for a grant of land in St Vincent, which he claimed as a reward for his achievements in the West Indies, but in this he was disappointed. Returning to England, he aspired to the lucrative governorship of Greenwich Hospital, which brought with it an imposing residence; but his accession to the post was delayed by the unexpected recovery from grave illness of the incumbent. However, Admiral Townsend died in 1765, and Rodney was duly appointed. By now he was married again, and a son was born that year, and a daughter in 1766. His financial position, though, was far from secure and his debts were mounting up.

With the coming of the general election of 1768, he unwisely stood for the seat of Northampton. After a tumultuous campaign he narrowly succeeded; but the election had been, literally, ruinous, costing him £30,000. His extravagant mode of living meant that his debts were now unmanageable. One way out of his troubles beckoned with the deepening of the diplomatic crisis with Spain, which called for naval rearmament, and Rodney worked hard to get the command of the Jamaica

2   N.A.M. Rodger, *The Command of the Ocean* (London: Allen Lane, 2004), p.344.

Sir George Rodney, depicted in younger days in a steel engraving by H. Robinson after Reynolds. (Anne S.K. Brown Collection)

station. Sandwich's return as First Lord made this possible, but to obtain the post Rodney was obliged, very reluctantly, to surrender his governorship of Greenwich Hospital. As for his debts, he entered into a remarkably disadvantageous loan, which temporarily brought some relief.

However, there was no war with Spain. As Rodney's three-year term at Jamaica began to draw to a close, he looked round for other opportunities. One was the governorship of Jamaica, but he was disappointed in this, and he returned to

England in 1774 to face his increasingly importunate creditors. He also faced enquiries by the Navy Board into alleged financial irregularities during his command in Jamaica. In September, he saw no alternative but flight; he had failed to find employment, and failed to find a seat in Parliament upon its sudden dissolution. From France he wrote a plaintive letter to Sandwich, expressing the hope that he could still count on the First Lord's friendship:

> All I wanted to be in Parliament for was only to have time to settle my private affairs, and if employed abroad to have resigned my seat whenever the King's Ministers pleased. Surely, after so long and faithful attendance in Parliament, I might have been indulged in such a request.[3]

As the American rebellion continued, Rodney continued to seek from his temporary exile in Paris a naval command, as well as release from the problems with the Navy Board, but there was little that Sandwich could do. Then, in March 1778, relief came from an entirely unexpected source. The venerable Marshal de Biron offered him a loan sufficient to overcome Rodney's immediate problems. The admiral at first refused to accept this generous offer, on the basis that he would be criticised for accepting help from a Frenchman; but there was no other source available, and when the offer was renewed it was gratefully accepted.

Returning to London in May 1778, Rodney was soon able to make the necessary accommodation to stave off his creditors, and thereafter eagerly pursued Sandwich for an appointment, as well as seeking support from Germain. Strongly sympathetic as he was to the policy to bring the American colonists to heel, Rodney certainly possessed in this the key qualification for the King's approval. Although there were still misgivings, at last in September 1779 it was resolved to appoint him to the command in the Leeward Islands. In seeking the royal sanction for this, Sandwich wrote to the King offering an important reassurance:

> [I] omitted to mention to your Majesty that, if Sir George Rodney should from his indigence have any temptation to make advantage of purchasing stores or anything else of that sort, he will have no means of doing it at present, as there will be a Commissioner on the spot through whose hands all that business must be transacted.[4]

Rodney had been on shore for the past five years and it was 17 years since he had last commanded a squadron, but in spite of the recent vicissitudes of his life, 'he still possessed a keen and active brain, and… whatever he might be in politics he

---

3   David Spinney, *Rodney* (London: Allen & Unwin 1969), p.270.

4   Barnes and Owen (eds), *Private Papers of John, Earl of Sandwich*, Vol.III, p.155.

was no reactionary where sea warfare was concerned'.[5] One intriguing aspect of his appointment was the selection of Walter Young as his flag captain. This hitherto obscure officer was promoted to post captain and appointed to Rodney's flagship, the 90-gun *Sandwich*, apparently on the First Lord's recommendation. David Spinney speculates that the choice was for a captain who would not only be reliable, but would also keep an eye on the admiral and report back to Middleton, the Controller of the Navy. Young was already middle-aged when he was appointed. He sent regular letters to Middleton, with candid observations on the subject of his admiral, frequently claiming credit for decisions that Rodney made and for which he was highly praised. On one occasion in 1780 he was to write of his relationship with the admiral: 'I have discharged my duty to him and my country, and will continue to do so, as far as my abilities extend, though my situation requires great patience with so unsteady and irresolute a man'.[6] Young seems to have been previously known to Middleton, since he was corresponding with him directly on minor administrative questions well before his appointment to the *Sandwich*. His correspondence with the Controller continued until his death on 2 May 1781.

In considering the strategy for Rodney's fleet, it is worth bearing in mind the point made by Nicholas Rodger, which was that there were serious disadvantages in the navy's traditional structure of 'stations' each with a separate commander. The separation into discrete areas of responsibility, each with its own squadron commander with an overall commander-in-chief 'made sense if there was sufficient control of home waters to minimise interference but carried considerable disadvantages in a fluid war of rapid movement'.[7] It seriously impaired the willingness of a station commander to enter the waters of another station; it also created problems of seniority if that happened. In 1779, there were, quite simply, insufficient resources to deal with each of the problems faced by British naval planners, with the fleets of both France and Spain to contend with. In Rodger's view, an opportunity had already been missed:

> If the King had been prepared to admit the logic of abandoning most of America until France was defeated – and the logic of abandoning Germain which went with it – the French folly in splitting their fleet when they might have united it would have opened the chance of a decisive victory before Spain could enter the war.[8]

5   Spinney, *Rodney*, p.296.
6   Sir John Laughton (ed.), *Letters and Papers of Charles Lord Barham* (London: Navy Records Society, 1908), Vol.I, p.62.
7   Rodger, *The Insatiable Earl*, p.274.
8   Rodger, *The Insatiable Earl*, p.278.

As it was, there was a serious threat to be faced from Spain in the siege of Gibraltar. As well, therefore, as dispatching a strong force to the West Indies, a way must be found to supply the beleaguered fortress. It was decided that, on his way across the Atlantic, Rodney should escort a substantial convoy carrying supplies, provisions and reinforcements to Gibraltar. Part of the convoy would go on to Minorca, while there would also sail with it another convoy with troop reinforcements for the West Indies. To ensure the security of these enormously vulnerable movements, Rodney would take a large part of the Channel Fleet under his command, which would accompany the convoys. Once into the Bay of Biscay, the West Indies convoy would part company, and the rest would sail on to Gibraltar. From there, the Channel Fleet would return home, and Rodney, with his squadron, would sail on across the Atlantic.

Rodney hoisted his flag on 21 November. Unfortunately, his ships were wind bound at Spithead; the West Indies convoy was at St Helens and the rest at Plymouth, with the wind firmly in the west. The delay in setting off caused Sandwich extreme anxiety; he wrote to Rodney on 8 December, evidently mistaking the direction of the wind:

> For God's sake go to sea without delay. You can not conceive of what importance it is to yourself, to me and to the publick that you should not lose this fair wind. If you do, I shall not only hear of it in Parliament, but in places to which I pay more attention… I must once more repeat to you that any delay in your sailing will have the most disagreeable consequences.[9]

There was nothing that Rodney could do about the winds, which continued adverse for a further two weeks. They finally abated on 23 December, and next day he was able to put to sea. Reaching Plymouth, he paused for a day to enable the ships there to join him. He then sailed with 22 ships of the line, one 44 and seven frigates, escorting not only 66 store ships, transport and victuallers but many merchantmen, a total of nearly 150 sail. On 8 January he enjoyed an unexpected success, when he snapped up a Spanish convoy of stores and provisions some 500 miles west of Cape Finisterre, heading for Cadiz, together with a 64-gun ship. Then on 16 January Rodney encountered off Cape St Vincent Don Juan de Lángara, who commanded a fleet of 11 ships of the line and two frigates. Opening fire at 4:00p.m., he chased Lángara all night on a lee shore, capturing his flagship *Fénix* and five other ships of the line; another Spanish ship of the line blew up. The engagement became known as the 'Moonlight Battle'. Walter Young, writing to Middleton with details of the battle, conveyed the suggestion that it was only due to his insistence on pursuing the enemy, against his admiral's irresolution, that the victory was secured. At the time Rodney was seriously afflicted by

9   Quoted in Spinney, *Rodney*, p.300.

gout; but as Spinney remarks, Young's claim does seem improbable. The weather continued foul after the battle, and two of the prizes were driven ashore. With odds of two to one in his favour, Rodney's victory was hardly surprising; Don Luis de Córdova, in Cadiz, did not venture out, and it meant that the relief of Gibraltar could proceed unmolested, although the weather delayed Rodney's entrance into the Bay. Meanwhile the Minorca convoy also successfully reached its destination, escorted by three of Rodney's fastest ships of the line. When they returned, he put to sea on 13 February, accompanied by Digby with the ships of the Channel Fleet, which sailed together with Rodney for three days before parting company for England with the prizes. Rodney, in defiance of his orders, left one ship of the line at Gibraltar, and got into trouble with the Admiralty for so doing.[10]

Rodney wrote a characteristically fawning letter to Sandwich to report on his proceedings:

> I most sincerely congratulate you on the great success that has attended his Majesty's arms. I hope your enemies will now be confounded and that you may long continue at the head of that Board you so ably direct, happy if by doing my duty I can again possess that confidence that was my boast, and the loss of which I have most sincerely felt.[11]

A few days later he wrote again, generously acknowledging the support which he had received from Walter Young:

> He proves himself the very man I could have wished, excellent, diligent, brave, good officer, endued with every quality necessary to assist a commander-in-chief. I think myself much indebted to him for the late action, and I am not ashamed to acknowledge it. He is entitled to every regard I can possibly show him.[12]

Reviewing the strategy to be adopted in the following year, Sandwich wrote a paper for the Cabinet in September 1779 in which he observed that in the West Indies 'the measure of all others that is most to be wished would be the reduction of Martinique'. He saw this as likely to lead to the capture of the rest of the French West Indies, adding that 'the stroke would be so sensibly felt by France that it would probably put an end to the war'. The responsibility to be placed on the new commander of the Leeward Islands, and his military counterpart Major General Vaughan, was therefore considerable. At the same time Sandwich was fearful for the security of Jamaica, remarking that he saw the danger 'with which

10   Mahan, *Navies in the War of American Independence*, p.126.
11   Barnes and Owen (eds), *Private Papers of John, Earl of Sandwich*, Vol.III, p.193.
12   Barnes and Owen (eds), *Private Papers of John, Earl of Sandwich*, Vol.III, p.195.

that island is surrounded without being able to suggest any effectual means of giving it relief'. It was the Spanish, with considerable forces based at Havana, that he saw as providing the main danger there.[13]

As Rodney sailed across the Atlantic, he was vexed to find evidence of disputes among the officers of his fleet; reporting this to Sandwich, he wrote:

> It is with concern that I must tell your Lordship that my brother officers still continue their absurd and illiberal custom of arraigning each other's conduct. My ears have been attempted to listen to the scandal; I have treated it with the contempt it deserved. In my opinion every officer did his duty to his King and Country. I have reported it so, and I hope to the satisfaction of your Lordship and the nation. The unhappy difference between Mr Keppel and Sir H Palliser has almost ruined the Navy. Discipline in a very great measure is lost, and that eager willingness of executing the orders given by the Board of Admiralty, or by those acting under their authority, is turned into neglect.[14]

When he received news of Rodney's successes, Sandwich was generous in his praise. In his letter of 8 March, he wrote:

> I scarcely know how to find words to congratulate you enough upon your late glorious successes, and upon the eminent services you have done your country. The worst of my enemies now allow that I have pitched upon a man who knows his duty, and is a brave, honest and able officer. I will not tire you with panegyric, but am not the less eager in dealing out to all around me the praises due to your merit. I have obtained you the thanks of both Houses of Parliament.[15]

Sandwich was not surprised to learn of the faction in Rodney's fleet, remarking that it was still very prevalent at home, though he hoped that 'time and moderation in those who are high in the naval department' would by degrees overcome the problem. He applauded Rodney's refusal to pay attention to comments of the kind that he had received. As to Rodney's request for coppered ships, he made him a firm promise that he should have 'copper enough,' and everything Sandwich could give to prove the truth and regard in which he held him. A week or so later Sandwich was able to tell Rodney that he had been granted a pension of £1,000 a year with immediate effect. This was later doubled on the orders of the King.[16]

13   Barnes and Owen (eds), *Private Papers of John, Earl of Sandwich*, Vol.III, p.166.
14   Barnes and Owen (eds), *Private Papers of John, Earl of Sandwich*, Vol.III, p.201.
15   Barnes and Owen (eds), *Private Papers of John, Earl of Sandwich*, Vol.III, pp.205-206.
16   Barnes and Owen (eds), *Private Papers of John, Earl of Sandwich*, Vol.III, p.207.

7

Martinique

The French had by no means given up hope of a successful campaign against the British possessions in the West Indies. With the return of d'Estaing to France, a new commander of the French naval forces there was appointed. This was the Comte de Guichen, who was highly regarded in the French navy. It was decided that a powerful reinforcement should be sent across the Atlantic, and de Guichen, when he sailed from Brest just before Rodney left Gibraltar, had with him 17 ships of the line. He was escorting a convoy of 39 transports carrying 4,500 troops, together with 22 merchantmen. With this fleet he would join the ships under de Grasse and La Motte-Picquet that d'Estaing had left in the West Indies.

Before de Guichen and Rodney arrived to take up their new commands, there had been a brisk action off Fort Royal on 18 December. At this point de Grasse, the senior French admiral presently on the station, had not yet arrived at Martinique, and La Motte-Picquet was in command of the ships there. The engagement came about when a French convoy, escorted only by a frigate, arrived off Martinique. It was spotted by the British lookout ship, the *Preston*, 50, which signalled its appearance to Rear Admiral Hyde Parker in St Lucia. The convoy's arrival found both the French and British entirely unprepared:

> Both the British and the French squadrons were in disarray, sails unbent, ships on the heel or partially disarmed, crews ashore for wood and water. In both, signals flew at once for certain ships to get under way, and in both the orders were executed with a rapidity gratifying to the two commanders, who also went out in person.[1]

Parker, with five ships of the line and a 50-gun ship, got out of harbour first, and was able to capture nine of the ships in the French convoy, driving another four ashore, before La Motte-Picquet could get out of Fort Royal with three ships of the line. He was to windward of Parker, which enabled the rest of the convoy to get

---

1   Mahan, *Navies in the War of American Independence*, pp.128-129.

in safely, and there followed an engagement for two hours before the British withdrew. The brunt of the action fell on the *Conqueror*, 74, whose captain was killed. A striking example of courtesy between enemies followed a few days later when Parker, exchanging a flag of truce with La Motte-Picquet, wrote to him:

> The conduct of your Excellency in the affair of the 18th of this month fully justifies the reputation which you enjoy among us, and I assure you that I could not witness without envy the skill which you showed on that occasion. Our enmity is transient, depending on our masters; but your merit has stamped upon my heart the greatest admiration for yourself.[2]

On 17 March Rodney arrived in Barbados with four ships of the line, a frigate and a sloop. He was not best pleased to find no communication from Parker awaiting him. He was, however, told that Parker was at Gros Islet Bay in St Lucia; he was also told that a large French convoy was due imminently to arrive, though it was incorrectly believed to have an escort of only four men of war. Rodney sent off his four ships of the line to cruise for the enemy convoy, and himself went on shore to recuperate from an attack of gout. Meanwhile de Guichen, unseen by Rodney's vessels, arrived safely at Fort Royal on 22 March. With the vessels there he now had 23 ships of the line, and he resolved to act immediately against St Lucia without disembarking his troops. However, when he reached the island, he found that Parker had drawn up his 16 ships of the line in so strong a position across the entrance to Gros Islet Bay that he deemed it unwise to attack. It was a sensible decision; the French might have won a victory, but it would have been at a cost which would have prevented them undertaking any further major operations.[3] De Guichen's next plan was to put together an expedition to other British islands, including Barbados, but in the meantime when he sailed on 13 April with his entire fleet, it was first to cover a convoy going to San Domingo, a move which was to bring on his first encounter with Rodney.

The British admiral had soon recovered from his gout, and left Barbados for Saint Lucia, arriving there on 27 March. When he learned that de Guichen had sailed from Martinique, he put to sea at once, having with him 20 ships of the line. Parker, in the *Princess Royal*, 98, was in command of the van with Rodney in his flagship *Sandwich* in the centre and Rowley in the *Conqueror* in the rear. The French fleet came in sight on 16 April to the west of Martinique, beating up against a north-east wind and heading for the channel between that island and Dominica. Rodney ordered a general chase, and as night fell he put his fleet into line of battle, careful to keep to windward of the enemy. On the morning of 17 April the wind was east by north, and the French fleet formed line of battle, heading

2   Mahan, *Navies in the War of American Independence*, pp.129-130.
3   E.H. Jenkins, *A History of the French Navy* (London: Macdonald & Janes, 1973), p.162.

south south-east on the port tack. De Guichen had 22 ships of the line, with his van commanded by de Grasse in the *Robuste*, 74; his flag in the centre was aboard the *Couronne*, 80, and the rear was led by de Sade de Vaudronne in the *Triomphant*, 80.

Manoeuvring fleets of this size was no easy matter. In line ahead, with each ship separated from the next by the usual two cables' length or 500 yards, the two fleets were each some six miles in length. The problem of signalling over such a distance was only partly overcome by stationing frigates down the disengaged side of the line to repeat signals. At 7:00 a.m. Rodney, considering that his line was too extended at

The Comte de Guichen. Engraved plate by Hardouin after Castelar. (Anne S.K. Brown Collection)

the normal distance, signalled that the fleet should close up to one cable's length. At this time the two fleets were passing on nearly parallel lines but in the opposite direction. It was Rodney's intention, as he signalled at 8:00 a.m, to concentrate on the enemy's rear, and to effect this he ordered the fleet to form line abreast towards de Guichen's line. The French commander at once divined Rodney's intention, and ordered his fleet to wear together on the starboard tack so that the threatened rear became the van. There followed a series of intricate movements, each commander being careful to maintain the discipline of his line, with the British still having the advantage of being to windward. By 11:00 a.m. the two fleets were steering parallel to each other on the same course, and Rodney made the signal to prepare for battle, followed by a signal to turn to port towards the enemy line. At 11:50 the crucial signal was made in accordance with Article 21 of the Additional Fighting Instructions 'for every ship to bear down, and steer for her opposite in the enemy's line'.[4] This, Rodney calculated, would bring about his desired concentration on de Guichen's rear, by cutting through the French line astern of its van.

This might well have happened, but the captains of the leading British ships, accustomed to the two lines engaging each other ship to ship, misunderstood Rodney's intention, and stretched ahead towards the van. As a result, the close fighting concerned only the rear and in particular the centre, where the *Sandwich*

4   Mahan, *Navies in the War of American Independence*, p.133.

was the only ship to break the French line and got so mauled in doing so that Rodney had to shift his flag. Mahan reckoned that it was not Rodney's intention to break the enemy line, although de Guichen, fearing that this was the case, signalled for his fleet to wear together. This order had been partly carried out when de Guichen, realising that after all Rodney was not going to break through, cancelled it and then gave orders to reform the line on those that had worn to leeward. This brought the action to an end, and each fleet returned to port to make good the damage suffered.

In his report of the battle, Rodney claimed that it was the effectiveness of his flagship that had caused de Guichen to execute this movement:

> The action in the centre continued to 4:15 p.m., when M. de Guichen, in the *Couronne*, the *Triomphant* and the *Fendant*, after engaging the *Sandwich* for an hour and a half, bore away. The superiority of fire from the *Sandwich*, and the gallant behaviour of the officers and men, enabled her to sustain so unequal a combat; though before attacked by them, she had beat three ships out of their line of battle, had entirely broke it, and was to leeward of the French Admiral.[5]

Rodney has been criticised for using, in his second attempt to engage the enemy, an ambiguous signal, which was couched in terms not clear enough to overcome the ingrained instinct of captains to aim for their opposite number in the enemy line. The full text of Article 21 of the Additional Fighting Instructions in use in 1780, on which Rodney was relying, appears in Volume I of Barham's published papers as a footnote to the evidence given in the court martial of Lieutenant Appleby, who was the acting captain of the *Montagu*:

> If the squadron be sailing in a line of battle ahead to windward of the enemy, and the commander-in-chief would have the course altered to lead down to them, he will hoist an union flag at the main top gallant mast-head and fire a gun; whereupon every ship of the squadron is to steer for the ship of the enemy which from the disposition of the two squadrons, it must be her lot to engage, notwithstanding the signal for the line ahead will be kept flying; making or shortening sail in such proportion as to preserve the distance assigned by the signal for the line, in order that the whole squadron may come into action at the same time.[6]

By 1782 the corresponding article in the Additional Fighting Instructions then in use had been slightly simplified, although both versions would have been

---

5   Mahan, *Navies in the War of American Independence*, p.134.
6   Laughton (ed.), *Letters and Papers of Charles Lord Barham*, Vol.I, p.376.

made clearer by distinguishing what was actually intended from the case where the leading ship was to engage the leading ship of the enemy. However, Sir John Laughton, reviewing the signals Rodney actually made and the text of Article 21, comes down firmly on the side of the captains. He notes that Rodney wanted his fleet, in close order, to come down on the enemy's rear, and with 20 ships against nine, to crush them:

> In his mind, the ship of the enemy which it was the lot of any ship to engage was that ship which was abreast her when the signal was made; and he conceived the former signal – to attack the enemy's rear – as strengthening and explaining the order. But in fact neither captains, nor commodores, nor junior admirals so understood it. To each of them, the ship which, by the disposition of the two squadrons, it was his lot to engage was the corresponding number in the enemy's line.[7]

Laughton goes on to ask the question: 'If it did not mean that, what could it mean?' If the British ships were more closed up than the French, it was certainly true that an attack on the rear might have yielded an overwhelming victory: 'But there was no instruction as to its being the 'lot' of two or three ships to engage one; the Fighting Instructions made no provision for any such thing'. And dealing with the suggestion that Rodney had explained all this to each of his captains, Laughton adds:

> If Rodney really did this, we can only say that power of exposition was altogether wanting to him; for it is quite certain that not one man to whom he thus explained his intention had the faintest notion of what Rodney wanted him to do, or how he wanted him to do it. It has often been said that the failure on this occasion must be attributed to the very inefficient system of signalling then in use. The facts before us scarcely seem to bear this out.[8]

The inefficiency, it would appear, was that of Rodney and Young. On the other hand, although the ambiguity inherent in the instructions explains why, at the head of the British line, the *Stirling Castle* led the van squadron towards the French van, Peter Trew points out that Rodney's signal that he intended to engage the enemy rear was still in force.[9]

Rodney was furious at the way he had been deprived of what he considered to have been the greatest opportunity of his life, and in his official dispatch excoriated

---

7   Laughton (ed.), *Letters and Papers of Charles Lord Barham*, Vol.I, p.xlviii.
8   Laughton (ed.), *Letters and Papers of Charles Lord Barham*, Vol.I, p.l.
9   Peter Trew, *Rodney and the Breaking of the Line* (Barnsley: Pen & Sword, 2006), p.69.

Captain Carkett of the *Stirling Castle* for not properly obeying his signal; had he done so, Rodney insisted, the battle would have begun sooner, the fleets would have been more compactly engaged, and 'the enemy's centre and rear must have been destroyed'. In his dispatch he expressed in the fiercest terms his frustration:

> I cannot conclude without acquainting their Lordships, that the French Admiral, who appeared to me to be a brave and gallant officer, had the honour to be nobly supported during the whole action. It is with concern inexpressible, mixed with indignation, that the duty I owe my sovereign and my country obliges me to acquaint your Lordships that during the action between the French fleet, on the 17th instant, and his Majesty's, the British flag was not properly supported.[10]

Rodney seems to have thought that he might have expressed himself rather too forcibly in this passage; before sending it to the Admiralty, he sent a copy to Major General Vaughan, with whom he had a warm and trusting relationship, asking him: 'Have I said too much? Tell me fairly'. Evidently Vaughan did not discourage him, for his dispatch went as drafted. The Admiralty, however, thought it best to excise this paragraph from the official publication of Rodney's dispatch; the navy was divided enough without pouring paraffin upon the flames of the factious disputes that already existed.

Rodney, however, did not confine himself to his official dispatch to express his fury at what had occurred. He wrote to Sandwich on 26 April:

> You may judge what extreme concern I feel, when my duty has obliged me to give to your Lordship's Board such an account of the battle with the French fleet, which though so honourable to the nation, has been attended with circumstances highly derogatory to the discipline of the Navy; but the barefaced disobedience to orders and signals, acknowledged by every ship, was such as calls aloud for strict enquiry.[11]

Although Carkett of the *Stirling Castle* was the only one of Rodney's subordinates to be specifically named in his official dispatch, his rage and frustration at his lost opportunity, as he saw it, led him to identify others upon whom blame lay. Among the captains, Bateman of the *Yarmouth* ended before a court martial. His ship had apparently unaccountably failed to support the *Sandwich* at a critical time when she was heavily engaged, and he was convicted of lying to windward and not engaging, and was dismissed the service. No formal action was taken against any other individual, apart from Appleby, the acting captain of the *Montagu*, who was

10   David Syrett (ed.), *The Rodney Papers* (Aldershot: Navy Records Society, 2007), Vol.II, p.473.
11   Barnes and Owen (eds), *Private Papers of John, Earl of Sandwich*, Vol.III, p.211.

acquitted, but Rodney found plenty of opportunity to express his opinions. Poor Carkett, of whom Rodney wrote that his leading had been in breach of his 'open and avowed indication of bringing the whole force of his Majesty's fleet against the enemy's rear' perished when the *Stirling Castle* was lost at sea with most of her crew in a violent storm in October 1780, wrecked on the Silver Keys.

Rodney also addressed the failings of his admirals. He wrote of three captains in Hyde Parker's squadron that 'they meant well and could have done their duty had they been permitted'. This emphatically laid the blame for their manoeuvres on Parker, with whom Rodney had a painful interview before the rear admiral returned home enraged at his treatment by the commander-in-chief. Rodney did not mince his words when writing to Sandwich on 31 May, expressing his pleasure at receiving orders to send Parker home:

> He is a dangerous man with a very bad temper, hostile in the highest degree to the administration and capable of anything, if he thinks he is within the pale of barely doing his duty. His cunning and art, however, has failed him; and if it is thought advisable to call him to account for his conduct during the action on 17 April, his head will be at stake for palpable disobedience of signals and daring to carry the van and his squadron two leagues ahead of their station.[12]

Rodney was scarcely less outspoken when he came to deal with Rowley's performance:

> I don't know which is of the greatest detriment to a state, a designing man or a man without abilities entrusted with command. Had not Mr Rowley presumed to think, when his duty was only obedience, the whole French rear with the centre had certainly been taken.

He was not quite as censorious of Commodore Hotham, whose head, he remarked, he could take for his conduct, and would do if he thought this proceeded from anything but mistake. Hotham did not take kindly to the criticism, and soon made up his mind that he should get away from Rodney's command. He wrote to Sandwich on 6 July:

> I can no longer wish to serve in this country; for where the chief in command will assume merit to himself, and aim to aggrandise his own reputation by depreciating indiscriminately the character of every officer below him, service will become irksome and all confidence will cease. The

---

12   Barnes and Owen (eds), *Private Papers of John, Earl of Sandwich*, Vol.III, p.216.

account published by authority of the affair of 17 April, although ludicrous enough in itself, has nevertheless given much cause of discontent here.[13]

Rodney's trenchant criticisms of his subordinates had, not surprisingly, made him many enemies in his fleet. Sandwich was evidently aware that not all his strictures were entirely just, for he soon complied with Hotham's request; the commodore came home in the following year and served in the Channel Fleet to the end of the war.

The British fleet had sustained more damage than the French; the *Sandwich* had been particularly knocked about, having received 80 shot in her hull. British casualties were 120 killed, and 354 wounded; the French lost 222 men killed and 537 wounded. Both commanders claimed the battle as a victory: Rodney wrote that 'at the conclusion of the battle the enemy might be said to be completely beaten'. De Guichen, on the other hand reported: 'It was unnatural to think that they could have broken off action so early, and he that retires is the loser; consequently we had the advantage of the day's work. We remained masters of the field of action'.[14]

Walter Young, reporting to Middleton on the outcome of the battle, was on this occasion generally supportive of Rodney's view of it. He warned, however, of the state of the ships of Rodney's command:

> The fleet is in a shattered condition. For God's sake and our country's send out copper bottomed ships to relieve the foul and crippled ones, with masts and stores of all kinds. With those, everything will be done; if you do not, nothing but misery and distress must ensue.[15]

To Rodney, Sandwich wrote a sympathetic and encouraging letter on the subject of the battle and the performance of his subordinates, saying that he was 'exceedingly obliged to you for the circumstantial though unpleasant account you give me of the behaviour and principles of some of the officers of high rank under your command'. Conscious that Rodney responded well to flattery, he went on:

> We are in hourly expectation of hearing of more glorious actions from the fleet under your command (for you must be aware that, from the sample you have given us, we almost expect impossibilities from you); and I am certain that I may safely venture to say that no man before you was ever so popular as you are, who acquired his popularity by real merit.

Sandwich concluded with a postscript as to an important decision which he had to make, and which he was very much aware was by no means straightforward:

13   Barnes and Owen (eds), *Private Papers of John, Earl of Sandwich*, Vol.III, p.219.
14   Both quotations from James, *British Navy in Adversity*, p.204.
15   Laughton (ed.), *Letters and Papers of Charles Lord Barham*, Vol.I, p.55.

I know not what to do to find a good second-in-command for you, but you may depend on my having that matter in my very serious consideration, and that I will endeavour to pitch upon a person who I think will be likely to second you properly and with proper subordination.[16]

The reason for the failure on 17 April arose from a failure to understand orders transmitted through the system of signalling to which a commander was limited. David Spinney, observing that it is hard to believe that Rodney had failed to inform Parker or Carkett of his general plan, but that no imputation could be laid against their courage and capacity, finds an explanation in the inherent conservatism of the British navy:

Such men do not always take kindly to new ideas. It is possible Sir George's plan was perfectly clear to them but that, in a cross grained, independent way, they deliberately mismanaged it, not for political reasons (Parker's subsequent employment by the government disproves this), but because it was unorthodox.[17]

Spinney notes also that an important contributory factor was that Rodney had not had much time to get to know his officers, or to train and exercise the fleet, which was clearly the case.

There were to be to further engagements between the two fleets, but although Rodney certainly was looking for action, and de Guichen was prepared to fight if he could do so with advantage, the latter's instructions made a decisive engagement unlikely These were 'to keep the sea, so far as the force maintained by England in the Windward Islands would permit, without too far compromising the fleet entrusted to him'.[18]. It is not surprising therefore that de Guichen conducted his fleet extremely cautiously.

Following the battle the French commander made in the first instance for Guadeloupe. It was necessary, however, if he was properly to refit his fleet that he get into Fort Royal, but Rodney was there before him. De Guichen refitted his fleet as best he could at Guadeloupe, and landed his sick and wounded men. Rodney was still between him and Fort Royal for several days before he was himself obliged to withdraw to St Lucia to refit the fleet and land his sick and wounded. While there he kept a constant watch on Fort Royal, with a screen of frigates also covering the other nearby islands. On 6 May the frigate stationed off Pointe Salines in Martinique arrived in St Lucia with the news that de Guichen was at sea. The French admiral's intention was to launch an assault on the latter island, but when

16   Barnes and Owen (eds), *Private Papers of John, Earl of Sandwich*, Vol.III, pp.220-221.
17   Spinney, *Rodney*, p.332.
18   Mahan, *Navies in the War of American Independence*, p.141.

he arrived it was to find Rodney's fleet already coming out to meet him. For the next few days the fleets were constantly in sight of each other, with de Guichen skilfully manoeuvring to retain the windward position and thus keep the initiative. Although he had a superior force, with 23 ships of the line to 20, he did not close in upon Rodney's fleet. To the French suggestion that during this period that the British were avoiding action, Mahan writes:

> Both admirals showed much skill and mastery of their profession, great wariness also and quickness of eye; but it is wholly untenable to claim that a fleet having the weather gauge for five days, in the trade winds, was unable to bring its enemy to action, especially when it is admitted that the latter closed the instant the wind permitted him to do so.[19]

Rodney was mindful of the command problems which he had encountered on 17 April, and in order to ensure the discipline of the fleet he transferred his flag on 13 May to the frigate *Venus*, aboard which he could supervise the fleet more closely, as he reported to Sandwich:

> It is impossible for your Lordship to conceive the infinite utility of this resolution. Men conscious of their bad behaviour in the battle of the 17th of April, and who would have been glad to have watched every opportunity of contributing to my disgrace as an officer, even at the risk of a defeat of the British fleet, were by this resolution thunderstruck, and found themselves under the absolute necessity of doing their duty and that my eye was more to be dreaded by those who betrayed their country's honour than the enemy's cannon. It is inconceivable in what awe it kept them. No regard was paid to rank. When either admiral or captain were out of their station the signal was instantly made and a frigate dispatched with orders.[20]

The bitterness which Rodney felt about his subordinates had evidently not in the least subsided.

On 15 May, in an effort to lure de Guichen closer, Rodney feigned a retreat, which did tempt the French to approach, so that their leading ship came within long range. At this point, however, the wind changed from east to south east, which allowed Rowley, in the van, to get to windward. De Guichen's response was to order his ships to wear together. The wind then backed to easterly, allowing the French to come about on the port tack to windward, crossing the 'T' of the British line. Rodney's leading ship, the *Albion*, 74, suffered severely, before tacking

19   Mahan, *Navies in the War of American Independence*, p.142.
20   Barnes and Owen (eds), *Private Papers of John, Earl of Sandwich*, Vol.III, p.215.

to the north, leading the British van onto a parallel but opposite course to that of the French. As darkness began to fall the British van tacked to the south to get to windward, but the French then tacked to the north, and regained their advantage. Rodney explained that 'as the enemy were under a press of sail, none but the van of our fleet could come in for any part of the action without wasting his Majesty's powder and shot, the enemy wantonly expending theirs at such a distance as to have no effect'.[21] British losses in this engagement amounted to 21 killed and 100 wounded.

The two fleets remained in sight of each other, continuing to manoeuvre with great care, until 19 May, when the third and final engagement between them took place. As dawn broke on that day the two fleets were both in line ahead, the British following the French at a distance of 12 to 15 miles, gaining slowly and trying to get to windward. The wind was south-easterly. At noon, as the British got closer, de Guichen ordered his fleet to tack together, crossing ahead of the British line, having ordered his ships to close up to half a cable apart. The fleets engaged in a passing action for about an hour, de Guichen concentrating in particular on the British van. When that had passed the French rear, he ordered his fleet first to tack together to avoid being weathered, and then to turn on to the same course as Rodney. As night fell the French drew ahead. British losses on this occasion were 47 killed and 113 wounded. Next day the two fleets were well out into the Atlantic, with the British some six miles astern. Two of Rodney's ships were in danger of sinking, and the *Conqueror*, Rowley's flagship, was about to lose her mainmast. Rodney sent all three back to St Lucia and took the rest of his fleet to Barbados. In his report he wrote: 'The enemy stood to the northward with all the sail they could possibly press, and were out of sight on the 21st inst. The condition of his Majesty's ships was such as not to allow a longer pursuit'.[22] De Guichen returned to Martinique, his fleet being down to six days' provisions.

In the course of the fighting, de Guichen's son had been killed, and in his grief and with the stress of having been constantly in the presence of the enemy over a long period, he broke down under the strain, and applied for his recall: 'The command of so large a fleet is infinitely beyond my capacity in all respects. My health cannot endure such continued fatigue and anxiety'.[23] He was, at least, unlike his opponent, able to count on his subordinates, praising his officers' conduct in all three actions. If tactically de Guichen might be said to have had marginally the best of the three encounters, Rodney could justly claim that, over all, his was the strategic victory in preventing de Guichen carrying out his plans for an assault on Barbados and St Lucia.

21 Mahan, *Navies in the War of American Independence*, p.144.
22 Mahan, *Navies in the War of American Independence*, p.144.
23 Mahan, *Navies in the War of American Independence*, p.145.

Rodney might have been enthusiastic about the effect of his conducting the last two battles from a frigate, but the private account which Young sent to Middleton portrayed a rather different aspect of the matter:

> I have said in my letter that I made signals. This was settled with the admiral after he left me, to make such signals as I saw necessary for the good of the service; which signals I was to show him by hanging them out at where they were to be made; and continued so doing until I saw him blunder, and then I wrote him that I would not be responsible for errors, as I had his flag to defend as well as make signals, but that I would repeat any signals he made and give him any information I could.

Rodney, Young complained, had left the flagship in 'a confused state' and he did not approve of his going into the *Venus*: 'His being in the frigate was of no service, as he always kept to leeward of our line. The enemy being to windward, he could never be a judge of it; but at last, I got him persuaded to keep between us, which he attended to the last encounter'.[24]

The three engagements had taken their toll of Rodney's fleet, as Young reported in his next letter to Middleton on 24 June:

> Our squadron is in a distressed situation; the *Cornwall* sunk in the Carenage, the *Fame* ordered to share the same fate, from their leaks; and not the smallest possibility of disposing of them otherwise. The *Boyne* may be saved; but this I can with certainty assure you of, if you do not get home the *Princess Royal, Albion, Suffolk, Magnificent, Vigilant, Trident, Stirling Castle, Elizabeth* and *Grafton* – they will in four months share the fate of the two former, who are now totally lost. What Admiral Parker did respecting those ships last hurricane months, by keeping them in this country, he is to answer for; but we have found a nominal squadron only.[25]

Rodney might have had a better chance of forcing a decisive result if the reinforcements which he was expecting had arrived. Commodore Walsingham, with five ships of the line, was windbound for three months at Torbay. Instructions for three more to be sent down from the North American station went astray, and it was not until April that they were finally sent, arriving on 17 June. Meanwhile a potentially decisive reinforcement was on the way to join the enemy; a fleet of 12 Spanish ships of the line sailed from Cadiz at the beginning of May, escorting a convoy with a large force of troops. The news of the departure of this fleet reached Rodney in time for him to come out to look for it, but its commander, Don José de Solano,

24 Laughton (ed.), *Letters and Papers of Charles Lord Barham*, Vol.I, pp.61-62.
25 Laughton (ed.), *Letters and Papers of Charles Lord Barham*, Vol.I, p.62.

pursued a more northerly route than was usual, and was able to effect a junction with de Guichen unmolested. It proved, however, not to be such a valuable reinforcement after all. Solano's crews were wasted with disease, and provisions were running low. His orders were to go to Cuba, and instead of supporting a French initiative against British islands he demanded that de Guichen escort him towards his destination. De Guichen did so, and then proceeded to Cap Francais in Haiti, where he found pressing appeals that he sail to North America to support the war there. However, his orders were to sail for Europe before the beginning of the hurricane season, and in mid-August he put to sea with part of his fleet for Cadiz, leaving 10 ships of the line at Haiti.

At home, Sandwich had been obliged to find a new commander for the Channel Fleet when Hardy died on 18 May 1780. Barrington was his first choice, but he refused the command, and instead Admiral Francis Geary was appointed, Barrington agreeing to serve as second-in-command. There was continued anxiety about the threat from the Combined Fleet. In June, Geary cruised off Ushant until receiving orders to send part of his fleet into the Atlantic to seek two enemy squadrons that had been reported. A Council of War aboard his flagship decided, however, that the fleet should not be separated, and that it should cruise off Cape Finisterre. In August, Córdova emerged from Cadiz, and succeeded in capturing all but two or three of a large convoy destined for the West Indies. It was a catastrophic setback; apart from the military consequences, it had a major political impact in scuppering secret contacts with Spain intended to lead to peace talks. Geary brought the fleet home in August; his health was breaking down, and since Barrington refused to take the fleet to sea in his absence, a successor had to be found. This was Vice Admiral George Darby, who sailed on 12 September to take up a position in the Bay of Biscay to try to prevent the junction of the French and Spanish fleets. There was a brief contact with de Guichen's squadron as it returned to Europe from the West Indies, but nothing came of it, and the Channel Fleet returned home on 21 December.

8

Charleston

Throughout 1779 Germain had been pressing Clinton to launch an attack on Charleston. A major effort in the south would, he hoped, enable the restoration of British authority in Georgia. There were other apparently persuasive reasons for choosing this sector for an offensive. The Carolinas were sparsely populated; there were said to be a substantial number of loyalists there calling for action; and the climate was suitable for a campaign during the winter months. In addition, Germain believed that a successful offensive there would release the valuable indigo and tobacco production to be sent to England which might very well pay for the cost of the expedition.[1] On the other hand, of course, the dispatch of a significant force to the south meant weakening the British army in New York, which would be directly contrary to the policy of concentration which Clinton was applying. Germain, however, whose opinion of Clinton continued to deteriorate, brushed this aside.

Clinton, who was always inclined to pessimism, had grave reservations. There had, in fact, been no real activity on the part of either army in the northern colonies for the best part of a year, but in July 1779 Washington launched a successful attack on the British post at Stony Point. This was followed up by the capture of the post at Paulus Hook in the following month. Neither these, nor the series of British raids on communities as far south as Virginia, affected the strategic situation, although the latter had caused heavy losses of property and terrorised the civilian populations in the areas affected.

Clinton expressed his reluctance in a series of letters to Germain. He was personally sceptical about the level of support to be expected from the loyalists in the Carolinas:

> I have as yet received no assurances of any favourable temper in the province of South Carolina to encourage me to an undertaking where we must expect so much difficulty... The small force which the present weakness

---

1 Valentine, *Lord George Germain*, p.366.

of General Washington's army would enable me to detach might possibly get possession of Charleston...but I doubt whether they could keep it... [the move]... would reduce me to the strictest defensive in this country.[2]

This was in April 1779. Germain's response was a blunt appeal to Clinton's sense of duty:

In times like these every officer, every subject, is called upon to stand forth in the defence of his sovereign, and of his country; and if a general declines the service because the force he commands is not adequate to his wishes, or may not enable him to extend his offensive operations with that rapidity he might expect, by whom is this country to be served in dangerous and critical situations?[3]

Mackesey has calculated that in the autumn of 1779 Clinton had all told some 32,000 troops under his command, of which some 27,000 were fit for service.[4] These were, however, scattered over a wide area, in spite of Clinton's desire to concentrate his forces, because there were a large number of points between Nova Scotia and the Bahamas which he was required to defend. Such a total might well be enough for him to take offensive action if, and only if, the British had effective command of the coastal waters of North America, and sufficient logistical resources to keep their widely separated armies properly supplied.

Very reluctantly, Clinton gave in to Germain's pressure, and began assembling a force with which to descend on Charleston. A combined operation of this kind called for the fullest cooperation with the naval commander and this, having regard to the latter's personality, might well not be forthcoming. Vice Admiral Mariot Arbuthnot was arguably one of the most obstreperous of all the quarrelsome admirals to be found at the top of the British Navy at this time. Born in 1711, he entered the navy in the late 1720s, was a lieutenant by 1739, and reached the rank of commander in 1746, when in command of the sloop *Jamaica* he distinguished himself by capturing two French privateers in the English Channel. In the following year he was appointed to the frigate *Surprise* as a post captain. During the Seven Years War, when in command of the *Portland*, he took part in Hawke's victory at Quiberon Bay. At the start of the American war he was Lieutenant Governor of Nova Scotia, holding the rank of rear admiral. In 1779 he was promoted to vice admiral and appointed to the command of the North American station.

2   Valentine, *Lord George Germain*, p.367.
3   Mackesy, *War for America*, p.339.
4   Mackesy, *War for America*, p.339.

Mariot Arbuthnot. Etching signed and dated by H.B. Hall, Morrisania, 1874. (Anne S.K. Brown Collection)

It has been said that rather than being a centre of naval activity deserving of having the best admirals, the North American station was a strategic backwater where only small forces of ships of the line were maintained; 'what was needed there was primarily an experienced naval administrator to run the immense logistical effort required to support the army'.[5] Arbuthnot was not an easy personality, being described as 'a coarse blustering, foulmouthed bully … destitute of even a rudimentary knowledge of naval tactics'.[6] Rodger however takes a different view, describing him as a man of initiative who was not frightened of taking big decisions, while Mackesy said of him that he 'was a rough old diamond who would not have been appointed to the command in ordinary circumstances,' adding that he wrote 'in a style so muddled as to make his dispatches obscure and ambiguous'.[7]

Arbuthnot was certainly careful to keep on the right side of the First Lord, to whom he wrote gushingly if somewhat incoherently on becoming a rear admiral:

> Words cannot convey the sentiments of my heart for your condescending goodness … Your Lordship's hand first lifted me into the world as a captain may I never forfeit it by any means one I am sure will always stand by me namely a grateful heart for favours received from a nobleman who could have no other inducement by his assistance to a man but who he conceived would endeavour to merit it by a faithful discharge of his duty.[8]

There is no doubt that Arbuthnot was always quick to take offence, and was always ready to take any dispute into a long-lasting feud, and his relationship with Clinton was generally very bad indeed. On the other hand, the King was impressed with

5   Rodger, *The Insatiable Earl*, pp.283-284.
6   Valentine, *Lord George Germain*, p.365.
7   Mackesy, *War for America*, p.341.
8   Tilley, *The British Navy and the American Revolution*, p.164.

him, describing him as 'a judicious as well as zealous officer,' and being especially pleased with the way in which, having set off for America, he proceeded first to the Channel Islands to deal with an attempted French invasion of Jersey.[9]

Sir Henry Clinton had been commander-in-chief in North America since Sir William Howe had returned to England in 1778, having previously served as second-in-command. Born in 1730, Clinton was brought up in New York in a family with aristocratic connections. At the age of 19 he came to England, and joined the army; during the Seven Years War he served as aide-de-camp to Prince Charles of Brunswick, and gained a reputation for gallantry in action. When he came to America as second-in-command he grasped, as Howe did not, that the proper strategic objective was the enemy's army, and not merely the occupation of territory. To inflict a decisive blow, the army must be sufficiently strong, and as commander-in-chief Clinton pressed constantly for reinforcements. In May 1779 he had, according to the Colonial Office return, 47,661 men under his command; but this was not his combat strength, as the figure included all those sick and injured and even those held by the enemy as prisoners, which Clinton pointed out. This did not go down at all well with Germain, who wrote: 'I do not like Clinton's dispatches as well as I had expected; he is magnifying the force of the rebels and diminishing his own by the new fashioned way of computing his army by the number of rank and file fit for duty'.[10] Clinton did not enjoy a great deal of political support in England, although the King generally approved of him. He was a reasonably competent commander, though lacking in inspiration. His was a mission that was beyond his military ability to carry out successfully with the limited resources available to him.

Clinton and Arbuthnot had intended that the proposed operation against Charleston should take place in the autumn of 1779, and at this time were working quite well together, as Arbuthnot observed in a letter to Sandwich of 19 September. Clinton, he wrote, 'has hitherto coincided with every idea of mine, and the utmost harmony subsists between us'.[11]

The plan for a southern expedition had to be put on hold due to d'Estaing's appearance in North American waters, and emergency steps had to be taken to deal with the threat. Arbuthnot reported on 30 October that in order to defend New York, he 'set about sinking ships on the bar of this place, and using every method I could think of to prevent him from entering this harbour'. In the same letter, he described another, more controversial decision which he and Clinton had taken:

9   Barnes and Owen (eds), *Private Papers of John, Earl of Sandwich*, Vol.III, p.129n.
10   Valentine, *Lord George Germain*, p.335.
11   Barnes and Owen (eds), *Private Papers of John, Earl of Sandwich*, Vol.III, p.135.

Under these circumstances it was not possible to give the smallest assistance to Rhode Island, which must inevitably have fallen if attacked, and from which place is no retreating; and after seriously reflecting on the consequences of capturing so great a part of the Kings troops and a large quantity of military stores, both the General and myself agreed in the measure of withdrawing the garrison.[12]

When news arrived of d'Estaing's return to Europe, Clinton and Arbuthnot could resume planning for the expedition to Charleston. This finally sailed from New York on 26 December. Violent gales off Cape Hatteras dispersed the fleet before it was able to concentrate off Savannah as planned. In the course of these gales several transports were lost, with most of the siege train and horses. The losses were made good by the arrival of mortars and ordnance stores from St Kitts, and the navy assisted by landing and manning 45 guns. The first landing was made on Johns Island, south of Charleston on 11 February. Moving with great caution, Clinton then slowly crossed to James Island, along the Ashley River, to the west side of the city. By the end of March he was able to cross the river there and now stood on the same peninsula as Charleston, where he began to put in hand the necessary siege works. He was opposed by Major General Benjamin Lincoln who commanded a force of some 6,000 men, including a reinforcement of 1,500 Continental troops sent to him by Washington from Virginia and North Carolina. Of Lincoln it has been written that as a soldier he 'had all the traditional virtues of a New Englander – reliability, sobriety and common sense'.[13] He had been in command in the Southern Department since the end of 1778 where he had enjoyed mixed fortunes in the engagements with British forces in Georgia. In particular he had led the unsuccessful attack on Savannah in the autumn of 1779.

When Clinton landed his army to begin his careful advance on Charleston, Lincoln was faced with a dilemma. He could see that he had little chance of successfully withstanding a siege, and that the correct military decision would be to pull out of the city. If he did so, however, the consequence might well be that South Carolina would make a separate peace with Britain. While he hesitated, Clinton sent a force around Charleston and invested the place. Lincoln rejected Clinton's first demand that he surrender, and also the second, made on 9 May; but the following day the inhabitants insisted that he accept the British terms, and on 12 May Lincoln capitulated, surrendering some 6,000 troops and 300 guns, together with five ships. Among those taken were seven generals, in what was the greatest victory of the war for the British army. It appeared to have ended, for the

12   Barnes and Owen (eds), *Private Papers of John, Earl of Sandwich*, Vol.III, p.137.
13   Clifford K. Shipton, 'Benjamin Lincoln: Old Reliable' in George A. Billias (ed.), *George Washington's Generals and Opponents* (New York: William Morrow & Co, 1969), p.193.

time being, American resistance in South Carolina, and Clinton sailed from New York on 8 June, leaving Lord Cornwallis in command in the south.

Clinton left Charleston in an optimistic frame of mind, believing that South Carolina and Georgia had now been securely regained. Before departing, he wrote on 30 May to William Eden, a private adviser whom Lord North particularly trusted, setting out the position as it then appeared to him:

> If a French or Spanish fleet does not interfere, I think a few works if properly reinforced, will give us all between this and Hudson's River... I leave Lord Cornwallis here in sufficient force to keep it against the world, without a superior fleet shows itself, in which case I despair of ever seeing peace restored to this miserable country.[14]

The war had already lasted five years; the fighting on land was now being conducted on both sides with increasing barbarity, and it is no surprise that war weariness prompted many American patriots to fear the worst. The loss of Charleston led many to believe that in the South at any rate the war was as good as lost. In June, there was a widespread rumour that the Continental Congress was preparing to make peace, and would as a term of the settlement abandon Georgia and South Carolina to Britain. The Congress moved at once to put paid to talk of this kind by passing unanimously on 3 June a resolution:

> That this Confederacy is most sacredly pledged to support the liberty and independence of every one of its members; and … will unremittingly persevere in their exertions … for the recovery and preservation of any and every part of these United States that has been or may hereafter be invaded or possessed by the common enemy.[15]

Although Clinton had been, before he left for New York, very hopeful of the position in the South; he left behind him a local commander who was rather more offensively minded than he could have wished. The relationship between the two men had steadily declined. It was Cornwallis's third tour of duty in North America, and he had returned there in the expectation that he would succeed Clinton in the chief command. Clinton, too, had been expecting this, believing that his request for relief would now be favourably received. He was still waiting for a reply to this when the Charleston campaign opened, but as Clinton observed, Cornwallis began increasingly to behave as if the post was already his. When in due course Clinton's resignation was not accepted, Cornwallis became thoroughly disenchanted, and the discord between them steadily intensified. Being left in

14   J.R. Alden, *The American Revolution* (New York: Harper & Row, 1954), p.232.
15   Alden, *American Revolution*, p.232.

sole command in the South, however, cheered Cornwallis up, and for a while he executed Clinton's orders efficiently. He reported to him at the end of June that a number of engagements had 'put an end to all resistance in South Carolina'.[16]

It was a premature judgment; in August Horatio Gates advanced with an army of 3,000 men. Cornwallis's response was immediate and characteristic; he moved out at once at the head of a force of 2,400 men to intercept him. They met at Camden on 16 August; Cornwallis won a stunning victory, shattering the American army, whose commander, riding a particularly fast horse, escaped, not stopping until he reached Charlotte in North Carolina after a journey of some 60 miles.

The victory enabled Cornwallis to put into effect a plan which he had been contemplating for some time, which was to advance into North Carolina. It was not a proposal which appealed to Clinton, but Cornwallis told him it was necessary to keep on the move, because if the army remained behind the fortifications of Charleston, both Carolinas would soon be lost.[17] On 8 September he began his march northwards, plagued not only by sickness among his troops but also by guerrilla activities on the part of rebel partisan bands.

Cornwallis crossed the border into North Carolina, and reached Charlotte on 25 September, where he paused to rest his troops after their lengthy march. His further progress was, however, abruptly checked by news of a battle fought some 40 miles to the west at King's Mountain on 7 October, in which a force of loyalist militia under Major Patrick Ferguson had been effectively wiped out by a detachment of 900 rebels, including riflemen from Virginia and North Carolina and a group of 'over the mountain men' from East Tennessee. Cornwallis had, belatedly, sent up a battalion of regulars to support Ferguson, but recalled it because he was becoming anxious about the reports of rebel militia gathering around him. After hearing of the disaster at King's Mountain, Cornwallis retreated to Winnsboro in South Carolina which he made his headquarters for the winter.

Clinton, meanwhile, had wanted to establish a base in the area of Chesapeake Bay, and had dispatched Major General Alexander Leslie by sea to establish himself there. Cornwallis thwarted this move by hijacking Leslie's force, sending word to him to come to Charleston in order to reinforce his own army in South Carolina. With this addition to his strength, and his troops having largely recovered their health, Cornwallis was buoyant about his prospects, exulting that 'for the numbers there never was so fine an army'.[18] There was not a lot that Clinton could do about this, but he still wanted a base in Virginia, so he assembled a fresh detachment with orders to establish itself at Portsmouth, and placed this under the orders of Benedict Arnold, now a British brigadier general. The notion of a base

16   Hugh F. Rankin, 'Charles Lord Cornwallis' in Billias (ed.), *George Washington's Opponents*, p.205.
17   Rankin, 'Charles Lord Cornwallis', p.207.
18   Rankin, 'Charles Lord Cornwallis', p.208.

Charles, Lord Cornwallis. Colour stipple-engraving by Smith after Copley. (Anne S.K. Brown Collection)

on the Chesapeake was one, at least, in which Cornwallis and Clinton were of the same opinion.

For some time, it had been apparent that the Continental Congress was running out of resources, which obliged George Washington to adopt a largely passive strategy. In the winter of 1779-1780 his army had been encamped on Morristown Heights, where it blocked any British advance from New Jersey in the direction of Philadelphia. The route to New England was similarly covered by a force at White Plains, while on the Hudson River the fortifications at West Point were being constantly strengthened, but more than this Washington could not for the moment do, and throughout 1780 his small army remained at Morristown Heights. As an old man, he looked back at his strategy during that year: 'Time, caution and worrying the enemy until we could be better provided with arms and other means, and had better disciplined troops to carry on, was the plan for us'.[19] Like Clinton, he perfectly understood that it would only be by attaining command of the sea along the American coast that the war could be won, and for that he depended entirely on the French.

Rodney had annoyed Arbuthnot by writing to him, after his arrival in the West Indies, to express surprise that he had not been reinforced with ships of the line from North America. Arbuthnot wrote huffily that Rodney should have waited until he knew that he, Arbuthnot, had actually received orders to send such ships or until after Rodney himself had asked for them. What had happened was that the orders from the Admiralty had gone astray, not reaching Arbuthnot in due time. Peace between Arbuthnot and Rodney was for the moment duly restored, when the explanation was known, and Rodney wrote on 18 June with an account of his engagements with de Guichen. He also emphasised the condition of his ships, describing his fleet as 'crippled,' and reported the arrival of Solano's fleet in the West Indies.[20]

Arbuthnot had returned with Clinton to New York in June after the taking of Charleston. His readiness to take pen in hand when meeting with an apparent affront was soon to be seen. He had expected to find there his second-in-command, Commodore Francis Samuel Drake, but to his astonishment New York harbour was almost empty of ships. What had happened was that in Arbuthnot's absence an order had arrived from the Admiralty, which Drake had opened. It contained the direction to send the three ships of the line to the Leeward Islands. Since Drake had three at his disposal, and Rodney had already called for reinforcements from New York, he went off with them to join Rodney. Arbuthnot was furious, writing to Rodney on 25 June:

> I wish I could draw a veil over Mr Drake's conduct who having opened my dispatches from the Admiralty, instead of hesitating with respect to any order, or at least calling off Charleston, has abided by the latter, and very improperly proceeded to join you who I hope will keep him and send any other ship in his stead.[21]

Quite why Arbuthnot should have been so cross about all this is far from clear, since in his letter to Rodney of 25 April he referred to the orders which he had given to Drake to sail to join Rodney with the *Russell* and *Robust*.

However, Drake was evidently concerned that his decision to open the dispatch from the Admiralty might attract some criticism, since he sent on ahead of him a

19   James Thomas Flexner, *Washington: The Indispensable Man* (London: Little Brown, 1976), p.131.
20   Syrett (ed.), *The Rodney Papers*, Vol.II, p.575.
21   Syrett (ed.), *The Rodney Papers*, Vol.II, p.594.

letter explaining what had occurred, and why he thought that he should as soon as possible sail from New York to the Leeward Islands: 'Under these circumstances and the great necessity there appears to me for the *Russell's* service in the West Indies, from the particular strong manner of your wording your orders, I cannot presume to doubt the necessity of my proceeding immediately'.[22]

Rodney was not fortunate in the matter of reinforcements in the summer of 1780; in addition to the failure of the orders to Arbuthnot, the squadron of five ships of the line under Commodore Walsingham which had been wind bound did not reach the West Indies until July. Rodney therefore had to make the best of what he had, and in June began a blockade of Fort Royal, where there were five French ships of the line. His intention was to prevent a junction between them and the main French fleet at Dominica, or at least bring on a battle. A defensive measure such as this blockade was really all that Rodney could safely do, as he had written to Hyde Parker on 15 June:

> This junction is of such consequence as behoves me to be extremely cautious and to take care to act in such a manner with the remains of the shattered fleet under my command, that the British flag may not meet with disgrace, or his Majesty's islands fall a prey to the greatly superior force of his enemies in these seas.[23]

In fact, the threat was not as serious as Rodney supposed. Solano's fleet was still suffering from epidemic diseases which for the time being rendered it completely ineffective. In any case, Solano maintained his refusal to join in action against the Leeward Islands, while de Guichen intended to carry out his orders to go home before the start of the hurricane season. The one point in the West Indies about which Rodney felt there might be particular concern was Jamaica, and on 22 July as a precaution he sent Rowley there with 10 ships of the line to reinforce Sir Peter Parker. The possibility of a move by Solano was obvious, although Rodney thought that in practice there was little likelihood of a Spanish attack. This reinforcement would in any case ensure that the homeward bound convoy from the region could sail with a more than adequate escort, which would be composed of ships that it was necessary to return to England to refit.

22   Syrett (ed.), *The Rodney Papers*, Vol.II, p.480.
23   Syrett (ed.), *The Rodney Papers*, Vol.II, p.566.

9

Graves

The preparation of a squadron intended to serve overseas was not something that could easily be concealed. Long before it was ready to sail, news of what was planned would have reached the enemy, frequently in considerable detail. This applied to both French and British operations, enabling steps to be taken to counter what was planned. Sometimes, but not always, it was possible to keep the actual destination secret.

Thus, when preparations began in France to send a squadron, escorting a substantial expeditionary force, to North America, it was not long before the British Admiralty became aware of it. The work of fitting out the squadron had begun as soon as de Guichen had sailed for Europe in mid-August 1780. Command of the squadron was given to the Chevalier d'Arsac de Ternay. He enjoyed a considerable reputation in the French navy, not least due to the skill and enterprise he had displayed in getting the stranded ships out of the River Vilaine following Hawke's defeat of Conflans at the Battle of Quiberon Bay in 1759. He had also, before the Seven Years War ended, led a successful raid on Newfoundland with two ships of the line and two frigates.[1] The squadron which de Ternay was now to lead was to consist of seven ships of the line, two frigates and two smaller ships. The military force, which initially was planned to be of 8,000 men, would be under the command of the Comte de Rochambeau. Unfortunately, it was soon found that there was insufficient shipping readily available for such a large force, and in the end it was found necessary to reduce it by one third.[2]

The need to bring help to the American armies was seen as vital. By the middle of 1780, Washington had no more than 10,500 men with him in the north, while Horatio Gates, the newly appointed commander of the Southern Department, had only 8,000. However urgently Clinton might be calling for additional troops, those he already had certainly outnumbered the enemy to a considerable extent. As it

---

1   Jenkins, *French Navy*, p.141.
2   Dull, *The French Navy and American Independence*, p.190.

was, the decision to send de Ternay's squadron with Rochambeau's troops across the Atlantic set in motion a chain of events that was to prove crucial.

British awareness of the planned expedition naturally led to anxious consideration of the steps that should be taken to counter it. There was for some time considerable uncertainty as to its intended destination. At first it had been supposed that it was to go to the Indian Ocean. Thinking about this, the King wrote to Sandwich on 6 March:

> The more I reflect on the fleet now equipping at Brest under the command of M. de Ternay, the more I am led to fix on North America as the most probable object; every account from whence paints in the strongest colours the distress, factions, and every other calamity, is now got to so great a height that necessity might drive the step of submission, if some change is not soon effected.[3]

He concluded his letter with a call for boldness: 'By keeping our enemies employed, we shall perplex them more than by a more cautious, and consequently less active, line of conduct'.

On the following day the Cabinet agreed that six ships of the line should be sent to North America. There was, however, still some debate as to where they should actually go; on 11 March Germain was reporting to Sandwich, who had not attended the latest meeting, that many in the Cabinet thought that the squadron should go to Halifax, thinking that the French might be intending to launch a thrust at Quebec. On 14 March, however, the Cabinet decided that New York should be its destination, and that it should be composed of eight ships of the line.

Earmarked to command the squadron was Rear Admiral Thomas Graves, currently serving with the Channel Fleet. He was the second son of Admiral Thomas Graves and thus the nephew of Vice Admiral Samuel Graves. Born in 1725, Thomas Graves joined the navy at an early age and by the time that he was 18 had already become a lieutenant. It took him a further 10 years to progress to the rank of master and commander, but in 1755 he made post captain. In the following year, commanding the frigate *Sheerness*, 28, he encountered what he thought was a French ship of the line, but which was in fact an Indiaman, and he took avoiding action. As a result, he faced a court martial, which found that he ought to have identified the enemy vessel by engaging her. He was, however, acquitted of the grave charge of avoiding action 'by reason of negligence, disaffection or cowardice,' and was found guilty only of an error of judgment for which he was reprimanded.[4]

3   Barnes and Owen (eds), *Private Papers of John, Earl of Sandwich*, Vol.III, p.243.
4   Rear Admiral French Ensor Chadwick (ed.), *The Graves Papers* (New York: Naval History Society, 1916), p.lxxvi.

In spite of this setback to his career he continued in command of frigates throughout the Seven Years War, until, before it ended, he was sent to Newfoundland as governor, a post he held from 1761 to 1763. Thereafter, in the years of peace, he was captain of a guard ship in Plymouth harbour. During the first half of 1775 he sat in Parliament as the member for East Looe. When war broke out in 1775 he went back to sea, and was appointed to command the *Conqueror*, 74, in 1778. She was part of Byron's fleet which had been sent in pursuit of d'Estaing across the Atlantic. The *Conqueror* became separated from the rest of the fleet in the violent Atlantic storm which it encountered, and in which she was heavily damaged, before making her landfall in America and re-joining Byron's fleet, which subsequently proceeded to the West Indies. On 29 March 1779, Graves was promoted to Rear Admiral of the Blue. In June he was appointed to take charge of the large convoy assembled in St Kitts and with this he returned to England to serve in the Channel Fleet.

After receiving his appointment to the squadron for North America, Graves took up with Sandwich on 21 March an issue with which the latter was all too familiar:

> Your Lordship will pardon me for taking notice that there is only one frigate allotted to eight sail of the line going on foreign service. Frigates are not inapplicably called the eyes of the squadron; they certainly are the scouts and voice of it. To have but one eye is certainly too little; and have but one scout deprives you of half your active powers, since upon any second occasion you must either detach a capital ship, to the weakening a small squadron, or remain in a very uninformed state.[5]

His plea fell on deaf ears. So frequent were the further requests made to the Admiralty over so long a period for more frigates that it is surprising that orders were not placed sooner for additional construction to meet the demand, though of course there was then the problem of manning them.

When Graves next reported to the Admiralty, it was to convey his concerns about payments due to the crews of his squadron. He wrote to Philip Stephens, the Secretary to the Admiralty, on 7 April: 'There is a disposition in my ship's company to require two months advance before they go to sea. But if it is not within the Rules of the service I hope to be able to keep them within the bounds of their duty'.[6] Under the current legislation such a payment was indeed a seaman's due; next day, when Graves made the signal to put to sea, five of his eight ships failed to move. Their crews shut themselves up between decks, with their ports closed. Graves took the view that prompt and effective action was essential, as he explained to

5   Barnes and Owen (eds), *Private Papers of John, Earl of Sandwich*, Vol.III, p.245.
6   Chadwick (ed.), *Graves Papers*, p.8.

Stephens: 'In my opinion mutiny was to be suppressed at the instant, though it might cost some lives, and justice would then take her seat with propriety'.[7] Arming his officers, his marines, and those crew members who joined them, he acted on that opinion and suppressed the mutiny; 16 men were subsequently tried by court-martial and two were sentenced to 500 lashes, of which only half were inflicted. The King was impressed, writing to Sandwich on 10 April: 'The conduct of the Rear Admiral on this occasion shows that he is both a man of sense and of resolution'.[8]

Putting to sea, Graves got as far as Plymouth before he was wind bound. On 17 May he finally got away, with six ships of the line and the *Amphitrite*, 24, and reached New York on 17 July after what had been a swift passage. He

Sir Thomas Graves. Engraving by Conde after Northcote. (NYPL)

reported to Philip Stephens that his squadron had arrived 'in pretty good health,' except the *Prudent*, 64, which was suffering from fever and scurvy. Arbuthnot did not accept Graves's opinion about the condition of his crews, writing to the Admiralty that the squadron had arrived 'in a sickly state'.

In spite of the fast passage which he had made, Graves found he was being criticised for having delayed his progress in order to take a prize. This was the French Indiaman *Farges*, which reached New York eight days after the squadron, escorted by the *Amphitrite*. The incident occasioned a good deal of correspondence, with Graves seeking to defend himself to the Admiralty; the argument was still going on in the following year, when Graves was writing to Sandwich to express his concern about the enquiry into the matter which had been ordered. He was later mollified by a letter from Sandwich dated 3 May 1781, in which the First Lord reassured him:

7   Chadwick (ed.), *Graves Papers*, p.10.
8   Barnes and Owen (eds), *Private Papers of John, Earl of Sandwich*, Vol.III, p.246.

It was obvious to every person who knew anything of naval matters, and of your character as an officer, that you was incapable of delaying your progress by any advantage that might accrue to you; but it was necessary that your friends should have authentic materials in their hands to silence the malice of the disturbers of the public welfare. This was the sole object of the enquiry.[9]

It was a trivial matter; but it illustrates just how touchy admirals could be, and the extent to which Sandwich, like all First Lords, had to go in order to satisfy them.

While Graves was making his way across the Atlantic, Sandwich wrote to Arbuthnot to commend him for his part in the taking of Charleston. It was a very upbeat letter:

I am happy that at such a crisis as this our naval affairs in America are in hands that may be depended on. The reduction of Carolina is a most fatal blow to the rebel cause; if you can baffle the efforts making by France to revive their hopes in consequence of the reinforcements sent to them by M. de Ternay, this campaign in your part of the world will have been a glorious one indeed, and will, I am firmly persuaded, put an end to the war … I flatter myself that when you are joined by Admiral Graves, you will be master of the American seas without wanting any further assistance.[10]

Sandwich was still experiencing difficulty in finding enough ships to meet the needs of each of the theatres in which the navy was engaged, and both in North America and in the West Indies, the local commanders in chief were at a numerical disadvantage.

Nevertheless, during 1780, with de Guichen confining his operations to the Caribbean, the Royal Navy enjoyed an effective command of the waters around the American coast. At one time no less than 27 frigates were operating there, and faced no opposition, enabling them to move at will, to raid or occupy such points on the coast as they chose. It was a time of the greatest danger to the American Revolution. Benjamin Lincoln's fear, that if he abandoned Charleston the state of South Carolina might make a separate peace, was not without foundation. Each of the states was sovereign; Congress could only request, not command, and any state could withdraw at any time. Washington was painfully aware that his troops were practically starving and in rags, and was amazed that their privations had not led to a general mutiny. He had though, high hopes of the effect of the arrival of de Ternay and Rochambeau.

9   Barnes and Owen (eds), *Private Papers of John, Earl of Sandwich*, Vol.III, p.270.
10   Barnes and Owen (eds), *Private Papers of John, Earl of Sandwich*, Vol.III, p.248.

10

Rodney at New York

While en route to North America, de Ternay encountered a British squadron under Commodore William Cornwallis. This force had been escorting a convoy from Jamaica bound for England as far as Bermuda, and was returning to its station when sighting de Ternay. Cornwallis had two 74s, two 64s and one 50-gun ship, so de Ternay's seven ships of the line (one 80, two 74s and four 64s) represented a much superior force. At this point two of de Ternay's ships were with his convoy, with the rest to windward of it, so in order to concentrate his force he stood on across the bows of the British before hauling his wind and standing towards Cornwallis. One of the latter's ships, the *Ruby*, 64, had become detached to leeward, so Cornwallis wore his squadron and formed line of battle before edging down towards the *Ruby*. De Ternay could still have cut her off, but bore up, allowing the *Ruby* to re-join Cornwallis. He then tacked, and there was a short engagement at long range as the two squadrons sailed on parallel courses. However, with the odds so heavily against him, Cornwallis declined to close and de Ternay went on his way. He was, however, the subject of criticism from some of the officers of his squadron for his caution. That said, Mahan notes that de Ternay had to take account of the possibility that he might face a superior force when he reached America, and he had also to consider the safety of his own convoy and the 6,000 troops which it carried. These considerations would certainly seem to justify his avoiding a close action.[1]

Accordingly, de Ternay proceeded to Newport, Rhode Island, where he was able to land Rochambeau and his troops on 11 July. This powerful reinforcement for the American Revolution was obviously a crucially important and entirely new factor in the balance of forces; but, in the event, it was to be a long time before Rochambeau's army, or de Ternay's squadron, achieved very much. Washington entirely grasped their potential, which would be enormous if – but only if – the allies could make effective use of sea power. In his first letter to Rochambeau he had spelt this out: 'Whatever efforts are made by the land armies, the navy must

---

1   Mahan, *Navies in the War of American Independence*, pp.155-157.

have the casting vote in the present contest'.[2] It was a principle which he set out again, in a memorandum to the French general dated 15 July 1780: 'In any operation, and under all circumstances, a decisive naval superiority is to be considered as a fundamental principle, and the basis upon which every hope of success must ultimately depend'.[3]

De Ternay's arrival with Rochambeau called for speedy action by the British if the French were to be prevented from establishing themselves in a defensive position at Newport. Clinton could see this perfectly clearly; he had known for some time that the French fleet was expected, and one way of dealing with the problem would have been to pre-empt it by reoccupying Rhode Island before the French arrived. Alternatively, Arbuthnot might have put to sea in order to intercept de Ternay, though the size and condition of his squadron was such for that to be an extremely risky course. Failing either of these, a promptly mounted combined operation might catch the French before they had been able effectively to fortify their position at Newport. As it was, Clinton did not move quickly enough to anticipate the French at Rhode Island, and Arbuthnot, who was awaiting the arrival of Graves, failed to keep an adequate watch off Newport, which enabled de Ternay to slip in unmolested. The arrival of Graves with six ships of the line gave Arbuthnot numerical superiority, and he was able to get to sea after only six days. At first, the admiral had agreed with Clinton that troops should be embarked and moved up Long Island Sound, to be ready for an assault after the fleet had carried out a reconnaissance of Narragansett Bay. This might have been promising, since an urgent strike was what was required. However, although Arbuthnot and Clinton had managed to cooperate effectively in the taking of Charleston, the relationship had now largely broken down again, and there was an atmosphere of mutual mistrust. When Clinton came to embark his troops, it was found that the transports lacked water, Arbuthnot having used it to replenish his fleet. By the time this had been remedied, the wind changed, and the transports only reached Long Island Sound on 27 July.

Arbuthnot now told Clinton that there was no chance of a successful attack on Newport, which the French had been able strongly to fortify, and the fleet could not provide a siege train; in addition, the French had been reinforced by American militia and artillery. Discouraged, Clinton gave up the idea; but then an officer who had been to Newport under a flag of truce reported that in his opinion the harbour could be forced if troops were landed on one side of the entrance. Arbuthnot suggested a meeting, and Clinton hastened to the rendezvous, but when he arrived he found only a note from Arbuthnot to say that he had sailed to intercept de Ternay, who was believed to have put to sea. This turned out to be a wild goose chase. By now the chance had finally gone for a successful assault on

2   Chadwick (ed.), *Graves Papers*, p.lii.
3   Chadwick (ed.), *Graves Papers*, pp.l-lii.

Newport, and Rochambeau was thus able to winter there undisturbed. De Ternay was, however, now a sick man, and he died at Newport on 15 December, and was succeeded temporarily by the Chevalier des Touches. This wasted opportunity on the part of the British was not the first time that the cause of American independence had benefited from a clash of personality; and it would not be the last.

Predictably enough, Clinton and Arbuthnot blamed each other. The admiral wrote on 20 August to Sandwich with an angry and not altogether accurate account of what had transpired:

> Sir Henry Clinton's amusing me with his situation in Huntington Bay, with his troops in transports and aides-de-camp dancing backwards and forwards with reports of intelligence with respect to the enemy, kept me in the constant hope of an eclaircissement one way or other, till time slipped from under my feet and obliged me at last to retire to Gardiner's Island Bay, as my public letter will inform your Lordship, after loitering away my time 19 days to no purpose. I am at last honoured with a letter from the General informing me that he has given over all thoughts of attacking the enemy.[4]

For his part, Clinton by now cordially detested Arbuthnot, and went so far as threatening to resign if the admiral was not removed. He was entirely aware of the extent to which his position depended on the fleet's ability to command the sea; without this, Cornwallis's position would become extremely vulnerable. This anxiety led him to intervene at the end of 1780 when Arbuthnot proposed to send Graves to the Leeward Islands with six ships of the line. Arbuthnot was prepared to accept the force of this protest, and Graves remained, but by December the admiral was telling Sandwich that his health would not permit him to remain in post much longer.

Each year a major factor in the naval strategy to be adopted in the West Indies was the hurricane season between August and October. It was during this period that a fleet hitherto engaged in the Caribbean should seek safer waters, and thus become available for operations off the coast of North America. Thereafter, once the winter set in there, the pendulum of convenience swung the other way, and all or part of a fleet active on the American coast might then usefully be transferred to the West Indies.

By the end of July Rodney had been able, correctly, to conclude that the French and Spanish fleets had given up any further offensive plans in the West Indies for 1780, and mindful of the approaching hurricane season he decided to put to sea, rather than risk being caught by a storm while at anchor or on a lee shore. He had already begun to consider the possibility of sailing north, reasoning, incorrectly,

---

4   Barnes and Owen (eds), *Private Papers of John, Earl of Sandwich*, Vol.III, p.249.

that de Guichen was likely to have departed in that direction. News of de Ternay's arrival there seemed to confirm the likelihood of this. Accordingly, when he sailed on 31 July he headed first to South Carolina, and then, to the astonishment of both friend and foe, went north and dropped anchor off Sandy Hook on 14 September with 14 ships of the line.

His arrival caused Arbuthnot extreme dismay; although he was commander-in-chief of the North American station, he was painfully aware that Rodney was senior to him. He 'showed plainly and with insubordination his wrath at this intrusion into his command, which superseded his authority and divided the prize-money of a lucrative station'.[5] Arbuthnot dashed off an angry letter to Sandwich on 5 October to protest at what he called Rodney's 'very extraordinary' conduct. Still apparently hopeful of persuading Rodney to go away, he wrote:

> I need not point out to your Lordship the necessity of putting a stop to such unlimited licentiousness, not only for the sake of good order and obedience, but it will not be possible for the Board to know how to proportion the stores and provisions for the different stations, of which this will prove a severe example. What other evil consequences will ensue is yet to be known; but I expect, if he means to return to the West Indies, he will carry away the greatest part of the useful frigates at his departure.[6]

Rodney, Arbuthnot thought, used the seniority of his flag improperly 'to confront and supersede wherever he chooses to be'.

The subject of this diatribe had, of course, much to say in justification of his unauthorised move, writing on 10 October to Sandwich:

> Your Lordship I am sure will not be surprised at receiving a letter from me at this place, when you learn the motives that have brought me here; and that nothing could have induced me to leave the West India station but the imminent danger of America, I am convinced your Lordship will believe.

Rodney did not offer the hurricane season as an explanation for his departure from the Caribbean, but went on to say that his move was prompted by concern that de Ternay would be reinforced by 10 or 12 ships of the line from de Guichen's fleet:

> Mr Graves was seen on the coast on 12 July with six sail of the line, and as I well know that Mr Arbuthnot had but three of the line, I concluded

5   Mahan, *Navies in the War of American Independence*, p.150.
6   Barnes and Owen (eds), *Private Papers of John, Earl of Sandwich*, Vol.III, p.252.

he must be overpowered if the French squadron joined. This consideration determined me to prevent so dire an accident if possible; and as it was impossible for his Majesty's Ministers to know the real situation of affairs, I was sure your Lordship and the rest of his Majesty's Ministers would approve of the conduct of an officer who had no other view than his Majesty's and the public service.[7]

He went on to add that he had thought himself to have arrived in time to attack Rhode Island, but was 'sorry to say the happy moment of destroying the French squadron had been lost, owing to the unhappy differences between the two commanders in chief'.

Arbuthnot remained extremely angry with Rodney, and kept up his complaints to Sandwich, writing on 11 November:

It gives me much concern that I have been necessitated to take up so much of their Lordships' time in representing the interference and proceedings of Sir George Rodney on the station. I have wished to avoid complaints, and nothing should have induced me to have troubled their Lordships with them but the necessity of the occasion. I believe I may safely pronounce that in no one instance has the conduct of Sir George Rodney been conducive to his Majesty's service, notwithstanding the powers he has assumed and exercised on this station.[8]

Rodney also continued his correspondence with Sandwich, offering his comments on various aspects of the way in which the war was being conducted:

I must freely confess that there appears to me a slackness inconceivable in every branch of it; and that briskness and activity which is so necessary, and ought to animate the whole, and bring it to a speedy conclusion, has entirely forsaken it … The evacuating Rhode Island was the most fatal measure that could possibly be adopted. It gave up the best and noblest harbour in America, capable of containing the whole navy of Britain, and where they could in all seasons lie in perfect security, and from whence squadrons in 48 hours could have blockaded the capitals of America, i.e. Boston, New York and Philadelphia. France wisely took advantage of our misconduct, and have used every endeavour to make it almost impregnable.[9]

7   Barnes and Owen (eds), *Private Papers of John, Earl of Sandwich*, Vol.III, pp.252-253.
8   Barnes and Owen (eds), *Private Papers of John, Earl of Sandwich*, Vol.III, p.259.
9   Barnes and Owen (eds), *Private Papers of John, Earl of Sandwich*, Vol.III, p.262.

As for Arbuthnot, Rodney loftily referred Sandwich to his official report to the Admiralty: 'I will not trouble you with my complaints relative to the conduct of Mr Arbuthnot. They are mentioned in my public letter to the Board; and I am convinced that any altercation between officers must give you concern'.[10]

This blazing row between two of his most senior admirals was naturally referred to the King; he, at any rate, was in no doubt which of them was in the right, observing on 1 December: 'Sir George Rodney's conduct seems as usual praiseworthy. I am sorry Vice Admiral Arbuthnot has lost his temper; the insinuation that prize-money has occasioned it seems founded'.[11]

That was the King's opinion; but Nicholas Rodger has pointed out that as a matter of law Arbuthnot had right on his side, and that Rodney's claim that his seniority gave him the automatic right to command wherever he pleased had no foundation. The commander-in-chief, he notes, commanded by virtue of orders from the Admiralty; it was possible for a more senior officer to be present but this did not interfere with the incumbent's command. Rodney's orders to command in the Leeward Islands were confined to that station, and he was not free to leave it whenever he chose. Orders to a commander-in-chief might contain an express power to enter another station, but, even then, he would not assume command there. Rodger concludes that in Rodney's character there was 'an element of gratuitous deceit' and that his smooth insinuations carried more conviction than Arbuthnot's blunt expostulations had.[12]

It should be noted, however, that Sandwich had seen nothing wrong in Rodney's going north; before the row exploded, he had written to him on 25 September to observe that it was impossible 'to have a superior fleet in every part; and unless our commanders in chief will take the great line, as you do, and consider the King's whole dominions as under their care, our enemies must find us unprepared somewhere, and carry their point against us'.[13]

The disputes between the respective commanders in chief in America meant, ultimately, that one of them had to go. The issue was one in which Sandwich and Lord George Germain were necessarily deeply involved. The latter was discontented with Clinton, and not particularly keen to please him by the removal of Arbuthnot, whose side of the arguments he had been hearing at first hand in a letter from the irate admiral:

> To say the truth my Lord, my task is not easy, nor my road pleasant; so many circumstances occur in the course of business, that I submit to only for peace: that keeps my command of temper so continually upon the

10   Barnes and Owen (eds), *Private Papers of John, Earl of Sandwich*, Vol.III, p.263.
11   Barnes and Owen (eds), *Private Papers of John, Earl of Sandwich*, Vol.III, p.264.
12   Rodger, *The Insatiable Earl*, pp.284-286.
13   Trew, *Rodney and the Breaking of the Line*, p.96.

stretch that I am apprehensive that I shall not able much longer to possess philosophy sufficient.[14]

At first sight it is a little surprising that Arbuthnot should have been corresponding with Germain direct, as well as with Sandwich who was his service chief, especially bearing in mind that the two Cabinet ministers were at loggerheads most of the time. Germain, however, as Secretary of State for the Colonies had an overall responsibility for the conduct of the war in America, though his authority stopped well short of being able to decide such an issue for himself.

In fairness to Rodney, it should be noted that he had always made clear to Sandwich the concern he felt for the situation in North America, about which he was continuously receiving information. On 31 July he had written to Sandwich to say that he thought Arbuthnot would need his assistance, and he was holding a large squadron of copper bottomed ships ready for this if necessary.[15] In reply, on 25 September, in the letter previously quoted, Sandwich had been at pains to endorse Rodney's willingness to assist: 'I am very glad that you tell me you shall hold yourself in readiness to assist in America, or where ever the enemy may endeavour to make their impression; for that is the only measure that can give us security'. Sandwich went on to say:

> I own I think that they are now gone to America, and am pampering myself with the idea of the glory you will acquire by pursuing them with your coppered ships and rendering their designs abortive. Our official letters will tell you what reinforcement is coming to you immediately, and also that Admiral Graves has positive orders to join you with five sail of the line as soon as the winter sets in.[16]

Furthermore, as Rodger points out in quoting from an order to Rodney from the Admiralty of the same date, the admiral was reminded that 'the whole of his Majesty's possessions on the continent of America' required the attention of all fleet commanders in those waters.[17]

In addition to writing letters home about their respective points of view, Arbuthnot and Rodney also engaged in some predictably acrimonious correspondence between themselves. Arbuthnot had taken his fleet to Gardiner's Bay in Long Island Sound, which was his idea of blockading de Ternay at Rhode Island. On 16 October he refused a suggestion from Rodney that he come to New York for a discussion with Clinton, adding angrily: 'Your partial interference in the

14   Valentine, *Lord George Germain*, p.369.
15   Barnes and Owen (eds), *Private Papers of John, Earl of Sandwich*, Vol.III, p.225.
16   Barnes and Owen (eds), *Private Papers of John, Earl of Sandwich*, Vol.III, pp.231-232.
17   Rodger, *The Insatiable Earl*, p.288.

conduct of the American war is certainly unaccountable upon principles of reason and precedence of service'.[18]

To this, Rodney politely replied on 19 October that he was sorry that he had given offence, which was not intended. He went on, however, to set out his position in terms which could not fail to enrage the combustible Arbuthnot:

> Your anger at my partial interference (as you term it), with the American War not a little surprises me. I came to Interfere in the American war, to Command by Sea in it, and did to do my best endeavours towards putting an end thereto. I know the dignity of my own rank, and the power invested in me by the Commission I bear entitled me to take the Supreme Command, which I ever shall do on every station where his Majesty's and the Public Service may make it necessary for me to go, unless I meet a superior officer, in which case it will be my duty to obey his orders.[19]

He added some sharp criticism of the way in which Arbuthnot had been conducting the affairs of his squadron. In the following week he sent copies of the correspondence between them to the Admiralty, deploring the fact that Arbuthnot's discontent was prompted by his concern over the potential loss of prize-money.

Arbuthnot did briefly make an attempt to be conciliatory in a letter of 2 November. Though reiterating that Rodney's conduct was 'in great measure obstructing the execution of the powers the King had vested in me,' he went on to trust that Rodney would impute his conduct 'to the novelty of your measures, and arising from no disrespect to your rank'.[20]

Rodney did not enjoy the weather in New York, adding a postscript to his letter to Sandwich of 10 October: 'This is a horrid climate,' and it was with considerable relief that he set off on 16 November to return to the Leeward Islands with 10 ships of the line. He wrote a farewell note to Clinton: 'God bless you, and send me from this cold country and from such men as Arbuthnot'.[21] When he put to sea, Rodney did not know that his original departure from the Leeward Islands had been extremely fortunate. In October, in a savage hurricane, three of the smaller ships he had left behind at St Lucia foundered, and three more were wrecked. To the west the *Thunderer*, 74, carrying the broad pennant of Commodore Walsingham, went down with all hands, and the *Stirling Castle*, with Captain Carkett, was wrecked on the Silver Keys. Three more 74s and a frigate were driven out to sea, dismasted, and only narrowly escaped destruction. However, Rodney's own fleet was itself

18   Spinney, *Rodney*, p.351.
19   Spinney, *Rodney*, pp.351-352.
20   Spinney, *Rodney*, p.355.
21   Spinney, *Rodney*, p.355.

badly damaged while en route southwards by a violent gale, and he only succeeded in returning to Barbados on 6 December.

In London the issues relating to the North American commands required a Cabinet decision; as a result of a bargain between Germain and Sandwich it was decided on 11 October to remove Arbuthnot and send him to Jamaica to replace Sir Peter Parker and to send another flag officer to take over the naval command in America. The Cabinet minute went on:

> If this arrangement, together with assurances of such a reinforcement of troops as can be spared from this country, does not induce Sir Henry Clinton to think that he can continue in the command, his Majesty though unwillingly does in that case permit him to resign his command to Lord Cornwallis.[22]

Although on this occasion Sandwich and Germain had been able to reach an agreement, the fundamental and ongoing struggle between them in the Cabinet continued to exercise a baleful influence on the direction of the war.

Sandwich, writing to Parker to explain the decision to relieve him, told him that it reflected no discredit on him, and that he would find the Board of Admiralty 'disposed to give you every proof of their approbation'. He went on to give him the reason for the move:

> The fact upon which this proposed arrangement is founded is the state of things in America between Sir Henry Clinton and Admiral Arbuthnot, who are under such violent animosities against each other that the very important service entrusted to them, and on which the fate of this kingdom very probably depends, cannot go on under their joint command.[23]

The extreme dissatisfaction felt around the Cabinet table about the proceedings of Clinton and Arbuthnot makes it surprising that such a situation should have been allowed to fester for as long as it did. Even after the decision had been taken, which Germain told Clinton would be of immediate effect, it was not, and Arbuthnot continued in post for the time being. Before he finally left, though, he was to be engaged in important action.

22   Barnes and Owen (eds), *Private Papers of John, Earl of Sandwich*, Vol.III, p.255.
23   Barnes and Owen (eds), *Private Papers of John, Earl of Sandwich*, Vol.III, p.257.

11

Hood

Sir Samuel Hood had been Commissioner of Portsmouth Dockyard since January 1778, and had been doing the job of getting the Channel Fleet to sea as efficiently as the grave shortage of naval supplies would allow. He was well thought of by the King, not least for the way in which he oversaw the arrangements for the young Prince William to enter the navy. Yet by the beginning of 1780 Hood was profoundly discontented. He saw his chance of a seagoing command beginning to slip away. As he set to work on his latest task, which was getting the squadron assigned to Graves ready for sea, his frustration burst out in a letter of 23 March to Sandwich in which he spoke of his 'painful feelings' at seeing others given favourable opportunities for distinction. He wanted, he said, to hoist his flag and be able to serve in the 'military line'.[1]

It was a First Lord's lot to receive an incessant flow of requests for promotions and appointments. Sandwich had the experience that was necessary for him to deal with this task effectively, as his biographer has noted:

> By the end of the American war he had been familiar with the Admiralty and the Navy for nearly 40 years. He had known even senior officers since their youth; he knew at least as much as they did about the people in the Navy, and a great deal more about its civil administration.[2]

When he received Hood's letter he dealt with it promptly and with characteristic firmness; there was no chance of a flag and in any case Hood was more valuable in his present post.

Hood had been, and remained, a loyal supporter of the administration, and in the light of this he felt that he deserved better. Naval officers were generally not shy when it came to seeking preferment, and Hood was no exception. Protesting

1   Colin Pengelly, *Sir Samuel Hood and the Battle of the Chesapeake* (Gainesville Florida: University Press of Florida, 2009), p.52.
2   Rodger, *The Insatiable Earl*, pp.173-174.

Sir Samuel Hood, Colour mezzotint by V. Green after Abbott. (Anne S.K. Brown Collection)

warmly at the injustice which he believed himself to have suffered, he wrote again on 25 and 26 March, to say that he was 'pained to the quick' at his treatment. Setting out his complaints in detail, he drew attention in particular to the fact that he had not been appointed to a colonelcy of marines, which others junior to him had achieved, and that he had not been given a commodore's position:

I have now served my Lord forty years, within a month, and in all that time I have never once been told I did wrong, but I have been honoured with many flattering testimonies of approbation from the Board at which your Lordship now presides ... I accepted the office I now fill, from a desire of giving accommodation to Government and to your Lordship (which I expressly said at the time) not conceiving it possible I should be forced to experience the very severe mortification of seeing junior officers brought forward to distinguished employments, when I was within four of the top of the list of captains. This my Lord is laying me by, and sorely afflicts me.[3]

An appeal to the King brought a sympathetic reply, with a Royal promise to use his best endeavours to see that Hood got a post. For the moment, however, there seemed no likelihood that Sandwich would change his mind, and Hood got on with the task of preparing Graves's squadron, a task which he said caused him to be 'worried from morning till night'. He wrote of his problems to his brother Alexander Hood, in which he described the way in which seamen were sometimes treated by captains at the start of a voyage:

When I have thought overnight I should have little to do next day; before daylight I have been informed of more than usual business... No sooner is the complement of a ship completed than such men as are not liked, are sent to the Hospital; and a demand made for more; and the poor devils of seamen are so turned from ship to ship, without the smallest consideration to them, that there is not a possibility of doing them justice respecting their wages.[4]

It was this kind of thing that created the mutinous discontent that Graves faced when he attempted to put to sea.

Hood could justly point out to Sandwich that he had served for a very long time. Born in 1724, he joined the Navy in 1741. He had served under Rodney as a midshipman when the latter was captain of the *Sheerness*, and followed him to the *Ludlow Castle*. As master and commander of the sloop *Jamaica* Hood served on the North American station, and then in the sloop *Lively*. With the outbreak of the Seven Years War he was made post captain, commanding first the *Grafton* and then the *Antelope*. Aboard her he fought a single ship action with the French *Aquilon*, battering her and driving her ashore in Audierne Bay. Later he commanded the *Bideford* and then, as captain of the *Vestal*, fought another distinguished single ship action against the French *Bellone*, which he captured. The *Vestal* later served under Rodney when the latter was in command of coastal

3   Pengelly, *Sir Samuel Hood and the Battle of the Chesapeake*, pp.52-53.
4   Dorothy Hood, *The Admirals Hood* (London: Hutchinson, c.1940), p.53.

operations in the Channel in 1759. During the peace Hood served as commander-in-chief on the North American station, flying his broad pennant as a commodore in the *Romney,* between 1767 and 1770. With the outbreak of the American war, he served in the Channel Fleet until in January 1778 he became Commissioner at Portsmouth, and Governor of the Naval Academy, a post which usually came at the end of a distinguished but not outstanding career. It was in that post that he had come into close contact with the King, who made him a baronet in 1778.

During the summer of 1778 the situation of the fleet in the Leeward Islands was causing a good deal of anxiety. The condition of its ships gave rise to the most serious concern, as Young's letters to Middleton continued to emphasise. On 28 June he wrote:

> I have pressed the Admiral, as much as my situation will admit of, to send all the leaky and crazy ships to England as soon as the enemy quits this country. I wish my Lord Sandwich would send out some more three decked ships, as they, if well-managed, are dreadful to the enemy.[5]

In addition, Young reported serious shortages of naval stores; the fleet was deficient in sails, cordage, masts, yards and anchors.

However, the gravest deficiency which was occupying Sandwich's attention was the need to find a successor to Hyde Parker, and in the postscript which he wrote to his letter of 14 July to Rodney he promised that he was giving the matter very serious consideration. He was under no illusion as to the difficulty of his task, given Rodney's behaviour to his senior subordinates. His propensity to fall out with them was much in Sandwich's mind, with the return to England of the indignant Hyde Parker, who was only with great difficulty restrained from publishing a pamphlet as a means of expressing his opinion of the conduct of his late commander-in-chief.

Looking for the ideal candidate was not made easier by what Sandwich termed the 'factious' conduct of some senior officers who, hostile to the administration, had made a point of refusing appointment at his hands. Reviewing those who might be suitable, Sandwich's first thought was that Vice Admiral George Darby might be the man; one particular concern was that if Rodney's health gave way, the appointee might have to take over command, and Darby was sufficiently experienced to be a safe pair of hands. On 23 July Sandwich wrote to him with an extremely diffident offer of the post:

> As it is my duty to employ officers of the best reputation on all important services, I would not fill up a station where an admiral of rank and distinguished merit is much wanted without knowing your sentiments,

5   Laughton (ed.), *Letters and Papers of Charles Lord Barham,* Vol.I, p.64.

and whether such service suited your ideas and situation. At the same time I desire to be understood that I do not mean to press this or any other service upon you ... The service in question is the going second-in-command to Sir George Rodney, the state of whose health is such that much must be left to the second-in-command at all times, and a great probability, from Sir George's infirmities, that the chief command will devolve soon on the next in rank to him.[6]

Darby, however, declined the post, though not on any 'factious' ground, so Sandwich had to look for an alternative. Vice Admiral William Drake seemed a possible choice, but on 22 August he too declined, on the grounds that his health might prevent him discharging the responsibilities of the post, writing to Sandwich:

I cannot express the high sense of obligation I feel for your Lordship's thinking of me as a fit person to serve in a station so important at this time. Nothing but the shattered condition of my constitution prevents my eager acceptance of your Lordship's kind offer.[7]

Thus thwarted again, Sandwich took a bolder course. Samuel Hood might still be only a post captain, but that could be remedied by promoting him to rear admiral in the next round of promotions. During his service he had worked closely with Rodney, and it appears that this was a decisive factor in choosing him as second-in-command, the assumption being that he was on good terms with the commander-in-chief. Accordingly, Sandwich wrote to Hood to offer him the post, a step which he took against the advice of Lord Mulgrave, who was just about his closest adviser; but he did have the approval of the Cabinet. He must have been astonished at the response which he received; on 16 September Hood wrote:

The very flattering offer of my flag and going to the West Indies I should have accepted with great joy and thankfulness some months ago; but now those bodily infirmities, with which I have been afflicted for near twenty years, are of late become so very heavy and severe that I have no spirits left and can scarce keep myself on my legs, and should only be the shadow of a flag officer.[8]

It was his duty, he said, therefore to decline the post and content himself with doing his duty as Commissioner 'for the short time I have left to live'. When he wrote this surprising letter Hood was 56 years old; he survived another 36 years.

6   Barnes and Owen (eds), *Private Papers of John, Earl of Sandwich*, Vol.III, pp.221-222.
7   Barnes and Owen (eds), *Private Papers of John, Earl of Sandwich*, Vol.III, p.227.
8   Barnes and Owen (eds), *Private Papers of John, Earl of Sandwich*, Vol.III, pp.228-229.

Pengelly suggests that the explanation for Hood's unexpected response is that it was a ploy to gain advantage for his brother Alexander, whom he hoped thereby to restore to the Admiralty's confidence. In his letter of refusal Hood had gone on to entreat Sandwich 'most humbly and earnestly' for the honour of his protection and favour to his brother Alexander.[9] Pengelly thinks it 'most likely' that Hood consulted his brother over the weekend before, on 18 September, writing to Sandwich:

> My Lord – feeling myself so much better than I was on Saturday, when I received the honour of your Lordship's letter of the 15th, and flattering myself that a warm climate will attend more to removing my complaints than any assistance I can get at home, I hope and trust I am not too late in signifying my very great readiness to accept my flag and to go to the West Indies at your Lordship's pleasure.[10]

Fearing that he might have missed his chance, Hood wrote again two days later to reiterate his willingness to go to the West Indies. He acknowledged that if the post had gone elsewhere, he had only himself to blame; but if it had not, he put forward the name of Captain John Walker to serve as his flag captain. Hood was not too late; his name appeared in the list of new rear admirals published on 26 September, which included Richard Kempenfelt and the younger Drake.

Sandwich wrote to Rodney on 25 September to tell him, in some detail, of the steps he had taken to identify suitable officers to join his fleet:

> It has been difficult, very difficult, to find out proper flag officers to serve under you; some are rendered unfit from their factious connections, others from infirmity or insufficiency; and we have at last been obliged to make a promotion in order to do the thing properly. Sir Samuel Hood is to have his flag and to bring out the next convoy to you … and with him and Admiral [Francis Samuel] Drake I hope everything will go on to your satisfaction.[11]

Sandwich added a reference to his interview with Hyde Parker; he hoped that he would follow the First Lord's advice 'and consider it as his interest to be quiet'.

Rodney received the news of Hood's appointment politely, writing to Sandwich to thank him for sending him 'so good a man'. To Hood, he wrote: 'I know of no one whatever that I should have wished in preference to my Old Friend Sir Samuel Hood'. He was, though, perhaps not as pleased with the appointment as

9   Pengelly, *Sir Samuel Hood and the Battle of the Chesapeake*, p.56.
10   Barnes and Owen (eds), *Private Papers of John, Earl of Sandwich*, Vol.III, p.229.
11   Barnes and Owen (eds), *Private Papers of John, Earl of Sandwich*, Vol.III, p.232.

these letters suggested; he is reported to have said privately: 'They might as well send me an old apple woman'.[12] The story is second-hand, at best; but if Rodney did make such a remark, it did not augur well for his working relationship with his new second-in-command. Hood was evidently not uniformly admired within the navy; Keppel wrote to Rodney on 10 November: 'I wish you joy of Sir Samuel Hood. It is impossible for me to say more than that'.[13]

It was to be some little time before Hood could set off for the West Indies, since he had to wait while the convoy which he was to escort was being assembled. David Hannay noted how tiresome a task this was:

> The difficulty of collecting the ships, the exacting demands of owners, the pigheadedness of skippers, the mere material toil of first collecting ships in roadsteads and then getting them out in the face of the tides and continually shifting winds, made the work as hard as it was thankless. Yet it had to be done …No English administration would have dared to subordinate the interests of trade to purely military considerations, as the French government could afford to do.[14]

It was a well-established and hugely important responsibility of the navy to provide merchant vessels with security from attack in time of war, by the organisation of convoys under the escort of warships. It was a priority even if at times it had an adverse effect on operations. The concept of providing an armed escort for vulnerable merchantmen is a simple one, but, for the reasons which Hannay identified, putting it into practice was far from simple, as had been amply demonstrated over the course of naval history. Although the protection afforded to merchantmen in this way was of crucial importance to their owners, not least because proceeding in convoy materially reduced insurance rates, neither they nor the captains of their ships made it easy for their protectors. At sea, the merchant vessels had great difficulty in keeping station, and frequently straggled, while they tended to be unresponsive to signals from the escort's commander, or obedient to the sailing instructions issued before departure. And as they approached their destination, they were frequently tempted to slip away with a view to selling their cargo before the arrival of the convoy brought down prices.

The war on trade was conducted not only by individual enemy warships, but sometimes also by whole squadrons, especially frigates, and all times by privateers operating under letters of marque, constantly on the lookout to snap up

---

12 Admiral Sir R. Hamilton (ed.), *Letters and Papers of Sir T. Byam Martin* (London: Navy Records Society 1903), Vol.I, p.2.

13 Spinney, *Rodney*, p.359.

14 David Hannay (ed.), *Letters Written by Sir Samuel Hood* (London: Navy Records Society, 1895), pp.xxi-xxii.

valuable prizes. These greatly increased the risk run by isolated merchantmen. For Great Britain, dependent on her seaborne trade, the threat was constant; the loss of individual ships was a serious matter, but the loss of an entire convoy was a national disaster.. A concern that everything possible should be done to ensure that convoys were unmolested was a recurrent preoccupation of the Cabinet and the Admiralty, and operational instructions, to the Channel Fleet in particular, frequently stressed the priority to be given to the protection of trade. Nevertheless, in spite of the continual losses, estimated at a total of 3,386 merchantmen during the course of the American war, the convoy system enabled Britain to maintain her seaborne trade, so that her overseas commerce increased even during the course of the war. As a result 'Britain was the only one of the warring nations involved in the American war to emerge from the conflict without serious financial problems and with her economy intact'.[15]

Hood, besides his flagship, the *Barfleur*, 98, took with him seven other ships of the line and four frigates as badly needed reinforcements for Rodney's fleet. The convoy which he was required to escort consisted of 118 ships of a total of 31,471 tons, carrying 801 guns and crews of 2,159 men. Managing such a considerable assembly of vessels required constant vigilance and above all patience. Hood's convoy was also carrying a large body of troops, and he was delayed as he waited at St Helens by the failure of their transports to arrive punctually. However, he finally got under way with his warships on 28 November, although even then a large part of the convoy was not able to join him, as he reported next day to Philip Stephens at the Admiralty:

> In the evening a great number of ships were seen coming from the Downs, which were mostly at anchor without us at daylight this morning, when I made the signal to weigh, and hoisted the topsails to quicken the masters of merchantmen on board for their instructions.[16]

At 10:00 a.m. the squadron put to sea, leaving some of the smaller vessels to hasten the convoy, for which he waited down Channel.

Meanwhile in the West Indies, while waiting for Hood to join him and with the French fleet reduced to four ships of the line, Rodney embarked on an attempt to recapture St Vincent. It did not go well. St Vincent was selected as a suitable target because reports suggested that it had been badly hit by the recent hurricane, that its fortifications were as a result in disrepair, and that the French garrison was few in number. Rodney subsequently told Sandwich that he 'put not the least confidence in the intelligence given by the interested inhabitants of the ceded islands',

15 David Syrett, 'The Organisation of British Trade Convoys During the American War 1775-1783', *The Mariner's Mirror* (May 1976), p.178.
16 Hannay (ed.), *Letters Written by Sir Samuel Hood*, p.7.

but he agreed to make the attempt as Vaughan seemed to believe the reports.[17] It was evident, though, that if the expedition were to succeed it must be mounted without delay, and on 9 December Rodney was at Gros Islet Bay in St Lucia to supervise the embarkation of the troops. Next day, however, the preparations unaccountably ceased. Young wrote to Middleton on 26 December to tell him what had occurred; he was sorry, he said, to be obliged to contradict Rodney's account of what transpired:

> His delineation of the expedition is very plausible, and although I detest detraction, yet I think it my duty to give you information of it, both as my friend, and a friend of our country, that we may not be imposed on by such plausible and pompous accounts.[18]

Young went on to explain what had been planned for the expedition, but then explained that 'an unsteady fit seized the admiral, and the whole was put a stop to, and orders issued accordingly'.

What had caused Rodney's sudden change of heart was not explained, but it only lasted 48 hours:

> On the 12th we were found in a different mood, and then the expedition was reassumed. Of course every effort was used to hasten it; but unfortunately, by its being put a stop to at first the secret was discovered, and the instant it was put *en train* again, the French inhabitants of the island gave information to the Marquis de Bouillé, and the Governor of Saint Vincent.[19]

De Bouillé, alerted to the threat, was able to supply the garrison with stores and powder. When the British expedition sailed, landing the troops on 16 December, it soon became clear that there had in fact been no hurricane damage, and that the citadel was intact and full of French troops. Vaughan ascended the position, but immediately realised that an assault would be fruitless: he therefore withdrew to the beach, and re-embarked his men.

Rodney's biographers hold different views of what to make of this fiasco. Peter Trew brushes Walter Young's account aside, commenting that there was no corroboration of this. David Spinney examines the question in some detail, noting Young's tendency 'to parade his own virtues and indispensability,' and remarking that his account would carry more conviction if General Vaughan had made any reference to Rodney's responsibility for the delay. Donald Macintyre, on the other

17   Barnes and Owen (eds), *Private Papers of John, Earl of Sandwich*, Vol.IV, p.145.
18   Laughton (ed.), *Letters and Papers of Charles Lord Barham*, Vol.I, pp.89-91.
19   Laughton (ed.), *Letters and Papers of Charles Lord Barham*, Vol.I, pp.89-91.

hand, puts it down to the sudden change in Rodney's fortunes having gone to his head.[20]

Young was certainly uncompromising in the picture he painted of Rodney, ending the letter previously quoted to Middleton by saying:

> I have many other matters to relate to you of inconsistency etc. etc, but shall suppress it on purpose to avoid giving uneasiness. I assure you I exert myself to the utmost of my power to keep our matters in order; at times they will get a little *outrée*, but in this I am obliged to you great men at home for, who have so poisoned my admiral that he really and *ipso facto* thinks and believes himself to be the very man you have represented him. God help us, how much mistaken you and he are![21]

20 Trew, *Rodney and the Breaking of the Line*, p.91; Spinney, *Rodney*, p.358; Donald Macintyre, *Admiral Rodney* (London: Peter Davies, 1962), p.160.
21 Laughton (ed.), *Letters and Papers of Charles Lord Barham*, Vol.I, pp.89-91.

12

Washington

For George Washington, 1780 had been a year of unrealised hopes. Looking back at the events that had transpired, he wrote on 20 December to Benjamin Franklin to summarise the campaign: 'Disappointed ... especially in the expected naval superiority, which was the pivot upon which everything turned, we have been compelled to spend an inactive campaign, after a flattering prospect at the opening of it'.[1]

Back in April the situation had indeed seemed extremely promising. The news which the Marquis de Lafayette had brought that the French government was sending Rochambeau and de Ternay to North America was a huge boost to Washington's morale. He determined to make the very most of the opportunity for a decisive stroke, and enquired about the possibility of getting in addition the support of de Guichen on the coast of North America. However, notwithstanding a letter written at Washington's instance by Lafayette to de Guichen, the French admiral resolutely adhered to his instructions to return to France at the start of the hurricane season, and he had departed on 16 August.

Washington remained in no doubt that it was in obtaining local naval superiority that was to be found the key to success. In a memorandum which he wrote for Lafayette to take with him to Rochambeau when he arrived, he set out his belief in the critical importance of sea power: 'In any operations, and under all circumstances, a decisive naval superiority is to be considered as a fundamental principle, and the basis upon which every hope of success must ultimately depend'.[2] In the detailed analysis which followed, Washington expounded his conviction that it was towards the capture of New York that the joint Franco-American operations should be directed. It was by some way the most important British position in North America; if it could be taken, such a victory would be a heavy blow to the enemy, and might be a means of ending the war by such a decisive stroke. As Washington saw it, the vicinity of New York was the location in which naval power might best be brought to bear.

---

1 Quoted in Knox, *The Naval Genius of George Washington*, p.70.
2 Knox, *The Naval Genius of George Washington*, p.64.

Disappointment with the proceedings of a major French fleet on the coast of North America was not a new experience for Washington; a similar situation had occurred in 1779 when he had prepared a substantial army to operate in conjunction with d'Estaing, only to learn of his return to France after the abortive attack on Savannah. Now, though, there was to be a French expedition intended specifically to operate in North America, and Washington made arrangements to meet with Rochambeau at Hartford on 20 September.

This conference, attended by Lafayette, de Ternay, and the Chevalier de La Luzerne, the French envoy to Congress, produced an agreement which acknowledged that there could be 'no decisive enterprise against the maritime establishment of the English in this country without a constant naval superiority'. For Dudley Knox, this discussion showed that Washington had 'the thoroughgoing support' of Rochambeau for his emphasis on sea power.[3] However, in fact, his French colleague was not being entirely candid in his exchanges with him.

Rochambeau had been instructed by his government to treat Washington as his commander-in-chief; but what the latter did not know was that this instruction did not mean that Rochambeau should allow this token acknowledgement of the command structure to lead him into any operation of which he disapproved. The French general had no present intention of moving from Rhode Island unless and until circumstances made this absolutely necessary. He had formed an unfavourable view of the size and state of Washington's army, and the situation of the colonists in general, as he reported home: 'Send us troops, ships and money, but do not depend on these people nor upon their means; they have neither money nor credit; their means of resistance are only momentary and called forth when they are attacked in their own homes'.[4] In particular, Rochambeau did not share Washington's conviction that the proper strategy was to mount an assault on New York. The Hartford agreement, such as it was, did restate that New York was the most important objective, and adopted in principle Washington's outline plan for its capture; but Rochambeau had already formed the view that an operation on the Chesapeake had greater possibilities.

At the conference it was agreed to apply to the French government for more assistance. An increase in the size of Rochambeau's army to a total of 15,000 men was called for, together with sufficient funds to enable the Congress to maintain an equivalent force. In addition, the French were asked to provide a fleet powerful enough to take control of the waters around the North American coast. Vergennes was already aware of Rochambeau's pessimistic appraisal, and these requests cannot have come as much of a surprise. Reviewing the situation, they gave him considerable grounds for concern. The situation of the Americans as it appeared

3   Knox, *The Naval Genius of George Washington*, p.70.
4   Flexner, *Washington*, p.139.

during the winter of 1780-1781 has been summarised by the American historian Edward S. Corwin:

> Despite the alliance, American independence had never been so near collapse. The British army now held New York, the Carolinas, and Georgia, while the British fleet ravaged the coast. Congress was bankrupt and forced constantly to resort to the most wretched expedients to obtain money or to dispense with its employment. The Continental Army, without pay, food or clothing and enlisted for short terms, was ever on the verge of dissolution. And the political situation was no better. With public spirit at the lowest ebb, the war had become throughout a great part of the country the desperate venture of a minority, sometimes a small minority.[5]

That winter called for the greatest determination from George Washington. Not only had he to cope with the sickening defection of Benedict Arnold, but also with the mounting discontent of his troops. This became so serious that it led to a mutiny over the right to discharge of men who had served for the three years of their original enlistment. The mutineers had some justification for their grievances, for they had been badly let down by the state governments. In the end, the problems were overcome; patient as ever, Washington published a general order calling on his army 'to bear present trials with fortitude, looking forward to the period when our country will have more in its power to reward our services'.[6]

He followed up his mournful letter to Benjamin Franklin by sending John Laurens, a member of his staff, to France to negotiate with the French government for the assistance which he regarded as indispensable. He set out in a letter of instructions what was required for the American Revolution to succeed. First, was money, and a lot of it. Loans were urgently needed which must be 'large enough to be a foundation for a substantial arrangement of finance, revive fallen credit and give vigour to future operations'. Such loans were essential if the next campaign was not to be the last. Washington went on:

> Next to a loan of money, a constant naval superiority on these coasts is most interesting. This would instantly reduce the enemy to a difficult defensive and, by removing all prospect of extending their acquisitions, would take away their motives for prosecuting the war. Indeed, it is not to be conceived how they could subsist a large force in this country, if we had the command of the seas to interrupt the regular transmission of supplies

5   Edward S. Corwin, *French Policy and the American Alliance* (Princeton New Jersey: Princeton University Press, 1916), pp.288-289.
6   Howard H. Peckham, *The War for Independence: A Military History* (Chicago: University of Chicago Press, 1958), p.158.

from Europe. This superiority, with an aid in money, would enable us to convert the war into a vigorous offensive. I say nothing of the advantages to the trade of both nations, nor how infinitely it would facilitate our supplies. With respect to us, it seems to be one of two deciding points, and it appears to be the interest of our allies, abstracted from the immediate benefits to this country, to transfer the naval war to America. The number of ports friendly to them, hostile to the British, the materials for repairing their disabled ships, the extensive supplies towards the subsistence of their fleet, are circumstances which would give them a palpable advantage in the context of these seas.[7].

This was a succinct account of the strategy to win the war, and it was clear to the French that it was on sea power that the emphasis must be placed. Vergennes was able to persuade Louis XVI to maintain and support the alliance financially, and by committing a fleet to the Americas. The request for additional troops made by the Hartford conference was, however, not accepted. When Laurens arrived in France he was able, by the force of his personality, and disregard of diplomatic protocol, to persuade the King to increase the commitments already agreed by giving a promise of greater financial support. By the time he arrived Laurens was pushing at an open door. He reached Brest on 9 March; on his way to Paris he met the Navy Minister, the Marquis de Castries, who was heading for the port, and frightened him into believing that the Americans were on the point of collapse, a suggestion which was supported by the mutiny in Washington's army.[8]

In one respect, the commitment of a new fleet was not entirely straightforward; it was complicated by the fact that Spain had joined the alliance against Britain, and the French were obliged to take account of Spanish interests. Quite apart from this general obligation, however, there was a practical reason for doing so, as Corwin pointed out:

> The Spanish marine was now in better fighting trim than it had been at any earlier period of the war. As between an ally able to contribute something to the common cause and one needing constant bolstering, good sense dictated the real work of the campaign should be undertaken in cooperation with the former.[9]

Writing to La Luzerne, Vergennes explained that the fleet to be sent had been ordered, at some time toward the approach of the following winter, to take part

---

7   Quoted in Gardner W. Allen, *A Naval History of the American Revolution* (New York: Houghton Mifflin, 1913), Vol. II, p.547.

8   Dull, *The French Navy and American Independence*, p.223n.

9   Corwin, *French Policy and the American Alliance*, p.294.

in operations on the coast of America in concert with the French and American generals. Its first objective, though, would lie in the Caribbean in support of the Spanish, who were making good progress with the siege of Pensacola in Florida.

In spite, therefore, of his very real misgivings about the military strengths and political effectiveness of his American allies, Vergennes remained determined to support them. Given the unpromising situation as it appeared, this was surprising. Edward Corwin put forward an explanation as to why 'to those Frenchmen who had come into contact with the American cause, that cause never appeared in more appealing light than at the moment of its greatest prostration'. He suggested that the reason for this was to be found in the personal ascendancy of Washington, 'whose integrity and fortitude naturally stood forth all the more strikingly as the other mainstays of the revolution fell away'.[10]

10   Corwin, *French Policy and the American Alliance*, pp.290-291.

13

Cornwallis

The retreat of Cornwallis's army to Winnsboro had been a fearful ordeal. He set out from Charlotte on 14 October, but was himself, like many of his men, almost at once struck down with fever. The march was conducted in appalling weather; it rained constantly, and the army lacked tents. Supplies were short. In particular, the sick and wounded suffered terribly as the march continued over bad roads and flooded streams. On its way the army was constantly harassed by small American detachments. In one more significant encounter Lieutenant Colonel Banastre Tarleton, the obnoxious commander of Cornwallis's dragoons and light infantry, fought an inconclusive engagement with an American force under Thomas Sumter on 27 November before the army finally settled down for the winter at Winnsboro. Even then there were frequent skirmishes with enemy forces which did not always end well, and Cornwallis faced continuing difficulties of supply, as well as the sickness of many of his troops.

Cornwallis was always a competent leader, and his spirits rose when he was finally joined in January 1781 by Leslie's force of some 2,500 men. He concluded that his best policy was to seek out and defeat the American Army of the South, now under a new leader, Nathanael Greene. Catching it, though, would be no easy task. Cornwallis secured his rear by leaving Lord Rawdon with approximately 5,000 men in garrisons at Augusta, Savannah, Charleston and Camden, as well as other posts in the hinterland of South Carolina. This left him with a force of about 3,200 men with which to deal with Greene; of these, some 2,050 were British and 450 German, with the rest being loyalist militia.[1]

Cornwallis had only the poorest intelligence about the enemy forces in the south, and much of the information reaching him was thoroughly unreliable hearsay. Greene had in fact split his army, sending a force under Daniel Morgan towards the key post in the Ninety Six district. Cornwallis detached Tarleton with about 1,100 men to deal with this threat; Morgan had about 1,000, and soon

---

1   Franklin and Mary Wickwire, *Cornwallis and the War of Independence* (London: Faber & Faber, 1971), p.252.

fell back with Tarleton in pursuit, coming up with him on 17 January at a position which Morgan had occupied at Cowpens. Characteristically overconfident, Tarleton suffered a crushing defeat, losing more than 700 men, killed, wounded and captured.

Cornwallis was utterly dismayed by the news of Cowpens, writing to Rawdon: 'The late affair has almost broke my heart'.[2] It cost him almost all of his light troops, without which his subsequent campaign laboured under a serious handicap. Tarleton, of course, admitted no blame for his defeat; vain as ever, he was offended by hearing of widely-uttered reproaches of his handling of the battle. He insisted that Cornwallis should expressly approve his conduct, threatening that otherwise he would retire until it could be considered by a court martial. Cornwallis could not afford to lose him, and whatever he might privately have felt, wrote a letter which satisfied Tarleton:

> You have forfeited no part of my esteem as an officer by the unfortunate event of the action of the 17th. The means you used to bring the enemy to action were able and masterly, and must ever do you honour. Your disposition was unexceptionable; the total misbehaviour of the troops could alone have deprived you of the glory which is so justly your due.[3]

From what he could gather about Cornwallis's movements, Rodney had been extremely sceptical about the campaign in North Carolina. In his letter to Sandwich of 15 November he had written: 'The whole expedition appears to me to have been an ill-conceived measure, and, in my poor opinion, could tend only to weaken the army, and give the rebels opportunity of destroying his Majesty's troops in detail'.[4] On the other hand, he was strongly in favour of establishing a base in the Chesapeake:

> For my part, I know no post in America where the squadron under Mr Arbuthnot (which he is ordered to keep with him in the winter months) can shelter themselves, but in the Chesapeake; or where the stationing a squadron would be more detrimental to his Majesty's rebellious subjects. But even then it would be necessary that his Majesty's troops had a post at Portsmouth or Norfolk, without which the squadron stationed in the Chesapeake would find it extremely difficult to get fresh water.

This was no doubt the subject of a good deal of discussion between Clinton and Rodney during the latter's sojourn in New York.

---

2   Wickwire and Wickwire, *Cornwallis and the War of Independence*, p.269,
3   Wickwire and Wickwire, *Cornwallis and the War of Independence*, pp.270-271.
4   Barnes and Owen (eds), *Private Papers of John, Earl of Sandwich*, Vol.III, p.261.

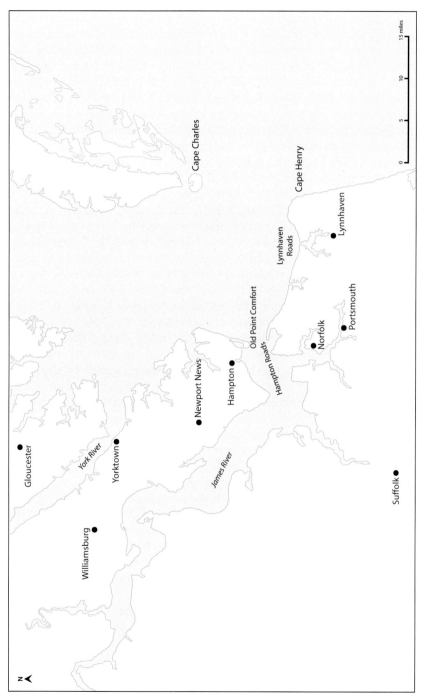

N

Cape Charles

Cape Henry

Lynnhaven
Roads

Lynnhaven

Old Point Comfort

Norfolk

Portsmouth

Newport News

Hampton

Hampton Roads

York River

Yorktown

Gloucester

James River

Williamsburg

Suffolk

0   5   10   15 miles

Chesapeake Bay and surrounding area.

There, Clinton had received such news as Cornwallis sent him, which was not a lot, with mounting concern. Apart from its immediate military consequences, the Battle of Cowpens was important in terms of the effect which it had on the uneasy relationship between Cornwallis and his commander-in-chief. Clinton was firmly of the opinion that his subordinate's practice of making detachments from his army had brought defeat on himself, as at King's Mountain and Cowpens. Clinton had become extremely concerned, ever since he left Cornwallis at Charleston, about the advances which the latter had been making into the hinterland of North and South Carolina. At the beginning of 1781 he was still more anxious about the suggestions that he received from Cornwallis that he was considering the possibility of marching north into Virginia and that Clinton should send an army there to meet him.

Before he could develop his plans for this, though, Cornwallis had first to deal with the enemy in his immediate front. Leslie had finally arrived on the day after the Battle of Cowpens, and it seemed clear to Cornwallis that he must now take the initiative. His first move was to chase Morgan, whom he thought he could catch and beat, and he moved at once, putting his troops in motion on 19 January, although losing some time by taking the wrong road. By 24 January he was some 36 hours behind Morgan, who had crossed the Catawba River the day before. Cornwallis was keeping Rawdon informed of his progress; he wrote to him: 'My situation is most critical. I see infinite danger in proceeding, but certain ruin in retreating. I am therefore determined to go on, unless some misfortune should happen to you, which God forbid'.[5]

Morgan was moving too fast to be caught, however. Joined by Greene, the rebels made their escape, crossing the Dan River into Virginia. Cheated of his prey, Cornwallis marched on Hillsboro, the capital of North Carolina, which he reached on 22 February. He did not remain there long, moving out three days later to resume his quest for Greene's army. This had begun to receive considerable reinforcements, and had moved back into North Carolina. On 14 March, outnumbering Cornwallis by two to one, Greene took up a position at Guilford Court House which he had chosen in advance. In spite of the odds he faced, Cornwallis characteristically decided that he would launch an attack on the following day.

After a brief skirmish between Tarleton's cavalry and that of 'Light Horse Harry' Lee, the British infantry began to advance towards the American position at noon. As they moved forward, Cornwallis could not immediately assess the position that Greene had taken up, but as his troops breasted the rise it became clear that it was extremely strong. In spite of taking heavy losses, Leslie launched his men in a bayonet charge. The British advance continued; in the centre the North Carolina militia retreated in disorder, but the American flanks held firm until the British infantry wheeled and drove them back to the second line of defence in the woods which Greene had prepared, which was held by the Virginia militia. After

---

5   Wickwire and Wickwire, *Cornwallis and the War of Independence*, p.273.

a prolonged struggle the British moved on to Greene's third line, in which he had posted his best troops. Here a savage battle developed; it is said that at one point Cornwallis had no alternative but to order his artillery to fire grapeshot into a thick crowd of struggling men, killing not only Americans but his own troops as well; in no other way could he prevent his troops being overrun. As the smoke cleared, the Americans fell back; more British troops came up and Cornwallis's line pressed forward. Greene retreated, abandoning his artillery. It had been a victory that cost Cornwallis a quarter of his effective force, and for the moment it deprived him of the possibility of further offensive action. Instead, he retreated all the way back to Wilmington, on the coast, a march of 175 miles, reaching there on 7 April. Clinton later wrote a bitter summary of the campaign:

> After forcing the passage of several great rivers, fighting a bloody battle, and running eight hundred and twenty miles over almost every part of the invaded province at the expense of above 3,000 men, he accomplished no other purpose but the having exposed by an unnecessary retreat to Wilmington, the two valuable colonies behind him to be overrun and conquered by that very army which he boasts to have completely routed a week or two before. [6]

Germain was one of those who had high hopes that Cornwallis would achieve a striking success in the Carolinas. As late as 7 March 1781 Germain was writing to him:

> I make no doubt but that your Lordship will, by this time, have had the honour to recover the province of North Carolina to his Majesty; and I am even sanguine enough to hope, from your Lordship's distinguished abilities, and a zeal for the King's service, that the recovery of a part of Virginia, will crown your successes before the season becomes too intemperate for land operations. [7]

Germain was on the same day writing to Clinton to urge the dispatch of a 'considerable force' to the Chesapeake. [8]

The problem was that the British had never determined on a consistent strategy for the conduct of the war in North America. The difference of approach between Clinton and his more adventurous subordinate was in large part to blame for this. Piers Mackesy ascribes it to Clinton's failure to exercise control: 'Throughout the three years of his command he had never laid down broad lines of policy or

---

6   Peckham, *The War for Independence*, p.155.
7   Valentine, *Lord George Germain*, p.415.
8   Valentine, *Lord George Germain*, p.415.

imposed a master plan; instead he had criticised the government's suggestions and grumbled at the size of his force'.[9] It is true, of course, that even between New York and the Carolinas communications took a long time, but Clinton should certainly have been in no doubt that Cornwallis had his own ideas, and was quite capable of pursuing them even if they were inconsistent with what Clinton wanted.

In Wilmington, Cornwallis was pondering his next course of action. The notion of a move into Virginia had been in his thoughts since the previous winter in Winnsboro. Now, turning his mind to the way he might most effectively carry out his plan to strike a blow there, it appeared to Cornwallis that the best move would be to link hands with the British force already operating out of Chesapeake Bay. Originally, before Cornwallis hijacked it for his own purposes, Leslie's force had landed in the Chesapeake and occupied Portsmouth. After he had left there to join Cornwallis, Benedict Arnold had been sent to the Chesapeake, arriving with some 2,000 men on 30 December. His orders were to establish a naval base, and then to make as much of a nuisance of himself as he could to the American forces in Virginia. The following month he raided up the James River as far as Richmond, destroying a great deal of property, which Thomas Jefferson, the governor of Virginia, was unable to prevent. Arnold then retired to Portsmouth, where he remained until Major General William Phillips arrived with a further 2,000 men, and assumed overall command. Thereafter a number of further raids were made into Virginia, proceeding up the James and Chickahominy Rivers. By the beginning of May a position had been taken up at Petersburg.

At the beginning of April Cornwallis wrote to Clinton to confess his discouragement at the events of the preceding months: 'My present undertaking sits heavy on my mind. I have experienced the danger, and distresses, of marching some hundreds of miles, without one active or useful friend, without intelligence, and without communication with any part of the country'.[10] A week later, though, on 10 April he wrote to Phillips to seek his support for his projected move into Virginia:

> Now, my dear friend, what is our plan? Without one we cannot succeed, and I assure you that I am quite tired of marching about the country in quest of adventures. If we mean an offensive war in America, we must abandon New York and bring our whole force into Virginia. We then have a stake to fight for, and a successful battle may give us America. If our plan is defensive, mixed with desultory expeditions, let us quit the Carolinas (which cannot be held defensively while Virginia can so easily be armed against us) and stick to our salt pork at New York, sending now and then a detachment to steal tobacco etc.[11]

9   Mackesy, *War for America*, p.409.
10   Valentine, *Lord George Germain*, p.417.
11   Wickwire and Wickwire, *Cornwallis and the War of Independence*, p.319.

The unassailable logic of his argument seemed perfectly clear to Cornwallis, although as he well knew it was never going to appeal to his commander-in-chief. There was no point at all in remaining at Wilmington; his concern about the need to be able to support Rawdon was shortly to be eased by the latter's victory over Greene at Hobkirk's Hill on 24 April, but he had already made up his mind that Virginia should be his objective. On the same day that he wrote to Phillips, he followed up his previous gloomy letter to Clinton with another to put his case as strongly as he could:

> I cannot help expressing my wishes that the Chesapeake may become the seat of war, even (if necessary) at the expense of abandoning New York. Until Virginia is in a manner subdued, our hold of the Carolinas must be difficult if not precarious. The rivers in Virginia are advantageous to an invading army; but North Carolina is of all the provinces in America the most difficult to attack.[12]

Germain was entirely persuaded that Cornwallis was right, and on 2 May he embodied his opinion in what amounted to an express order to Clinton. He was mystified, he wrote, to find that the commander-in-chief did not share his view of the importance of recovering Virginia:

> I am commanded by his Majesty to acquaint you that the recovery of the southern provinces and the prosecution of the war, by pushing our conquests from south to north, is to be considered the chief and principal object for the employment of all the forces under your command.[13]

Meanwhile during the winter of 1780-1781 the Admiralty had been facing the difficult task of resupplying Gibraltar. It was decided that the relief convoy, together with another convoy bound for Minorca, should be escorted by the whole of the Channel Fleet. It finally sailed under Darby on 13 March 1781. It was a risky venture; not only did it leave the Channel exposed, but it would have to pass Brest, where the French were preparing their fleet for the West Indies, and Cadiz, where Córdova had 25 Spanish ships of the line and a French squadron. However, these threats did not materialise, de Grasse having sailed for the West Indies by the time Darby left the Channel, and Córdova failed to appear. Accordingly, Darby was able successfully to relieve Gibraltar and to send on the Minorca convoy before returning home on 21 May.

12   Wickwire and Wickwire, *Cornwallis and the War of Independence*, p.320.
13   Valentine, *Lord George Germain*, p.416.

14

St Eustatius

St Eustatius is a small island, no more than six miles long, lying some 10 miles to the north-west of St Kitts. Its existence, or rather the activities conducted there, had been a running sore for the British since the outbreak of war. The Dutch had taken full advantage of neutrality to develop the trade of the island to the point where it had become the crucial centre of the international commerce of the West Indies. Along the waterfront, stretching for a mile and a quarter, stood a range of stone-built warehouses through which passed an enormous volume of produce, both raw materials and manufactured goods. To St Eustatius from America came cotton, tobacco, salt cod, bacon, maize, furs and lumber. Destined for the American market, there came sugar and rum from other West Indian islands, while from Europe came manufactured goods of all kinds. During 1780, 3,217 ships had visited the port, which was 'a unique convenience for all who wished to evade the many tiresome restrictions imposed by warring nations on international trade'.[1]

It was bad enough that its existence enabled the Americans to avoid the worst effects of the British naval blockade. What made the activities of St Eustatius far worse was that British merchants availed themselves of the opportunity which it provided to trade with the enemy. Nor, it seemed, were the Dutch even-handed in their dealings with the combatants. De Guichen had been able to obtain materials and shipwrights from the island after his battle with Rodney off Martinique; but on the other hand, Rodney's requests for rope and other stores after the great hurricane of 1780 were not met, although great quantities of stock were held by the merchants there.[2]

In a paper which Sandwich wrote for the Cabinet in September 1779 he had drawn attention to the effect which St Eustatius had on the British campaigns in the West Indies:

---

1   Spinney, *Rodney*, p.360.
2   James, *British Navy in Adversity*, p.255.

There is one circumstance concerning the Leeward Islands that deserves our most serious attention; and without something is done in that point, the French will always maintain their fleets and islands in good condition, and be free from the innumerable distresses which we are subject to. From conversing with Admiral Barrington and from what I knew before, I am convinced that two thirds of the provisions that we carry out under convoy from England and Ireland is, on its arrival in our islands, immediately shipped off for St Eustatius and from thence to Martinique, without which the French could not keep their fleet in a condition for sea. It is idle to talk of restraining such abuses by laws; the rapacity of merchants overbears all legal obstructions, and nothing but more forcible coercion can restrain them from anything in which they find their immediate interest.[3]

Britain's relationship with the neutral Dutch during the war was an important aspect of her diplomacy. Efforts were made constantly to apply pressure to the Dutch to discourage them from supplying strategic naval stores to France. When in 1779 the Dutch refused to discuss the matter, the British government announced that it would no longer permit Dutch vessels to carry such stores through the Channel. The Dutch response to this was simply to send such vessels through as part of their general convoys. Another source of friction was the help and support given to the American John Paul Jones during his operations off the coast of Britain. In April 1780 Britain suspended its commercial treaty with the Dutch, and subjected their ships to the rigour of its blockade.

Meanwhile, led by Russia, other neutral countries had been coming together to defend their commercial interests, and in the summer of 1780 the League of Armed Neutrality was established, the effect of which was to open French and Spanish ports to naval stores from the Baltic. The first nations to join Russia in the League were Sweden and Denmark; together these three powers could assemble a powerful fleet. The key development so far as the British government was concerned was whether the Dutch joined the League; if they did, and thus obtained uninterrupted access to enemy ports, it would be impossible to prevent the supply of critically important naval stores from reaching the enemy. At first, the Dutch hesitated to join the League; but in November 1780 the States General voted in favour of this. The British government acted quickly to pre-empt this, skilfully devising a *casus belli* that arose from the capture of Henry Laurens, the father of John Laurens, who had been taken when on his way to Holland. He was found to be carrying papers which revealed Dutch contacts with the Americans. Since the issue did not involve neutral rights, and had arisen before the Dutch had joined the League, its existing members declined to be drawn in. Britain, however, had thus acquired a fresh enemy.

3   Barnes and Owen (eds), *Private Papers of John, Earl of Sandwich*, Vol.III, p.167.

Whatever may have been the disadvantages of thus adding to the forces ranged against Britain, war with the Dutch provided considerable opportunities in the form of the weakly-defended colonies of the Dutch Empire. The British Cabinet lost no time in deciding that the first targets lay in the West Indies, ordering an immediate embargo on the export of salt provisions to foreign ports there. Even more important was the prompt dispatch to Rodney of orders dated 20 December:

> The islands which present themselves as the first object of attack are St Eustatius and St Martins, neither of which it is supposed is capable of making any considerable resistance against such a land and sea force as you and the General can send against them … And as the enemy have derived great advantage from these islands, and it is highly probable considerable quantities of provisions and other stores are laid up there or are on the way there, which may fall into our hands if we get possession speedily, it is his Majesty's pleasure that we should recommend to you the immediate attack and reduction of these islands as of very great importance to his Majesty's service.[4]

These orders were sent by a fast-sailing sloop and reached Rodney on 27 January.

The task was one which he undertook with unconcealed relish. It should be noted that in 1779, when considering steps that might be taken to prevent the Dutch supplying the French fleet with provisions and ammunition, Rodney had unctuously declared his preference for the public service 'to any emolument that might accrue to himself by the capture of the Dutch vessels attempting to succour the enemy'. It was an assertion that would have convinced nobody; Rodney's avarice was widely known.[5] Meanwhile, before the news of the outbreak of war with the Dutch had reached Rodney, Hood had finally arrived in Barbados on 7 January, after a slow crossing of the Atlantic, having pressed on ahead of his convoy with a number of ships; the convoy dropped anchor a week later.

Rodney, as soon as he received his orders, began preparations with Major General Vaughan for the expedition to St Eustatius. Steps were taken to ensure secrecy, so comprehensive that de Bouillé, in Martinique, began to suspect that something was going on, concluding that it must be an attempt to recapture Grenada, to which he hurried with 500 men. Rodney was able to put to sea on 30 January; Hood, with six ships of the line, was sent to hover between Montserrat and Nevis until the main fleet reached St Eustatius, and Drake, with six of the least seaworthy ships of the line, blockaded Fort Royal. Rodney took the fleet up the west side of Martinique to alarm the French garrisons in the island. On 2 February

---

4   Barnes and Owen (eds), *Private Papers of John, Earl of Sandwich*, Vol.IV, p.178.
5   Barnes and Owen (eds), *Private Papers of John, Earl of Sandwich*, Vol.III, p.188.

Hood reported that there were some 150 ships anchored in the roadstead of St Eustatius, and that there were no more than 100 troops on the island.

Rodney's fleet arrived off St Eustatius on the afternoon of 3 February, and within an hour an officer was sent ashore with a summons to surrender. The governor realised at once that he had no choice but to do so, and Rodney and Vaughan took possession of the island and of the 150 ships anchored in the roadstead. Twelve of these were British merchantmen which had formed part of Hood's convoy. On learning that a Dutch convoy had cleared the port only 36 hours before, Rodney sent a squadron after it, which took all the 30 ships of which it consisted. Congratulating Sandwich on the blow that had been struck against Britain's latest enemy, Rodney wrote in triumph to the First Lord on 7 February:

> The capture is beyond conception; and I have reason to say that St Eustatius, for its bigness, was the richest island in the world. Notwithstanding the very rich convoy, valued at the least at £500,000, which was taken by Captain Reynolds, every store house was full of rich goods, and every part of a very extensive beach covered with sugar, tobacco and cotton.[6]

Rodney wasted no time in getting the first tranche of his booty on its way to England. Commodore William Hotham, aboard the *Vengeance*, 74, with two captured Dutch men of war, and later the frigate *Alcmene*, escorted some 30 merchant vessels carrying goods which Rodney estimated as being worth more than £1 million. Hotham put to sea on 19 March and made a relatively swift passage. Unluckily for him, when he reached the Soundings, he encountered La Motte-Picquet, who was cruising there with a squadron of six ships of the line, several frigates and some cutters. There was nothing that Hotham could do other than to signal the convoy to scatter; with his warships he escaped to Berehaven with six merchantmen. A handful of others also escaped to other ports in Ireland, but La Motte-Picquet was able to return home with 18 prizes. Vice Admiral George Darby, who was returning with the Channel Fleet after a successful relief of Gibraltar, heard of the disaster to Hotham's convoy and tried but failed to intercept La Motte-Picquet before he returned to Brest.

With St Eustatius secured, the next Dutch possession to be considered for attack was Curaçao. According to Hood, Major General Vaughan had taken him aside to persuade him to put the project before Rodney. When he did so, the commander-in-chief was favourably disposed, telling Hood that he should have five ships of the line and some frigates. When Hood next took up the question with Vaughan he found to his surprise that the general had abandoned the idea, saying that he had no men available. Hood was in no doubt that the real reason for the change of heart

---

6   Barnes and Owen (eds), *Private Papers of John, Earl of Sandwich*, Vol.IV, p.148.

originated with the commander-in-chief, writing on 2 June to George Jackson, his regular correspondent at the Admiralty, to explain Rodney's real motives:

> The truth is, I believe, he could not bear the thoughts of leaving St Eustatius, where he fancied there were 3 millions of riches, as his letter to Lord G Germain expressed; and I dare say he would have been there to this hour had not the arrival of de Grasse obliged him to decamp.[7]

Rodney subsequently gave as the reason for not attacking Curaçao the receipt of a report, which turned out to be groundless, that the French fleet was about to arrive.

What is certain is that the vast quantity of booty taken at St Eustatius presented Rodney and Vaughan with a hugely intricate problem. That it was worth over £3 million seems to be generally accepted; the value of the goods which regularly passed through the island may be judged from the fact that the warehouses were let at an annual rent of £1.2 million. The King assigned to the army and navy the benefit of the captures made, and Rodney and Vaughan concluded an agreement that all should fall into one aggregate sum, rather than for the army to have what was captured on land and the navy the ships that had been taken. A joint committee was set up to oversee the process of disposal. The complexity of the problem of dealing with the goods, and shipping them, was almost at once enhanced by the claims of some British merchants for the release of their goods which, they said, had been stored at St Eustatius because of the lack of security elsewhere in the West Indies; and there soon followed a flood of other claims and counter claims. David Spinney has described the plight of Rodney and Vaughan in dealing with the situation:

> With a bench of learned judges to decide questions of ownership, a team of independent assessors and valuers, some capable accountants, and an efficient police force, the job *might* have been done. But as things were it is hardly surprising that the two commanders, unaided except for their committee and two secretaries, soon found themselves in deep water.[8]

Since it had been very much in Sandwich's mind that whoever he sent out to the Leeward Islands as second-in-command might very well, due to Rodney's state of health, have to take command, his selection of a newly appointed rear admiral with no experience of handling a fleet had been extremely bold. The coming years were to show, however, that Sandwich had made an inspired choice. Now, in the spring of 1781, the situation which he had foreseen had come about. Partly by

---

7   Hannay (ed.), *Letters Written by Sir Samuel Hood*, pp.21-22.
8   Spinney, *Rodney*, p.365.

reason of his health, and partly due to his absorption in the affairs of St Eustatius, to which he gave a high priority, Rodney had left Hood to command the fleet and to watch for the anticipated arrival of the French, while he remained ashore to deal with these problems for some three months. The false report of the imminent arrival of the French fleet caused Rodney to order Hood to put to sea at once with eleven ships of the line, to pick up Drake's six ships of the line off Fort Royal, and to take up a position to intercept the French. As time passed, though, and the French did not appear, Rodney became convinced that the sighting of the French was of a squadron intended for elsewhere. He now ordered Hood to take up a position blockading Fort Royal in order to ensure that the four French ships of the line there should not be able to get out and attack Hotham's precious convoy. Rodney's orders meant that Hood would be to leeward of Martinique, which effectively deprived him of the advantage of engaging the French fleet from a position of his choice, while still enabling him to prevent a junction of the new arrivals with those in Fort Royal. Hood pleaded with Rodney to change his mind:

> I most humbly beg leave to suggest, with all the submission to your better and more enlightened judgment, whether it would not be more advisable when the whole of the very respectable force you have done me the honour to commit to my charge are watered, stored and victualled, and collected together was stationed to windward, with a proper number of frigates to look out, the chance would not be abundantly more in my favour for effectively crushing any squadron of the enemy's coming to Martinique rather than by cruising before Fort Royal.[9]

To Jackson, Hood wrote bluntly to complain of Rodney's policy: 'But doubtless there never was a squadron so unmeaningly stationed as the one under my command, and what Sir George Rodney's motive for it could be I cannot conceive, unless it was to cover him at St Eustatius'.[10]

Rodney, however, was not to be moved. At this time his judgment had fallen to pieces under the stress of dealing with the problems at St Eustatius. Just how far this was so can be seen from the terms of the extraordinary and explosive letter which he wrote to his son George on 7 March, just after he had heard that Sandwich had appointed the hated Hyde Parker to another command:

> What can I think of that man who, after receiving the most confidential letter from me as one of HM ministers, and where I had pointed out to him a man who ought to have forfeited his head for his treasonable behaviour in the battle of 17 April, and that I was ready to bring the charge, has

---

9   Hannay (ed.), *Letters Written by Sir Samuel Hood*, p.17.
10   Hannay (ed.), *Letters Written by Sir Samuel Hood*, p.17.

since given that man the command at Plymouth, tho' he was well assured that Ministry had not a more bitter or inveterate enemy … If Lord S–h provokes me I will show to the World, and prove it too, that during his whole administration of naval affairs he has been totally ignorant of the duty of a First Lord of the Admiralty.[11]

Rodney was by now a very sick man, in considerable pain, which may explain the almost demented fury with which he greeted any opposition.

Rodney was particularly incensed by the evidence of treasonable activities on the part of British merchants trading through St Eustatius. In an article on the subject of the capture of the island, Randolph Cock quoted a letter which Rodney wrote to Captain John Laforey on 27 February. Laforey was the naval Commissioner who had been appointed, at least in part, to ensure that Rodney did not have to deal with the purchase of stores during his command, and thus not be subject to any temptations. Rodney wrote:

I have daily experience of iniquitous practices, and the treasonable correspondence carried on by those calling themselves British merchants settled in this Dutch, and the neighbouring islands, and am fully convinced, by intercepting hundreds of letters, that had it not been for their treasonable correspondence and assistance, the American war must have been long since finished.[12]

While there is no reason to doubt Rodney's genuine indignation about the activities of such merchants, Cock makes clear the extent to which Rodney and Vaughan hoped and expected to enrich themselves from the booty of St Eustatius. He also explains very clearly how it all went wrong, and the two men became mired in a complex web of litigation, which went on for a considerable time, and threatened to ruin them. The claims made of more than £300,000 amounted to practically all of the commission which Rodney and Vaughan had received; their defence to the claims was wrecked by the disappearance of the books and papers which had been seized, and were supposed to be in the possession of Germain's department. The story of St Eustatius itself came finally to a sad end, when the French recaptured the island in November 1781 in a daring operation which resulted in the court martial of the officer commanding the garrison.[13]

11 Spinney, *Rodney*, pp.366-367.
12 Randolph Cock, "The British Capture of St Eustatius, 1781", *The Mariner's Mirror* (August 1980), p.275.
13 Andrew O'Shaughnessy, *The Men who Lost America* (London: Oneworld Publications. 2013), p.308.

15

De Grasse

The choice of commander of the French fleet for the West Indies presented Minister of Marine de Castries with a problem. By reason of his seniority de Guichen would have been entitled to the command; instead he was offered the command of the port of Brest, but refused it. Another candidate was the Comte de Latouche-Treville; he, however, also submitted his resignation partly on health grounds but partly also under duress because it was felt that the size of the fleet was too large for him to manage.[1] De Castries accordingly returned to de Grasse, partly because he was known to get on well with de Bouillé. There is some dispute as to whether de Grasse actively lobbied to get the command, or whether on the other hand he did his best to avoid it, not least on the grounds of his health. At all events, the King insisted that he should be appointed. As his second-in-command de Castries would have chosen the capable La Motte-Picquet, but he was at the time suffering from a disabling attack of gout and in his place the less experienced *Chef d'Escadre* Louis de Bougainville was appointed. This may have been all for the best; La Motte-Picquet apparently did not enjoy a good relationship with de Grasse.[2]

Two other key appointments which de Castries made at this time were in respect of the squadron which was to go to the Indian Ocean, and the squadron currently at Newport, Rhode Island. For the former, de Castries selected the brilliant Chevalier de Suffren, evidently on the recommendation of Vergennes. It was necessary to find a new commander for the Rhode Island squadron because de Ternay was known to be seriously ill; in fact, he had died on 15 December. To replace him, de Castries appointed the Comte de Barras; pending his arrival in North America the squadron was under the command of des Touches.

---

1   Dull, *The French Navy and American Independence*, pp.221-222.
2   Dull, *The French Navy and American Independence*, p.222n; Charles Lee Lewis, *Admiral de Grasse and American Independence* (Annapolis Maryland: Naval Institute Press, 1945), p.96; J.G. Shea, *The Operations of the French Fleet under the Count de Grasse in 1781-1782* (New York: Da Capo Press, 1864), pp.27 and 139.

The Comte de Grasse. Copper-engraved plate from *London Magazine*, August 1782. (Anne S.K. Brown Collection)

The rise to the top of his profession of the man selected to lead the crucial mission to the Caribbean and North America had been steady rather than meteoric. François Joseph Paul de Grasse was born on 18 September, 1722 in Provence, about six miles from the town which bore the family name. He was the fifth son of the Marquis de Grasse, who had been a captain in the French army. At the age of 11 the boy was enrolled in the Gardes de la Marine, which existed to educate young noblemen to become officers in the French navy. After a year, the young de Grasse was appointed as one of the pages to the Grand Master of the Knights of St John at Malta. He remained there for six years; in 1740, with the outbreak of the War of the Austrian Succession, he returned to France to join the French navy. In 1744 he served at the indecisive battle of Toulon, the outcome of which led to the court martial of Admiral Mathews, the commander of the British fleet, and several of his captains, who were controversially dismissed the service. By 1747, with the rank of *enseigne de vaisseau*, de Grasse was serving aboard the 44-gun ship *Gloire*. He was severely wounded at the Battle of Cape Finisterre, and was taken prisoner when his ship was captured after fighting for three hours against heavy odds.

De Grasse was promoted to *lieutenant de vaisseau* in 1754, and then served in the navy of the Knights of St John for two years, prior to returning to France on the imminent outbreak of the Seven Years War. He served in India until 1760. In 1762 he was promoted to *capitaine de vaisseau*. His first command appears to have been the *Protée*, 64; although the records of his service at this time are conflicting, it is said that his ship was part of the French squadron operating in the West Indies, and took part in the campaign which ended with the loss of Havana. A succession of defeats had left the French navy greatly demoralised; when peace was signed it still possessed some 40 ships of the line and about 10 frigates, but these were widely scattered and many were in a state of disrepair, and the arsenals were empty. Nevertheless, Choiseul had already put in hand plans for the rebuilding of the fleet in readiness for the next war against England.[3]

De Grasse had remained a bachelor; but in 1764 he abandoned the vows of celibacy which he had made on becoming a Chevalier of the Order of Knights of St John, and married Antoinette Rosalie Accaron, a lady of the court of Louis XV. De Grasse's biographer has written that he was considered to be one of the handsomest men in the country, quoting a French historian who described him as 'large and handsome, and of a height admired by Anglo-Saxons who, like other people of the North, admire tall men'.[4] De Grasse, after his marriage, purchased the Château de Tilly, a manor house near Versailles. Later in life, Louis XVI was to grant him the title of Marquis de Tilly.

Returning to sea in 1765 de Grasse commanded the frigate *Héroine* in what proved to be an unsuccessful campaign against the Moroccan pirates. His next

3   Jenkins, *French Navy,* p.142.
4   Lewis, *Admiral de Grasse*, p.41.

command was the frigate *Chimére*; then came the corvette *Isis*, which was part of the 1772 *escadre d'evolution* commanded by d'Orvilliers, who wrote of de Grasse:

> He was the best skilled captain in the squadron. Although his vessel was very inferior in quality, he nevertheless gave to the evolutions all the precision and brilliance possible. His frequent collisions with other ships during the cruise seem to demand something more perfect in his estimate of a situation at a glance but they show his confidence in approaching vessels; and whenever the King may confide a squadron to me, I shall always choose the captains who prefer to risk a collision rather than abandon their position with the certainty of failing to execute a movement.[5]

De Grasse was next appointed in 1773 to the command of a brigade of marines based at St Malo. By now the process of rebuilding the navy which Choiseul had begun was showing effective results. That year domestic tragedy struck de Grasse, when his wife died, leaving him with five children. In 1775 he went to sea again, taking command of the frigate *Amphitrite*, stationed in the West Indies. There he met and married his second wife Catherine de Pien, the widow of a nobleman. When he returned to France in 1776 he was appointed to command the *Intrépide*, 74.

The war for American independence was by then well under way. King Louis XVI may have hoped that France would be able to stay out of the war, but it was evident to his ministers that this might not be possible, or even desirable. In the period before France did enter the war, in order to improve the French navy's readiness, there were again assembled each year *escadres d'evolutions*, to cruise principally in French and Spanish waters. From time to time ships were detached to escort convoys heading for the West Indies. In the French navy of the time promotion to the highest ranks was slow; d'Orvilliers did not reach the equivalent rank of rear admiral until he was 64 years of age. De Grasse reached that rank on 1 June, 1778 at the age of 55, slightly younger than de Guichen. Sartine, while Minister of Marine, had been unable to accelerate promotions as he would have wished, mainly because the size of the French navy did not provide sufficient command opportunities. War, and the build-up of the French fleet, gave more chance for the senior officers to gain experience.

De Grasse, with his flag in the *Robuste*, 74, had led the second division of the third squadron in d'Orvillier's fleet at the Battle of Ushant. He did not have much opportunity to distinguish himself, due principally to the fact that the Duc de Chartres, his squadron commander, proved an ineffectual leader. In January 1779 de Grasse, with four ships of the line, sailed to join d'Estaing in the West Indies. He took part in all d'Estaing's operations; when the latter returned to France after the

5   Lewis, *Admiral de Grasse*, p.49.

abortive attack on Savannah, de Grasse was sent back to the West Indies with four ships of the line and four frigates, to await de Guichen's arrival as commander-in-chief. In the campaign against Rodney in 1780, de Grasse had continued to fly his flag in the *Robuste* as commander of the blue squadron.[6]

When de Guichen decided to return to France, it had been intended that de Grasse should command the squadron of nine ships of the line which were to remain in the West Indies, but by then he had been taken ill, and the command of the squadron was conferred on the Baron de Monteil. De Grasse accompanied de Guichen when, on 16 August, he set sail to return to France. After a slow crossing they first reached Cadiz where they found a large fleet under d'Estaing; their arrival brought the total number of French ships of the line there to 40. Among others with the fleet were La Motte-Picquet and Suffren. D'Estaing had reached the conclusion that an attempt to take Gibraltar could not possibly succeed, and he had already decided to take the fleet back to Brest, where it arrived on 3 January 1781.

De Grasse now went on leave in an effort to recover from his recent illness. He travelled to Paris, where he was well received by the King and his family. While he was there de Castries was considering the appointments to be made in respect of the naval operations planned for 1781. After the King had insisted that he should accept the command of the fleet to go to the West Indies, de Grasse left Paris, arriving at Brest on 26 February. There, in spite of the fact that he was supposed to be convalescing from his illness, he threw himself into the task of overseeing the fitting out of his fleet, arriving for work each day at 5:00 a.m. As the time approached for the fleet's departure, however, he encountered a problem similar to that which had faced Graves during the previous year. The seamen, still unpaid for their previous voyages, were extremely discontented. One of his officers, in a not necessarily reliable journal, which he wrote under the pseudonym de Goussericourt, described the situation:

> I can say in truth that we sailed unsupplied with most of the articles absolutely necessary for a long voyage and manned moreover with wretched crews. We were ready to sail, but the sailors being underpaid were screaming like eagles, when M. de Castries, Minister of the Navy, ex-general officer of cavalry, arrived and found means to satisfy them, after knocking at a hundred doors, the Treasury being exhausted.[7]

The fleet was to consist of 20 ships of the line and three frigates. It was to escort a convoy of some 150 merchant vessels. De Grasse flew his flag in the *Ville de*

6   Lewis, *Admiral de Grasse*, p.85.
7   Shea, *Operations of the French Fleet*, p.30. Shea was unable, after extensive researches, to identify the writer.

Paris, which with 104 guns was one of the largest ships in the French navy. The orders which de Castries issued to de Grasse on 7 March gave him a considerable discretion:

> According to these, he was to go to the American coast on the approach of winter, after he had supplied the French West Indian islands with provisions. There he was to cooperate with Generals Washington and Rochambeau as far as possible. The number of ships he would take to the North American coast would depend upon the aid needed by the Spanish allies in the West Indies, and would be decided by de Grasse on his arrival at Sainte Domingue.[8]

The fleet finally put to sea on 22 March, seen off by an enormous crowd, which included de Castries and his suite, who watched from the fort commanding the roadstead, as the *Ville de Paris* got under way and fired the appropriate number of signal guns. It was the start of a voyage that was to have momentous consequences. In addition to his 20 ships of the line de Grasse was accompanied by Suffren and his squadron of five ships of the line, which were destined for the East Indies; and by the *Sagittaire*, 56, which was to escort a convoy of 30 ships direct to North America. Aboard this convoy was a reinforcement of 660 troops for Rochambeau's army at Rhode Island, the government having partially relented from its refusal to send more troops.

Suffren parted company on 29 March, when some 450 miles south-west of Madeira. De Grasse sailed on in favourable winds, and on 5 April detached the *Sagittaire* and her convoy. She carried a letter from de Grasse to Rochambeau which was to prove immensely significant:

> The force which I command is sufficient to fulfil the offensive plans, which it is the interest of the Allied powers to execute, that they may secure an honourable peace. If the men of war are necessary for fulfilling the projects which you have in view, it will be useful to the service that M. de Barras or M. des Touches be apprised of it, and that pilots be sent to us, skilful and well instructed, as the French ships have a greater draught than the British …It will not be until the 15th July, at the soonest, that I shall be on the coast of North America, but it will be necessary, by reason of the short time that I have to stay in that country, also being obliged to leave it on account of the season, that everything necessary for the success of your projects should be in readiness, that not a moment for action may be lost.[9]

---

8   Lewis, *Admiral de Grasse*, p.98.
9   Lewis, *Admiral de Grasse*, p.99.

16

Cape Henry

One by one, a series of largely unrelated decisions and events were leading inexorably to the area of Chesapeake Bay becoming the critical focus of operations in North America, just as Cornwallis had advocated. In putting this forward as the strategy to be adopted, he, and Germain, had taken for granted the continued British command of the sea, and it was this which was to prove the flaw in their argument. Germain had always been interested in taking action in that area, particularly with regard to the establishment of a naval base at Portsmouth, writing to Clinton as far back as September 1779:

> The other Enterprize you meditate on the side of the Chesapeake Bay, cannot, I am persuaded, fail of accelerating the great end of all the King's American measures, the suppression of the Rebellion; and I shall hear with particular pleasure that you have found measures to establish a post at Portsmouth in Virginia.[1]

When Benedict Arnold landed at the Chesapeake, and during his incursions into Virginia, from his base at Portsmouth, he had been supported there by a squadron of frigates and smaller vessels under Commodore Symonds. Clinton had ordered him to maintain himself at Portsmouth at all costs, but Arnold soon realised that it was a very difficult post to defend, spread out and broken up by waterways. Another potential threat came from the French squadron at Newport, Rhode Island. In addition, Washington had on 15 February sent the Marquis de Lafayette down to Virginia with a force of 1,200 Continentals, in order to check Arnold's raiding of the province. At the same time Washington wrote to Rochambeau to say that it was essential that there be cooperation between the land and naval forces. Since it appeared from the reports reaching him that the British squadron opposed to des Touches was inferior, he wrote that 'it has appeared to me probable that he would prefer going with his whole fleet, rather than separating it, as by

---

1   John O. Sands, *Yorktown's Captive Fleet* (Newport News: University of Virginia Press, 1983), p.7.

making a detachment he would lose his superiority and would give Mr Arbuthnot an opportunity to escort his disabled ships to New York, and follow his detachment with the remainder'. He went on to inform Rochambeau of the dispatch of Lafayette's forces to the Head of Elk River.[2]

If des Touches was to go south, he would have to evade the blockade of Newport which Graves, with nine ships of the line, was continuing to maintain, Arbuthnot having retired to New York due to illness. Since de Ternay's death, des Touches had made no offensive moves, but on 20 January he tested the effectiveness of the blockade by sending out three ships of the line. This was merely a feint; but since such a move could only be directed towards the Chesapeake, Graves felt obliged to respond, and he sent three of his own ships of the line to follow the enemy, reporting to Arbuthnot that he had done so. Des Touches had in mind that the deteriorating weather was so threatening that he would not in any case have been able to get to the Chesapeake with his whole squadron, and his three ships soon returned. They had lured Graves into sending out his own three ships in response, and by the time the French got back safely into Newport the rising gale had got up so strongly that one of the three British ships, the *America*, 64, was blown far to the south; a second, the *Bedford*, 74, was dismasted during the storm, and the remaining vessel, the *Culloden*, 74, ran aground in Portpond Bay. High on the rocks, and pounded by the seas, she soon became a hopeless wreck. Arbuthnot now made his way painfully to re-join his squadron. When the weather began to improve, work to repair the *Bedford* was put in hand, by using the masts and rigging of the *Culloden*. It was a long and difficult task. Meanwhile the storm battered *America* finally returned to Gardiner's Bay on 8 February.

When the gale had passed over, des Touches sent out the *Eveillé*, 64, with two frigates and a cutter to go south to Chesapeake Bay. Arbuthnot, having for the moment only six effective ships of the line, was now on level terms with des Touches, and dared not weaken his remaining force. All he could do was to send a frigate south to Charleston to order up to Chesapeake Bay the available forces there.

The *Eveillé* and her companions reached Hampton Roads on 8 February. When they arrived, Symonds withdrew his ships into the safety of the shallow waters of the Elizabeth River. There, they also enjoyed the protection of the shore batteries that had been established at Portsmouth. There was little that the French ships could do, and after 10 days in Hampton Roads they gave up and returned to Rhode Island. On the way back they encountered the *Romulus*, 44, which had been sent up from Charleston to relieve the flagship of Symonds' flotilla. Against such overwhelming odds, the *Romulus* was obliged to strike her colours, and the French took her back to Newport, where des Touches was pleased to add her to his squadron.

2   Knox, *The Naval Genius of George Washington*, p.73.

At Gardiner's Bay, Arbuthnot had been working hard to supervise the repairs to his damaged ships. It was the kind of task that he did well. His secretary, William Green, who did not usually have a good word to say of him, recorded that 'on this occasion and crisis Admiral Arbuthnot appeared to resume the ardour and energy of his ancient character as an officer and to exert himself with a zeal, rectitude, and activity suitable to the call of his country, and he was nobly seconded by every officer and man in the remaining ships'.[3]

The strain of command was getting to Arbuthnot, however, and on 16 February he sent a letter to the Secretary of the Admiralty to ask leave to retire before the summer campaigning season, following it with a characteristic personal letter to Sandwich:

I am flattered with the accounts that my Royal Master, his confidential friends, and my country have been satisfied with my endeavours to serve it. But such have been the fatal Consequences to myself in the pursuit, that my constitution is destroyed. I have lost almost totally the sight of one eye, and the other is but a very feeble helpmate, constantly almost obliging me to call in assistance to its aid in discovering particular objects. Besides this I have been seized with very odd fits, resembling apoplexy.[4]

Clinton, meanwhile, sent a prudent warning to Arnold that the threat from des Touches might not be over, telling him that 'appearances at Rhode Island give some reason to suppose that the ships seen last Wednesday were the Avant-Garde from that place,' adding that Arnold might be assured that every attention would be paid to his situation.[5] Arnold had concluded that to defend Portsmouth effectively more troops must be sent; this was the genesis of the decision to send down Phillips by way of reinforcement. Before they could arrive, Arnold had to persuade Symonds to accept his view of how the place should be defended, and this, with some difficulty, he succeeded in doing, as he reported on 12 March:

Commodore Symonds at my earnest request has at last consented to attempt to stop the enemy ships at the bar, below Craney Island, should they attempt to come up here. He is preparing ships to sink for that purpose, and was to have moved his frigates down to the place two days ago. They are (for what reason I know not) still remaining in their old station.[6]

3   Tilley, *The British Navy and the American Revolution*, p.214.
4   Tilley, *The British Navy and the American Revolution*, p.214.
5   Sands, *Yorktown's Captive Fleet*, p.8.
6   Sands, *Yorktown's Captive Fleet*, p.19.

Arnold's continuing anxiety was entirely justified. His position was very exposed, and Washington was continuing to press des Touches to take effective action against the British occupation of Portsmouth; seeing that the work of repair in Gardiner's Bay was still continuing, it seemed to him an opportune moment to do so. Accordingly, des Touches yielded to Washington's pressure, and on the evening of 8 March he sailed from Newport with seven ships of the line and four frigates, carrying with him 1,200 troops and supplies.[7]

Arbuthnot received the news of the departure of des Touches on the following day, but it was only on 10 March that he was able to put to sea with eight ships of the line and three frigates. Des Touches, therefore, had 36 hours' start of him, which seemed to Washington to be sufficient to ensure that he got to Chesapeake Bay before Arbuthnot.

The historian Larrie de Ferreiro has made an extremely thorough study of the events of the week that followed the departure of Arbuthnot from Gardiner's Bay, in order to explain how it was that he was able to enter Chesapeake Bay ahead of des Touches, so that when the French arrived they found the British squadron blocking their entrance. De Ferreiro notes that several theories have been put forward to account for this. The first was that suggested by Mahan, who wrote: 'Favoured by a strong north-west wind, and his ships being coppered, he outstripped the French, only three of which had coppered bottoms'.[8] Another explanation came from Ludwig von Closen, a French army officer who sailed with the fleet; he blamed des Touches for making 'a great turn' out to sea, finding bad weather and a contrary wind. Finally, de Ferreiro observes that neither navy had at that time a clear sense of the location of the Gulf Stream, which runs opposite to the direction in which the fleets were heading.

Analysing these factors, after a detailed comparison of logbooks from each fleet, de Ferreiro concludes that each contributed to Arbuthnot's advantage. Arbuthnot, he reckons, was sailing about 10 percent faster, which gained him 15 hours or so; des Touches' less direct course cost him another 18 hours; the weather probably made not much difference; but fighting against the effect of the Gulf Stream part of the way may have cost des Touches a further 14 hours. Taken together, these factors explain how it was that Arbuthnot arrived at the entrance to Chesapeake Bay ahead of his opponent.[9]

It was crucially important that he did so. Once Arbuthnot stood in his way, des Touches would have to win a decisive victory if he was to enter the bay. At New York, meanwhile, Clinton had learned from the master of a vessel employed by the quartermaster general's department that there were no French warships in the

7   Larrie de Ferreiro, 'The Race to the Chesapeake between des Touches and Arbuthnot, March 1781', *The Mariner's Mirror*, 104.4 (November 2018) p 477
8   Mahan, *Navies in the War of American Independence*, p.171.
9   Ferreiro, 'The Race to the Chesapeake', pp.480-481.

Chesapeake. At that time this was certainly true, and Clinton gave orders that the convoy which was to carry Phillips and his troops to reinforce Arnold should sail to the Chesapeake. Fortunately, the convoy was delayed in port, and by adverse winds, and it was not until 20 March that it got away, escorted by eight warships and carrying 2,000 troops, and safely reached the bay a week later.[10]

At 6:00 a.m. on 16 March the frigate *Iris*, scouting to the rear of Arbuthnot's squadron, signalled that she had sighted six French ships almost directly astern. The weather was hazy, with a heavy sea running, with the wind in the west; both squadrons were steering slightly to the west of south. Des Touches, on becoming aware that Arbuthnot was ahead of him, reversed his course; Arbuthnot, still out of sight, but kept informed by the *Iris*, followed suit, and hoisted the signal to form line of battle, at one cable's length. Before sailing, Arbuthnot had issued to his captains a note of the order in which his ships were to form line: *Robust*, *Europe*, *Prudent*, *Royal Oak* (Arbuthnot's flagship), *London* (Graves' flagship), *Adamant*, *Bedford* and *America*. The frigates *Guadeloupe* and *Pearl* acted as repeating ships. Visibility remained poor, and it had begun to rain. The wind came around northerly, and the two fleets sailed north-east close hauled. As the morning went on, each endeavoured to gain the weather gauge; Arbuthnot, with five coppered ships, could sail the faster, and by 8:15 a.m. the enemy were in sight. Des Touches at first had hoped to avoid action and get into the Chesapeake; but, when it became clear that this was not possible, he ordered his fleet to come about in succession and form line on the starboard tack, steering south-east. By 10:15 a.m. the wind had come round to the north-east, and Arbuthnot signalled his ships to tack in succession, and as they approached the enemy there seemed a prospect of crossing his 'T', with the weather gauge.

However, des Touches, an hour or so later, again came about, heading south-east out to sea, giving him the chance to cross Arbuthnot's 'T,' before the latter abandoned the weather gauge and steered on a course parallel to that of the French. He was obliged by the weather conditions to wear rather than tack, and as a result lost ground, and had to resume a chase of the enemy. As the British gradually closed the gap, the leading ship *Robust* was almost in range of the last ship in the French line, which was their newly acquired *Romulus*. Des Touches realised that, with his ships heeling to starboard, they could not open their lower gun ports; at 1.30 he wore in succession, his line curling around the bow of the oncoming *Robust*. Arbuthnot, taken by surprise, had no choice but to wear also, since des Touches was now heading for the Virginia coast, and must be prevented from getting there.

Once his squadron was steering on the same course as the French, Arbuthnot might hope that the greater firepower of his squadron would prevail. Each had eight ships in line of battle, but Arbuthnot had a 98-gun ship (*London*), three 74s, three 64s and a 50 against des Touches who had one 80-gun ship, two 74s, four

10   Syrett, *American Waters*, p.167.

64s and the 44-gun *Romulus*. As Arbuthnot remarked in his report to Sandwich, 'nothing could be a more pleasing prospect than my situation'.[11]

Arbuthnot ordered the hoisting of a signal indicating that 'every ship is to engage the enemy as close as possible,' but even before he did so Captain Corby, aboard the *Robust*, did not wait for a signal, but soon after 2.00 p.m. swung to port, and began to engage the leading French ship, the *Neptune*. Seeing this, des Touches, aboard the second French ship, the *Duc de Bourgogne*, also closed on the *Robust*, followed by the *Conquerant*. The *Europe* and *Prudent* next came up to join issue. Arbuthnot, in his report, wrote that he had 'to form under the fire of the enemy's line; and as the van was by this means soon put into confusion, I was single in bearing down to connect the line, exposed to the fire of the admiral and his two seconds'.[12]

Des Touches, who was a skilful tactician, now ordered his leading ships to change to the opposite tack, steering east-south-east while the rest of his line tacked in succession on to the same course, delivering their broadsides into the three leading British ships, all of which were now badly damaged. Since they were to leeward, the French had been able to open their lower gun ports, and as usual the French fire was largely directed at the upper works and rigging of the British ships. Both the *Royal Oak* and *London* were suffering severely from this, as Arbuthnot noted:

> Soon after which the *London* had her mainsail shot down, and my ship's foresail was so torn with shot that it hung to the yard by four cloths and the earrings only, the maintopsail halliards, braces, ties, also the foretopsail and fore braces and bowlines, and in short (for a little space only) the ship was ungovernable.

By now the *Robust, Europe* and *Prudent* had been so damaged that when Arbuthnot attempted to pursue des Touches, they were drifting off to leeward and more or less out of control, while the *London* was unable to keep up with the French. Des Touches drew away; Arbuthnot detailed a frigate to follow, but he could do no more. The British gunners, firing at the enemy's hulls, had inflicted considerable casualties on the French ships, particularly among the soldiers being carried by them. French losses amounted to 72 dead and 112 wounded; the British had lost 30 dead and 73 wounded.

The battle had, in one sense, been drawn; on the other hand, des Touches had outmanoeuvred and out fought the British, taking advantage 'of his superior control over his ships and the prompt obeying of signals by their captains to outmanoeuvre Arbuthnot completely. He then lost the battle by breaking off

11   Barnes and Owen (eds), *Private Papers of John, Earl of Sandwich*, Vol.IV, p.169.
12   Barnes and Owen (eds), *Private Papers of John, Earl of Sandwich*, Vol.IV, p.169.

the engagement without attempting to enter Chesapeake Bay'.[13] As it was, therefore, Arbuthnot had won a strategic victory by preventing the French from gaining control of Chesapeake Bay, and by saving Arnold's force from being trapped between the French and the Americans.

The failure of the ships of the British line to come simultaneously into action was ascribed to the lack of a signal for close action, and Mahan was one of those who was severely critical of Arbuthnot for this:

> The British Vice Admiral, keeping the signal for the line flying, and not hoisting that for close action, appears to have caused a moment of indecision in the squadron – an evidence again of the hold which the line still had upon men's minds. Of this des Touches cleverly availed himself, by ordering his van ships, which so far had borne the brunt, to keep away together and haul up on the other tack, while the ships behind them would wear in succession; that is, in column, one following the other.[14]

After the battle Arbuthnot took his battered squadron, with the *Robust* and *Prudent* under tow, into Chesapeake Bay, and anchored in Lynnhaven Roads on 18 March. He went into Portsmouth to meet Benedict Arnold, who could for the moment now breathe freely. Lafayette was far up the bay at Annapolis, prevented by British sloops from moving by water, and no offensive moves were made against Arnold before Phillips arrived on 27 March.

Des Touches took his squadron back to Newport. It was always possible that he might reappear, and Arbuthnot, after effecting temporary repairs to his ships, and patrolling between Cape Charles and Cape Henry before being driven into the bay by bad weather for several days, was able to take his squadron back to New York, arriving on 10 April. Understandably, he put the best face he could on the outcome of the battle, concluding in his report to Sandwich that his arrival had been in time 'to save both Mr Arnold's forces here and also Lord Cornwallis, which must have cost us all our conquests to the southward';[15] but for this, the French would have landed the 2,000 troops they carried and occupied Norfolk and destroyed the ships there.

The effect of the battle was to enable Phillips to arrive with his force to reinforce Arnold, after which Arbuthnot, back in New York, reckoned that he would be ready to go to sea again by 25 April, and resume his blockade of the French in Newport. If for the moment the threat posed by des Touches had been met, it was plain that the position was still critical. The problem of cooperation between Clinton and Arbuthnot had not gone away. The commander-in-chief had been constantly

13 Syrett, *American Waters*, p.169.
14 Mahan, *Navies in the War of American Independence*, pp.172-173.
15 Barnes and Owen (eds), *Private Papers of John, Earl of Sandwich*, Vol.IV, p.169.

pressing Germain to get Arbuthnot removed, but got no satisfaction, not least because Germain was thoroughly disenchanted with Clinton. The proposal that Arbuthnot be appointed to relieve Sir Peter Parker on the Jamaica station raised Clinton's hopes; but not by much, as his letter to Phillips of 30 April made clear:

> Our Admiral is grown, if possible, more impracticable than ever. He swears to me, he knows nothing of his recall. To others, he says he is going home immediately. If the next packet does not satisfy me in this particular, I shall probably retire and leave him to Lord Cornwallis's management.[16]

16 Quoted in Valentine, *Lord George Germain*, p.374.

17

The Road to Yorktown

One of the factors which de Grasse had been required to take into account when considering his operations on the North American coast was the extent to which the Spanish needed his support in the Caribbean. In fact, in early 1781 the Spanish had been doing rather well. In 1779 and 1780 Spanish forces had captured British military posts at Manchac, Baton Rouge, Natchez and Mobile.[1] There was one more important prize to take. Pensacola was the only remaining British base in West Florida; it had no naval support and was effectively isolated from all other British forces in the region. Two Spanish expeditions to attack Pensacola had endured savage storms which had scattered the convoys carrying their troops, but they did not abandon the project. On 9 March, 1781, with the assistance of the French, the Spanish landed a force near Pensacola. It was commanded by the governor of Cuba, the capable Bernardo de Gálvez. Escorted by four French ships of the line and 16 other warships, several thousand Spanish troops were soon disembarked, and drove the defenders of Pensacola into the fortress. The total strength of the garrison was approximately 1,200 troops, led by Major General John Campbell. The ensuing siege lasted until 9 May, when Campbell surrendered:

> The British force in Pensacola was doomed from the moment that the Spanish and French arrived with overpowering military and naval forces. Isolated completely from other British forces, the only hope that the defenders of Pensacola had was that their enemies would make a colossal blunder, but Galvez was too good a commander for that to happen.[2]

While this was going on Cornwallis had been enduring an unpleasant march as he made his way unopposed northwards across North Carolina. His difficulties were principally due to a lack of supplies. He crossed the Roanoke at Halifax on 13 May, and continued his march through Virginia northwards to Petersburg to

---

1   Syrett, *American Waters*, p.174.
2   Syrett, *American Waters*, p.175.

effect his junction with Phillips' force there, arriving on 20 May. To his dismay he found that Phillips had died five days earlier from a fever, and that Benedict Arnold had for the moment assumed the command of the army, which was 4,500 strong. Shortly after this, further reinforcements arrived, which with Cornwallis's troops brought the total up to 7,000 men. It remained his belief that it was in Virginia that it would be possible to strike a major blow at the Americans, but he had set off without waiting for any orders from Clinton before doing so. Now, he found from the orders which the commander-in-chief had issued to Phillips that the intention was that the operations in Virginia were to be confined to raids, and the establishment and defence of a suitable naval base on Chesapeake Bay.

The proposal to create a naval base there had been in Clinton's mind since the middle of the previous year; it was on 5 July that he proposed Portsmouth as a suitable location, presumably on advice and after looking at a map, but he does not appear to have visited the place. Arbuthnot told him that he could not spare ships for such an operation at that time, and Clinton did not for the moment pursue it. In August, Clinton raised it again with Arbuthnot, telling him that he was 'entirely of opinion that some very early expedition into Chesapeake Bay is absolutely necessary'.[3] This was, of course, also the view of Germain, who continued to press for it, believing that it would have the effect of discouraging the Virginia and Maryland militia from supporting the campaign against Cornwallis in the Carolinas; in any case he wanted the establishment of a British presence there before the French turned up.

Clinton had in the meantime himself begun planning for the expedition to the Chesapeake, and had finally prevailed on Arbuthnot to release sufficient ships for this. He had written on 20 September to Cornwallis to tell him that the expeditionary force would now proceed:

> I have always thought Operation in the Chesapeake of the greatest importance, and have often represented to Admiral Arbuthnot the necessity of making a Diversion in your Lordship's favour in that Quarter, but have not been able till now to obtain a convoy for this purpose. I have communicated to Sir George Rodney my wishes to send an expedition there, and he has most cheerfully consented to grant every Naval Assistance.[4]

Major General Leslie was duly placed in command, and the convoy had sailed in 17 October; before the end of the month a post had been established at Portsmouth. It was not long, however, before Cornwallis had concluded that Leslie's force would be more useful in the Carolinas, and the troops had been re-embarked, sailing from Hampton Roads on 23 November. At first intended to go to the Cape Fear

---

3   Sands, *Yorktown's Captive Fleet*, p.9.
4   Sands, *Yorktown's Captive Fleet*, pp.10-11.

River, they were directed by a further order to Charleston. In due course they were embodied in Cornwallis's army, returning with him to Virginia.

On leaving Chesapeake Bay, Leslie confirmed to Clinton the value of maintaining a post there:

> I left the works entire, and I still hope you will be enabled to take up the ground, for it certainly is the Key to the wealth of Virginia, and Maryland, it is to be lamented that we are so weak in ships of war, for there is a fleet of 60 sail expected hourly from the West Indies, besides the valuable ships or craft ready to sail from the Chesapeake.[5]

Rodney, when he arrived in New York was, as has been seen, very much in favour of Portsmouth as a base, where he believed that the inhabitants were loyally disposed, and he regretted its abandonment. So did Germain, when he heard of it, writing to Clinton on 3 January 1781 to express his great concern at the news, and reiterating the reasons why it remained important to secure the Chesapeake. The first draft of what was an extremely emphatic letter was prepared for Germain by William Knox, his Under Secretary of State, to whom he had written that they should 'enforce as strongly as possible the establishing a port in the Chesapeake'. He wanted, though, to be careful not to give Clinton an alibi if things went wrong; 'We must be cautious not to give him an opportunity of doing a rash action, under the sanction of what he may call a positive order'.[6]

By then, however, Clinton had already dispatched Benedict Arnold with his force of 2,000 men to the Chesapeake, and Arnold had begun to carry out his orders both as to the base at Portsmouth, and the incursions into the surrounding countryside. He was largely unhindered in his successful operations, but it was not long before he had reason to fear interruption from des Touches' force at Rhode Island, as previously described.

The lack of effective communication between Clinton and Cornwallis had meant that the latter had been able to put into action his plans for a campaign in Virginia without having been explicitly forbidden to do so, though he could scarcely have had any doubt as to Clinton's views. Now, however, being in possession of unequivocal orders setting out what the commander-in-chief wanted done, Cornwallis was obliged to review his position. He had plenty of resources with which to carry out the raids which were required. As for Portsmouth, and the establishment of a naval base there, there was a serious problem. Lieutenant Colonel von Fuchs, left in command there by Phillips, wrote to Cornwallis on 23 May to tell him that the defensive works there were 'but slender,' and due to the sandy soil it was necessary to make daily repairs. In addition, the garrison had been suffering a high rate of

5   Sands, *Yorktown's Captive Fleet*, p.12.
6   Sands, *Yorktown's Captive Fleet*, p.13.

desertion due to the 'severity of the duty,' which required over 400 men every day.[7] The problem had been previously identified by Arnold, and Cornwallis suggested to Clinton that Yorktown would be a better location for the base, because it could provide better protection for warships, was healthier, and could be more easily fortified.

In his letter to Clinton, dated 26 May, Cornwallis went on to advise the desirability of keeping the army concentrated as far as possible:

> From the experience I have had, and the dangers I have undergone, one maxim appears to me to be absolutely necessary for the safe and honourable conduct of this war, which is, – that we should have as few posts as possible, and that wherever the King's troops are, they should be in respectable force. By the vigorous exertion of the present governors of America, large bodies of men are soon collected; and I have too often observed that when a storm threatens, our friends disappear.[8]

Based on this proposition, Cornwallis hoped that Clinton would take advantage of the substantial force of 7,500 men now assembled in Virginia, and allow him to use them to better purpose than merely raiding American towns and plantations: 'I shall take the liberty of repeating that if offensive war is intended, Virginia appears to me the only province in which it can be carried on, and in which there is a stake'.

The importance of Virginia was as plain to the Americans as it was to the British. Washington felt real concern about the prospect of an invasion of the province as Cornwallis made his way northward, leaving Greene and his army far behind. Virginia was the largest and most populous state in America. It provided between 10 and 15 percent of the troops which made up the Continental Army, and a large part of the food and other supplies required for its support. For all the combatants the strategic significance of Chesapeake Bay, with the waterways flowing into it, was obvious when the use of naval forces in North America was under consideration.

While waiting to hear from Clinton with the hoped-for authority to launch a major offensive in Virginia, Cornwallis identified the targets that he might attack in the meantime. The state assembly of Virginia was meeting in Charlottesville, in the shadow of the Blue Ridge Mountains, where the outgoing Governor, Thomas Jefferson, was coming to the end of his term. Here seemed an attractive objective at which Cornwallis's mounted troops could strike. Another was the substantial arsenal that had been established at Point of Fork, held by a small garrison under

7   Wickwire and Wickwire, *Cornwallis and the War of Independence*, pp.327-328.
8   Wickwire and Wickwire, *Cornwallis and the War of Independence*, p.328.

von Steuben, and which served as an important supply centre for the Continental Army.

Before striking these targets, however, Cornwallis resolved to deal with Lafayette, who had been sent into Virginia when Arnold had landed at Chesapeake Bay, with the task of putting a stop to British raids into the province and, if possible, to catch and hang the traitor who was leading them. In neither mission had Lafayette been notably successful. Cornwallis now sent Leslie to Portsmouth to take command of the garrison there, while he prepared to move against Lafayette.

In his important letter of 26 May to Clinton, he had announced his intention of chasing the Frenchman out of Richmond, and thereafter retiring on Williamsburg, the former capital of Virginia. This city was, he said, a healthy location, and well provided, and had the advantage of being near to Yorktown, which Clinton might prefer as a base to Portsmouth.[9]

Lafayette had arrived at Richmond on 29 April, and with the reinforcements which he had received now had about 3,000 men. Cornwallis crossed the James River at Westover, and advanced in the first instance to Hanover Court House on the North Anna River, which he reached on 1 June. Lafayette did not propose to linger to be dealt with, and this advance was sufficient to prompt him to evacuate Richmond. He retired northwards to meet 'Mad Anthony' Wayne, who had been sent down by Washington with 800 Continentals to reinforce the Marquis. Concluding that he was not going to be able to catch his adversary, Cornwallis turned to the two raids which he had in mind. He sent Lieutenant Colonel John Simcoe, in command of the Queen's Rangers, reinforced by 200 infantry, to destroy the stores collected at Point of Fork and, if possible, to catch Steuben, who had a force of about 1,000 militia. Steuben did not wait to be caught, and Simcoe was able to destroy a large quantity of army supplies. Cornwallis joined him there with the rest of the army on 7 June.

Tarleton, meanwhile, had ridden fast with 250 mounted men to Charlottesville, riding into the town on 4 June, where he surprised the Virginia assembly in session, and very nearly caught Jefferson in his mansion at Monticello. The Governor only narrowly escaped. Tarleton respected Jefferson's property, but destroyed a large quantity of stores in Charlottesville before returning to join the main army. Cornwallis, with these operations completed, now retired as planned to Williamsburg, followed at a respectful distance by Lafayette. On 25 June the Marquis sent forward an advance guard under Colonel Richard Butler towards Spencer's Ordinary, which caught up with the British rearguard retreating towards Williamsburg. After a brisk skirmish, Butler fell back when Cornwallis turned and came up with the main army.

While all this had been going on, Washington had held another crucially important conference with Rochambeau at Wethersfield, Connecticut, on 21 May.

9   Wickwire and Wickwire, *Cornwallis and the War of Independence*, p.339.

They had not been entirely candid with each other. Rochambeau had not told Washington of de Grasse's intention to operate on the coast of North America, while Washington did not disclose that he had already been privately made aware of this by Chastellux, an officer on Rochambeau's staff. Washington was much put out by Rochambeau's evasions on this vital point, complaining bitterly to the French minister La Luzerne: 'It is not for me to know in what manner the fleet of His Most Christian Majesty is to be employed in the West Indies this summer, or to enquire at what epochs it may be expected on this coast'.[10] This was in a letter of 23 May, in which he sought to persuade La Luzerne to do what he could to bring about the appearance of de Grasse on the coast. He went on:

> The Count de Rochambeau and the Chevalier Chastellux agree perfectly in sentiment with me, that while affrs. remain as they now are, the West India fleet should run immediately to Sandy Hook, where it may be met with all the information requisite, and where, most likely, it will shut in, or cut off, Adml. Arbuthnot; and may be joined by the Count de Barras. An early and frequent communication from the Count de Grasse would lead to preparatory measures on our part, and be a means of facilitating the operation in hand, or any other which may be thought more advisable.[11]

A concentration of French naval forces was obviously desirable; Washington did not, however, address the possibility that the British too might see the advantage of bringing their West Indies fleet north.

Washington had approached the Wethersfield conference in a decidedly pessimistic frame of mind, writing in his diary in early May:

> Instead of having everything in readiness to take the field we have nothing; and instead of having the prospect of a glorious offensive campaign before us, we have a bewildered and gloomy defensive one, unless we should receive a powerful aid of ships, land troops, and money from our generous allies, and these at present are too contingent to build on.[12]

At the conference Rochambeau did air the possibility that de Grasse would come to North America, and he and Washington exchanged a series of written questions and answers to record their intentions if this should happen. Rochambeau posed the question: 'Should the squadron from the West Indies arrive in these seas, an event which will probably be announced by a frigate beforehand, what operations will General Washington have in view after a union of the French army with his

10   Flexner, *Washington*, p.155.
11   Lewis, *Admiral de Grasse*, pp.125-126.
12   Knox, *The Naval Genius of George Washington*, pp.80-81.

own?' To this, Washington again insisted that New York should be the objective, not least because the British garrison there had been depleted. He did not rule out alternatives: 'Should the West Indian fleet arrive upon the coast, the force thus combined may either proceed to the operations against New York or may be directed against the enemy in some other quarter as circumstances shall dictate'.[13]

Dudley Knox, whose principal concern is to illustrate Washington's grasp of naval reality, has suggested that this exchange shows what were the intentions of the two generals: 'It was thoroughly recognised by both, and well understood between them, that future circumstances might make a major enterprise in the South advisable'.[14] All the same, Washington's letter to La Luzerne does rather suggest that he and Rochambeau were not yet entirely of one mind. The French general seems still to have been treating Washington with a degree of discourtesy during the conference, but he did agree that his army should move from Newport to join the American army on the Hudson. This took him nearer to what he regarded as the proper theatre for their joint action, which was the area of the Chesapeake, while still humouring Washington's wish to be ready for an attack on New York. The French army left Newport by sea to Providence, Rhode Island on 10 June and marched slowly through Connecticut, joining the Continental Army on 6 July at Philipsburg, New York. On 20 June the frigate *Concorde* left Boston for Cap Francais with seven pilots and three vitally important dispatches to de Grasse from Rochambeau.

The first of these outlined the military situation in New York and Virginia and, interestingly, discussed a suggestion said to have been made by Washington that Barras, who had now arrived to take over command of the squadron at Newport, should transport Rochambeau's army to Chesapeake Bay. This suggestion, Barras had said, was impossible to carry out. The dispatch went on to address the strategic options to be considered:

> There are two points at which an offensive may be made against the enemy: Chesapeake Bay and New York. The south westerly winds and the state of distress in Virginia will probably make you prefer Chesapeake Bay, and it will be there where we think you may be able to render the greatest service, whereas you will need only two days to come from there to New York. In any case it is essential that you send, well in advance, a frigate to inform Barras where you are to come and also General Washington, that the first may be able to join you and that the second may cooperate with you with his army.[15]

13   Knox, *The Naval Genius of George Washington*, p.82.
14   Knox, *Naval Genius of George Washington*, p.83.
15   Lewis, *Admiral de Grasse*, pp.120-121.

Rochambeau's second letter enclosed a memorandum as to the financial situation of his army, and which called on de Grasse to raise the sum of 1.2 million livres in the French Antilles and to bring it with him in specie. The third letter, written on 11 June, was a response to the letter sent by de Grasse while at sea, and which had been delayed by bad weather. In it, Rochambeau reported his move to join Washington and the plan, by threatening New York, to make a diversion in favour of Virginia. He went on to give a grave account of the situation of the Americans:

> I must not conceal from you, Monsieur, that the Americans are at the end of their resources, that Washington will not have half of the troops he is reckoned to have, and that I believe, though he is silent on that, that at present he does not have 6.000 men; that M de Lafayette does not have 1,000 regulars with militia to defend Virginia, and nearly as many on the march to join him; that General Greene has pushed a small force far in advance on Camden, where he was repulsed and that I do not know how and when he will rejoin M de Lafayette; that it is therefore of the greatest consequence that you will take on board as many troops as possible; that 4,000 or 5,000 men will not be too many.[16]

Rochambeau went on to reiterate the alternative objectives for an attack, concluding that he was quite persuaded that de Grasse would bring naval superiority, but that he must also bring the troops and the money. Even now, the tone of his references to Washington suggests that he did not altogether trust the information that he was getting from his ally.

De Grasse also heard from La Luzerne emphasising the importance of his arrival on the Atlantic coast, which was the only thing that might prevent a bad situation in the South from becoming still worse. As Lewis observed, a very great responsibility was being placed on Grasse: 'He alone had to decide where the attack should be delivered. Rochambeau had not committed himself in recommending any particular plan, though Washington definitely recommended that the French fleet cooperate in an attack on New York'.[17]

16   Lewis, *Admiral de Grasse*, pp.123-124.
17   Lewis, *Admiral de Grasse*, p.126.

18

Hood and de Grasse

Off Martinique, Hood had kept up his complaints to Rodney about the leeward station which he had been ordered to take up. He pointed out the poor condition of his ships, the difficulty of maintaining station close in to the land, the impossibility of preventing small vessels getting in and out of Fort Royal at night, and the danger from the French coastal batteries. Rodney was entirely unimpressed. Based on his own operational experience there, he did not accept that the difficulties were anything like as great as Hood was suggesting, and he had no doubt that a French fleet arriving at Martinique could be brought to action. As for his own plans, he told Hood that he would be re-joining the fleet in a few days. He did not, however appear, and Hood was left to maintain his vigil, awaiting an enemy that was sure to come.

Since leaving Brest on 22 March, de Grasse had been making a remarkably fast passage across the Atlantic, partly due to the expedient of towing his slower ships. It was at 7:00 a.m. on 28 April that the British frigate *Amazon*, cruising off Pointe Salines, sighted a large fleet and convoy to windward, and made the signal 'Enemy in sight'. This was repeated to Hood at 9:00 a.m, and he at once stood with his 17 ships of the line to the south-east. By early evening, from a position off the southern end of Martinique, the French had come in sight to the windward of the island.

De Grasse, with an enormous convoy to bring safely into harbour at Fort Royal, decided to delay action until the following day, and sent an officer ashore to get up-to-date information as to the situation; he returned at 8:00 p.m. with the news that the British fleet, of 17 ships of the line and five frigates, was off Fort Royal. De Grasse passed the night to windward of Pointe Salines. What happened next, as far as the British fleet was concerned, is a matter of some dispute. Rodney later claimed that Hood laid to for the night, when he should have been beating up to windward of Pointe Salines in readiness for action on the following day. David Spinney believes that this was the case, and that as a result Hood's ships became scattered, some drifting far to leeward during the night. Mahan, on the other hand, a great admirer of Hood, rejects the suggestion completely, writing indignantly that the charge was 'incredible of an officer of Hood's character,' and asserting that it was contradicted by the captain of the *Russell*, who noted that the fleet kept moving across Fort Royal bay during the night, in line of battle.[1]

Hood himself, in his official report to Rodney, wrote that 'just after sunset I tacked the squadron all together, stood to the northward, and kept close in to Fort Royal all night'.[2] In a complacent private letter to George Jackson, the Second Secretary of the Admiralty, he wrote: 'I never once lost sight of getting to windward, but it was totally impossible'.[3] Like much of Hood's correspondence it was a letter glowing with self-satisfaction, and cannot be regarded as altogether convincing evidence. Mahan, of course, thought that if Hood had not got the fleet to windward, it could only have been because it was impossible to do so.

The fact was that, for whatever reason, when de Grasse made his move early on the morning of 29 April, standing round the southern end of Martinique, Hood was still too far to leeward to be able to prevent the French from heading westward between Pointe Salines and Diamond Rock. As they did so, the convoy was between the fleet and the shore to the northward. Hood was sighted at about 8:00 a.m., sailing southward on the port tack. He was joined just before the engagement commenced by the *Prince William*, 64, from St Lucia, bringing him to 18 ships of the line.

Hood signalled to his fleet to close up and prepare for action. As the two lines of battle drew closer, each hoisted their colours. There was some firing, but at too great a range to be effective and then, at 10:35 a.m., Hood tacked his fleet all together and bore away northward. By now de Grasse had rounded the Diamond Rock and was headed on a similar course, with his van roughly abreast of the British centre. At 11:20 a.m. Hood tacked again together, standing to the south; de Grasse wore round to the same course, these manoeuvres bringing the fleets closer together. At this time the four French ships of the line lying in Fort Royal slipped their cables and emerged to join de Grasse's battle line, bringing his potential strength up to 24, but in fact they took no part in the engagement.

From his leeward position, Hood was finding it difficult to close the enemy fleet, so, in his words, he invited it to come to him by bringing his ships to under their topsails. By 12:30 p.m. the two flagships were more or less abreast of each other, and the *Ville de Paris* opened fire on the *Barfleur*, though still at very long range. In the light winds the two lines drew slowly away southwards. De Grasse, throughout these exchanges, was principally concerned with the safety of the convoy; as the battle moved away, it headed around the coast to the safety of Fort Royal Bay, and the French admiral could feel that his first objective had been satisfactorily achieved.

Hood described the closing stages of the action in his report to Rodney:

---

1   Spinney, *Rodney*, p.370; Mahan, *Navies in the War of American Independence*, p.163n.
2   Laughton (ed.), *Letters and Papers of Charles Lord Barham*, Vol.I, p.110.
3   Hannay (ed.), *Letters Written by Sir Samuel Hood*, p.13.

At 1.00 I made the signal for the van to fill, the French admiral having filled and drawing ahead; at 1.17 made the *Shrewsbury*'s signal (the leading ship) to make more sail, and set the topgallant sails; at 1.34 repeated the signal for a close line of battle; and finding not one in ten of the enemy's shot reached us, I ceased firing. The enemy did the same soon after; but their van and ours, being somewhat nearer, continued to engage; and though the French admiral had ten sail astern of him and three others to windward, he was backward in making a nearer approach.[4]

Firing finally ceased at 3:18 p.m. Particularly during the final period of the battle, four British ships (*Centaur, Russell, Intrepid* and *Shrewsbury*) had suffered severely. 'The *Russell*, having several shot between wind and water, was with difficulty kept afloat, the water rising over the platform of the magazine'.[5] The *Montagu* and the *Torbay* also suffered serious damage. At nightfall, Hood sent the *Russell* off to St Eustatius, where she arrived on 3 May, bringing Rodney the first news of the action.

On the following day the fleets remained in sight of each other, but in the light winds Hood was unable to close the gap of four or five miles which separated them, with de Grasse to the eastward. They both continued to sail on a southerly course, and by dusk were off the north end of St Vincent, with de Grasse still careful to keep his distance. By this time the *Centaur* and *Intrepid* had been pumping continuously for 24 hours, and could no longer keep station, while the *Montagu, Shrewsbury* and *Torbay* were in no fit state to renew the battle. It was clear to Hood that he could do no more, and he turned west, with de Grasse in pursuit of him a cautious six miles astern. De Grasse got to within cannon shot of Hood by nightfall, intending to attack on the following day, but, due to straggling during the night, on the morning of 1 May only 11 of his fleet were within range, and a rain squall obscured visibility. After a long-range bombardment, de Grasse abandoned the chase.[6] Both fleets now turned north, Hood heading for St Eustatius and de Grasse for Fort Royal, which he reached on 6 May. Rodney, meanwhile, on receiving the news of the engagement, put to sea and joined Hood with two ships of the line on 11 May, between St Kitts and Antigua. There are varying statements of the casualties of each side during this prolonged engagement; Lewis records the British loss as 39 killed and 162 wounded, with the French loss being 18 killed and 56 wounded.[7]

Very different views have been expressed of Hood's performance during the engagement. James considered that 'Hood did remarkably well. He took risks, he

4   Laughton (ed.), *Letters and Papers of Charles Lord Barham*, Vol.I, pp.111-112.
5   Mahan, *Navies in the War of American Independence*, p.165.
6   Lewis, *Admiral de Grasse*, pp.109-110.
7   Lewis, *Admiral de Grasse*, p.108.

manoeuvred skilfully awaiting opportunity to strike, and proved himself a bold and capable fleet commander'. Of de Grasse, on the other hand, he wrote that he had 'displayed the usual caution of French admirals,' and failed to take his chance of attacking with his superior numbers and metal when he chose.[8] Mahan, predictably, adopts the conclusion of a French writer, Captain Chevalier, who while noting the advantage Hood had in the speed of his copper-bottomed ships, wrote that 'homage is due to his skill and to the confidence shown by him in his captains. If some of his ships had dropped behind through injuries received, he would have had to sacrifice them, or to fight a superior force'.[9]

Hood himself thought he had done well. In the letter to Jackson previously quoted, he wrote: 'I am perfectly conscious of no one omission in the whole of my conduct, and of having done everything that was in my power for the support of the honour of the British flag'.[10] In his official report to Rodney he derided the performance of the French fleet: 'I believe never was more powder and shot thrown away one day before, but it was with Monsieur de Grasse the option of distance lay, and he preferred that of long shot'.[11]

An alternative view was put forward by David Spinney:

> It is hard to understand how Hood could congratulate himself on his performance ... as de Grasse achieved his object while Hood's casualties were 37 killed and 125 wounded, not to mention the *Russell* driven out of the line, the statement is certainly remarkable. Finally he dismissed his opponent with the breathtaking comment: 'He has, I thank God, nothing to boast [of].[12]

Charles Lee Lewis has also rejected the opinions of Mahan and some British historians, observing that Hood had failed to do what he had been ordered to Martinique to accomplish: 'He did not keep the French convoy from entering Fort Royal in safety. Not a single merchant vessel was captured or injured, and none of de Grasse's fighting ships were much damaged'. Lewis points out that during the engagement the odds were only 18 to 20 in ships of the line, while Hood had five frigates to de Grasse's three.[13]

For his part, de Grasse, although he could feel satisfied that he had entirely achieved his objective, was not pleased with the performance of some of his captains. The Swedish-born *Enseigne de Vaisseau* Tornquist, who was aboard the *Ville de Paris* during the engagement, recorded:

8   James, *British Navy in Adversity*, p.260.
9   Mahan, *Navies in the War of American Independence*, p.167.
10 Hannay (ed.), *Letters Written by Sir Samuel Hood*, p.13.
11 Laughton (ed.), *Letters and Papers of Charles Lord Barham*, Vol.I, p.111.
12 Spinney, *Rodney*, p.371.
13 Lewis, *Admiral de Grasse*, p.111.

All the chiefs of the ships were called on board by Count de Grasse, when he with the sharpest reproaches made known the dissatisfaction he felt with the behaviour of some of the captains, adding that another time he would lay down his command, unless they showed a better conduct in obeying signals and fulfilling their duties. The Admiral also had cause for this. Although his brutal character corresponded with his grim appearance, he was nevertheless a good seaman and known for bravery, but, besides, somewhat too careful.[14]

The engagement had, however taught de Grasse one important lesson, as he wrote to de Castries, remarking that it was 'only too true' that the British ships were sailing much faster than his. Once again, the advantages of coppering had been amply demonstrated.[15]

De Grasse had gained the initiative, and the strength of his fleet gave the French the chance to assert command of the sea in the West Indies. It would be for Rodney to prevent him from exercising it, and this would not be easy. De Grasse and the Marquis de Bouillé, the governor of Martinique, were determined to make the most of their opportunity. On the day after his arrival at Fort Royal de Grasse sent off the *Pluton*, 74, and the *Experiment*, 50, with several frigates and 1,300 troops to make a descent on the island of Tobago. Next day he escorted with his entire fleet several transports carrying 1,400 troops under the command of de Bouillé to land at Gros Islet Bay. The force was not strong enough to take Morne Fortuné, the fort covering Port Castries, but it was hoped to occupy and fortify a position at Gros Islet Bay and thus deny the anchorage to the British fleet.

On 12 May de Grasse returned to Gros Islet Bay with his whole fleet, and came to anchor under the mistaken impression that de Bouillé had taken the defences there. When the British batteries opened a heavy fire on his ships, de Grasse was obliged to beat a hasty retreat. De Bouillé now decided that his force was not strong enough for his purpose, and it was re-embarked, returning to Fort Royal on 18 May.

Rodney and Hood, meanwhile, had proceeded to Antigua where on 12 May they began taking on stores. News of the French attack on St Lucia had already been received, and Rodney was anxious to put to sea as soon as he could. He left St Lucia to fend for itself, and, on 14 May, sailed slowly, in light winds, to Barbados. This he feared would be the object of the next French attack, but on his arrival on 23 May was relieved to find that this was not so. However, three days later information arrived of the French attack on Tobago, where troops had gone ashore on 23 May. Rodney was in a quandary; reports suggested that the French force was small; on the other hand, most of his ships needed to take on water and fresh vegetables, and

14   Lewis, *Admiral de Grasse*, p.108.
15   Lewis, *Admiral de Grasse*, p.110.

he believed that the garrison should be able to hold out for some time. Accordingly, it was with only six ships of the line and a body of troops under Colonel Skene that Drake sailed from Barbados to Tobago on the evening of 28 May.

However, when Drake arrived on 30 May he sighted de Grasse in the offing. The French admiral had arrived with his entire fleet, and Drake prudently withdrew, returning to Barbados on 2 June. Soon after his departure, the island capitulated. Rodney put to sea next day with 20 ships of the line, five frigates and five smaller vessels, with which he arrived off Tobago on 4 June.

At 11:00 a.m. on 5 June the first elements of de Grasse's fleet were sighted, soon after followed by the remainder which were standing out from Great Courland Bay. At noon Rodney received news of the island's capitulation, to his extreme fury. By the afternoon the whole of the French fleet was in sight heading north. It consisted of 24 ships of the line, with three frigates and three cutters, and by 6:00 p.m. was nine or 10 miles to leeward in a very irregular line between Grenada and the Grenadines. Rodney had every chance to bear down and engage the enemy, but chose not to do so, as he explained in his official dispatch:

> The situation was such as rendered it impossible to attack them with a probability of success, as it was in their power (night coming on) to entangle his Majesty's fleet among the Grenadilles, to decoy them into the channel between Grenada and the Spanish Main, where the currents are so very rapid that his Majesty's fleet might have been drove far to leeward, while the enemy had it in their power to anchor under the batteries of Grenada and rejoice at the sight of the British fleet being caught in their deception and driving far to leeward.[16]

Given that he had the weather gauge, Rodney's caution is at first sight surprising, but the reasons which he advanced against attacking were sound, and in addition he was concerned for the safety of Barbados. Hood, though, was critical, remarking that 'there be some who say that we never shall have such another opportunity of attacking them'.[17] Attacking a superior fleet, in the conditions that Rodney described, meant the risk of significant damage to his own ships, for which there could be no hope of replacement, and his caution was justified. He did not give up hope that an engagement on more favourable terms might be possible on the following day, as he went on to explain in his dispatch:

> I was in hopes to draw them by the next morning to the windward of St Vincent, where we should have had sea room to have attacked them. With this in view, I gave orders that all the lights of the fleet should be

16   James, *British Navy in Adversity*, p.263.
17   Macintyre, *Admiral Rodney*, p.179.

particularly conspicuous to the enemy, that in case they chose an action, they might be sure their wishes should be complied with the next day.[18]

These proceedings were viewed rather differently from the deck of the French flagship. Tornquist wrote:

> The weather being beautiful and clear, the English fleet …under command of Admiral Rodney was sighted bearing down upon us; but it soon again held the wind to starboard at a distance of two leagues from us. Presumably he found our fleet in too good an order and therefore refused to fight. He continually maintained the same respectful distance and by aid of the night stole away. We did not see him in the morning, as he presumably returned to Barbados to relate the capture of Tobago.[19]

In a letter of 24 June to Jackson, Hood delivered a ferociously critical judgment on Rodney's conduct:

> It is quite impossible from the unsteadiness of the commander-in-chief to know what he means three days together; one hour he says his complaints are of such nature that he cannot possibly remain in this country, and is determined to leave the command with me; the next he says he has no thought of going home. The truth is I believe he is guided by his feelings on the moment he is speaking, and that his mind is not at present at all at ease, thinking if he quits the command he will get to England at a time that many mouths perhaps may be opened against him on the top of Tobago, and his not fighting the French fleet off that island after the public declarations he made to everyone of his determined resolution to do it; and again, if he stays much longer, his laurels may be subject to wither.[20]

David Hannay, the editor of Hood's letters, considered that Rodney's health had deteriorated to the point at which he was unfit to exercise command. In addition, he was undoubtedly mindful of his public prestige: 'Hood's sneering judgment, that he was nursing his popularity, is only an unfriendly way of stating the truth, that he was in no small fear for his reputation'.[21]

Returning from Tobago, de Grasse put into Grenada for water and provisions, and then on 15 June left for Martinique, where he set about preparing his fleet for the next stage of his operations. This was to take his fleet with a convoy of 160 merchant

---

18   Macintyre, *Admiral Rodney*, p.180.
19   Lewis, *Admiral de Grasse*, p.115.
20   Hannay (ed.), *Letters Written by Sir Samuel Hood*, p.18.
21   Hannay (ed.), *Letters Written by Sir Samuel Hood* p.xxxiii.

vessels to Cap Français, picking up en route the *Hector* and 15 more merchantmen from Grenada. De Grasse arrived at Cap Français on 16 July, where he was able to add Monteil's squadron to his fleet. This had been left behind by de Guichen when he returned to Europe, and had been making itself useful by cooperating with the Spanish in the operations against Pensacola. Cap Français, known as the most agreeable town in the West Indies, was called the Paris of the Isles. One of de Grasse's officers described the roadstead as 'very extensive, lying before the royal battery of 60 pieces of ordnance, which would not amount to much, I opine, if the town were attacked. I have seen 400 vessels anchored in the roadstead, and there was still room for 50 more'.[22]

On his arrival at Cap Français. de Grasse read the various letters from Rochambeau, Barras and La Luzerne which were awaiting him. Almost once he made up his mind what he should do, taking a decision that, in the words of his biographer, 'was to change the whole course of history'.[23] He decided to make Chesapeake Bay the point at which he would aim. He had the benefit of a very cooperative attitude from his Spanish allies. In particular, he had the support of Francisco Saavedra, a former army officer who was serving as director of customs, and who was in Cap Français when de Grasse arrived. Saavedra had played a significant part in ensuring that the Spanish expedition under Galvez against Pensacola was strong enough to undertake the operation successfully. Now, in discussion with de Grasse, he was emphatically of the view that to ensure a decisive result, the French admiral should take the whole of his fleet to North America. The meeting between de Grasse and Saavedra was held on 18 July aboard the *Ville de Paris*; according to the Spaniard's journal, they 'talked about the cordiality and good faith with which the Spaniards and the French must cooperate toward the humiliation of a nation that so openly claimed dominion of the seas'.[24] To take his whole fleet north would mean de Grasse leaving Sainte Domingue unprotected; Saavedra promised to cover this by proposing that four Spanish ships of the line be sent from Havana to Cap Français.

Above all, to take the whole fleet meant postponing the departure of the Europe bound convoy from Cap Français, since this would require a substantial escort. This was a bold decision from the political point of view, as Captain Thomas White observed: 'If the British government had sanctioned, or a British Admiral had adopted such a measure, however necessary to carry an important political operation, the one would have been turned out, and the other would have been hung: no wonder that they succeeded and we failed'.[25] It was Rodney's assumption that part of de Grasse's fleet would escort the convoy to Europe and part remain to cover the French islands, that led him to believe that only a section of the French fleet at any rate would go to North America.

22   Shea, *Operations of the French Fleet*, p.57.
23   Lewis, *Admiral de Grasse*, p.136.
24   Nathaniel Philbrick, *In the Hurricane's Eye* (New York: Random House, 2018), p.140.
25   White, *Naval Researches*, p.77.

On 28 July, de Grasse wrote to Rochambeau to announce his plans, sending letters also to La Luzerne and Barras aboard the frigate *Concorde*:

> I shall be obliged to employ the fleet promptly and to good purpose, so that the time may be spent to profit sufficiently against the enemy naval forces and their land forces; but I shall not be able to use the soldiers long; they are under the orders of the Spanish who will need them.[26]

His Spanish allies were continuing to be entirely cooperative, and raised no objection to de Grasse taking with him a force of some 3,300 men, which would not be required until the winter. De Grasse went on:

> All will be embarked on 25 or 26 ships of war which will leave this place on August 3 and reach as soon as possible Chesapeake Bay, the place which seems to me to have been indicated by Rochambeau, Washington, Luzerne and Barras as the surest to operate best as you propose …By these efforts which I have made you may realise the desire that I have to effect a change in our position and in the condition of affairs.

When he set about raising the required sum of 1.2 million livres required by Rochambeau, de Grasse ran into immediate difficulties. Even though he offered to pledge his own properties on Saint Domingue and back home in France as security, and *Capitaine de Vaisseau* Charitte of the *Bourgogne* did likewise, he found that those with the necessary resources were disinclined to make a loan to the French King. De Grasse turned next to Francisco Saavedra to ask his help in raising the money in Havana, who at once agreed to do so, sailing for the city in the frigate *Aigrette*. When he got to Havana, the whole sum was raised, with the assistance of private contributions, within a few hours.

With his whole fleet, minus the ship of the line *Intrépide* and the frigate *Inconstant*, both of which had been separately destroyed by accidental fire, and taking with him as requested the necessary troops, de Grasse sailed from Cap Français on 5 August. The specie raised by Saavedra was to come from Havana in the *Aigrette*. To facilitate her safely re-joining the fleet, and to conceal as far as he could his intentions from the British, de Grasse chose to sail along the north east coast of Cuba between that island and the Bahamas, a notoriously difficult and dangerous route which had never before been used by a French fleet.[27] On 18 August, some 10 miles off Matanzas, the *Aigrette* joined the fleet from Havana, and her cargo was distributed throughout the fleet to ensure that the loss of a single ship did not result in the loss of all the vital funds.

---

26   Lewis, *Admiral de Grasse,* p.138.
27   Shea, *Operations of the French Fleet*, p.152.

19

Indecision

After the clash at Spencer's Ordinary on 25 June, Cornwallis had a clear idea of the strength of Lafayette's force opposing him, and felt confident in his ability to defeat it. However, when on the following day he received two letters from Clinton, it became clear to him that he could not undertake the offensive against Lafayette which he had in mind. In the first of these letters, the commander-in-chief made plain what Cornwallis was to do, which was to take up a defensive position of his choice at Williamsburg or Yorktown and then, keeping in hand what was needed to hold the position and to annoy the enemy, send back the rest of his force to New York. The second letter was more emphatic, telling him that he was immediately to embark a part of the troops.[1]

Cornwallis rode to Yorktown, and concluded that the position there would not be suitable. After examining the alternatives, he returned to Williamsburg, intending to march to Jamestown and there cross the James River en route to Portsmouth, where he would embark the troops for which Clinton had called. Before setting off, he wrote the commander-in-chief a lengthy report of his operations against Lafayette, adding his own view as to the strategic options to be pursued, and reiterating his motives in coming to Virginia. While confirming that he would carry out Clinton's intentions, he questioned the wisdom of holding Portsmouth or any other small base: 'I submit it to your Excellency's consideration, whether it is worthwhile to hold a sickly defensive post in this bay which will always be exposed to a sudden French attack, and which experience has shown makes no diversion in favour of the southern army'.[2] He went on to suggest that if Clinton still insisted on the naval station in the Chesapeake, he himself might be allowed to return to Charleston; there, he would certainly have the opportunity to conduct aggressive operations against Greene's army.

Back in New York, Clinton had been left in no doubt of the serious risks involved in continuing to conduct military operations in the Chesapeake. On 17 June he

---

1   Wickwire and Wickwire, *Cornwallis and the War of Independence*, p.339.
2   Wickwire and Wickwire, *Cornwallis and the War of Independence*, p.340.

had a meeting with Vice Admiral Arbuthnot and Commodore Affleck, and the minutes which he took of the discussion show that he perfectly understood that the security of Cornwallis's army depended on the navy maintaining command of the sea on the North American coast:

> The Admiral and Commodore expressed their fears that de Grasse might get possession of the Chesapeake before us, particularly York River. But I told them, I had, I hoped, provided against that by advising Lord Cornwallis to take Post at York Town. That I had left his Lordship at liberty with respect to operations; I had however recommended one in particular. But if his Lordship should not find that of mine expedient and had none of his own to propose I had ordered great part of his Troops to return to me during the sickly season.[3]

The reassurance that Clinton supposed he was offering to his naval colleagues appears on the face of it to be something of a non sequitur.

In Virginia, Lafayette had naïvely convinced himself that Cornwallis's movements were dictated by the need to retreat from the American army. By 4 July, including the Continental troops brought by Wayne, his army had increased to a strength approximately equal to that of Cornwallis, and he moved forward in the hope of cutting off part of his retreating enemy. Cornwallis, however, had expected Lafayette to attempt something of the sort, and by planting false intelligence he deceived Wayne, whose force now constituted the American vanguard, into thinking that the bulk of the British army was over the river and that only a rearguard remained. On 6 July Wayne advanced to attack. After two hours of skirmishing this movement had brought him, all unaware, to a point close to the main body of Cornwallis's army, which launched an attack taking Wayne entirely by surprise. Nevertheless, he boldly attempted a counter-attack, but this quickly broke down with heavy loss, and the American troops reeled back towards Green Spring Farm. Cornwallis was unable to finish off Wayne's force, since such cavalry as he had was unable to gallop through the woods and bogs in the darkness.

Having taught Lafayette a sharp lesson, Cornwallis now took his army over the James River. On 8 July, however, he received another letter from Clinton, which conveyed a very different message from those sent earlier. He now appeared much less concerned about the safety of his position at New York, and raised the possibility of launching a raid on Philadelphia. Accordingly, he suggested that the troops for which he had originally called should be employed in this task, and thereafter be sent to New York. He was himself planning to attack the French in Newport. He still wanted to see a naval base established in the Chesapeake. To the idea of raiding Philadelphia Cornwallis was entirely opposed, as he made clear in

---

3   Sands, *Yorktown's Captive Fleet*, p.33.

reply to Clinton's letter on the same day; but, under protest, he was prepared to carry it out.

As for the proposed base in the Chesapeake, he wrote that a defensive position in Virginia 'cannot have the smallest influence on the war in Carolina, and … only gives us some acres of an unhealthy swamp, and is forever liable to become a prey to a foreign enemy with a temporary superiority at sea'.[4] Cornwallis, like Clinton, was perfectly aware of the possibility that the arrival of the French fleet could mean disaster; but in spite of this, neither man seemed able to draw the obvious conclusion. In the case of Clinton, this was due to the pressure from the navy and, still more, to the pressure from Germain. In the case of Cornwallis, his complacency is harder to explain, but may in part have been due to a sulky reaction to the denial of his wish to conduct offensive operations in Virginia.

Having told Clinton what he thought, Cornwallis ordered Leslie at Portsmouth to prepare for the expedition to Philadelphia to be carried out by the troops summoned by Clinton, which must await the arrival of the necessary transports. He put his army in motion towards Suffolk, where on 12 July he received three missing letters from Clinton dated 29 May, 8 June and 19 June; these did not though, change the situation. The first complained about Cornwallis's unauthorised move to Virginia; the two following stressed Clinton's fears about the security of New York. On 20 July, by which date the army had arrived at Portsmouth, and troops had begun to embark for the assault on Philadelphia, a message arrived at 1:00 p.m. from Clinton abruptly countermanding his previous instructions. It was couched in emphatic terms; Clinton said that he could not be more explicit in setting out what he desired. The expedition to Philadelphia was cancelled; Cornwallis was to reoccupy the Williamsburg Neck. The troops were to remain; if they had sailed they were to be recalled. Finally, Clinton wrote, 'it is the admiral's and my wish at all events to hold Old Point Comfort which secures Hampton Road'.[5]

These instructions astounded Cornwallis, and made him very angry indeed. He had been fighting hard for a year and endured considerable privations in an unsuccessful attempt to subdue the South. Although he was in Virginia without orders, once he had arrived he had obeyed Clinton's instructions faithfully. Now, after all the trouble to which he had gone to carry out those instructions, he had been told abruptly to cancel everything, and to employ his whole army to fortify a post. Nevertheless, though regarding the order as absurd, he set about complying with it, halting the embarkation and ordering a survey to be made of Old Comfort Point.

Next day there came yet another letter from Clinton repeating the need for the naval station in the Chesapeake, adding that Rear Admiral Graves agreed with him about this. Graves had now assumed command of the North American station, upon Arbuthnot having sailed for England. This command was, however,

---

4   Wickwire and Wickwire, *Cornwallis and the War of Independence*, p.348.
5   Wickwire and Wickwire, *Cornwallis and the War of Independence*, p.249.

only temporary, pending the arrival of Rear Admiral Robert Digby, who had been selected for the post. Graves was firmly of the opinion that he must have an anchorage in the south, as he explained in a letter to Cornwallis of 12 July:

> I need only say to your Lordship that there is no place for the great ships during the freezing months on this side the Chesapeake, where the great ships will be in security, and at the same time capable of acting – and in my opinion they had better go to the West Indies than be laid up in Halifax during the winter. If the squadron is necessary to the operations of the army, Hampton road appears to be the place where they can be anchored with the greatest security and at the same time be capable of acting with most effect against any attempts of the enemy.[6]

What was more, of course, if the British fleet had a secure base in the Chesapeake, it would deny it to the French.

Graves had been very put out to learn that Digby, whom he incorrectly believed to be junior to himself, had been appointed to succeed Arbuthnot. He wrote to Sandwich to express the hope that he would not be asked to 'serve abroad in an inferior station after being superseded by a junior officer'. It was a subject on which he felt deeply and he raised it again in a letter to Sandwich of 20 July.[7] In deciding to appoint Digby, Sandwich presumably regarded him as an abler man. Rodger, though, observes that Graves 'was an excellent manager of men, associated with the new ideas of initiative and delegation which were to be the key to future tactical development,' and quotes Jervis as having remarked of Graves that he was 'very knowing in his profession, distinct and clear in his understanding'.[8]

None of the reasons put forward for the occupation of Chesapeake Bay assuaged Cornwallis's fury at the way in which he had been treated, and he allowed his feelings to become known to those around him. To Rawdon, in Charleston, he wrote that Clinton 'is determined to throw all blame on me and to disapprove of all I have done, and that nothing but the consciousness of my going home in apparent disgust would eventually hurt our affairs in this country could possibly induce me to remain'.[9]

Clinton's order allowed Cornwallis, if he thought it advisable, to occupy Yorktown in order to cover Old Point Comfort, and to emphasise the importance now attached to the establishment of the base, Clinton told him that he was now 'at full liberty to detain all the troops now in Chesapeake … which very liberal concession will I am persuaded convince your Lordship of the high estimation

6   Sands, *Yorktown's Captive Fleet*, p.37.
7   Barnes and Owen (eds), *Private Papers of John, Earl of Sandwich*, Vol.IV, p.177.
8   Rodger, *The Insatiable Earl*, p.290.
9   Rankin, 'Charles Lord Cornwallis', p.216.

in which I hold a naval station in Chesapeake'.[10] Clinton thought that Cornwallis would actually need only about 3,000 troops to hold the position, and that those which were not required should be sent to New York, a requirement directly contradictory to his previous 'concession'.

Three captains of ships stationed in the Chesapeake were asked to report on the suitability of Old Point Comfort. They were unanimously of the opinion that it would not serve; the width of the channel and the depth of the water were such that enemy ships could pass any works erected there with little damage. This was on 24 July; next day Lieutenant Sutherland, the engineer ordered to survey the site from a military standpoint, reported that it was 'attended with many inconveniences,' and could not afford much protection to an inferior fleet, while the time and cost of building a fort there would be very considerable.[11] Reporting the outcome of these surveys to Clinton, Cornwallis went on to repeat his reasons for his march to Virginia, and explained why he had not hitherto fortified a post. He observed that he had not previously appreciated the importance attached to doing so, and said that there was really no suitable location. The only places suitable for anchoring larger vessels were Yorktown and Gloucester, which was on the opposite bank of the river. Accordingly, he would pull out of Portsmouth and fortify these places, while warning that they were 'easily accessible to the whole force of this province'.[12]

Since Clinton's orders had, more or less, permitted him to do so, Cornwallis resolved to employ his whole army in the task of constructing the necessary fortifications. There were three principal reasons for doing this. First, Yorktown and Gloucester were on low-lying ground, and the building of the necessarily strong fortifications would require considerable labour. Secondly, while the work was going on, he would need strong enough forces available to send out foraging expeditions. Finally, such large forces would be necessary for the protection of the working parties engaged on the fortifications. By 2 August, Cornwallis's troops were disembarking at Yorktown to start work. Leslie was now sent to Charleston to take over the command there from Rawdon, who had been taken seriously ill, and O'Hara, now in command at Portsmouth, was ordered to dismantle the works that had been erected there. Cornwallis's army went on to spend a hot August at work on the fortifications at Yorktown, while Clinton and Cornwallis continued their correspondence; the commander-in-chief repeatedly asked what troops might be spared to go to New York, and Cornwallis invariably replied that he needed every man to complete the fortifications at Yorktown.

News that the troops at Portsmouth had been embarking on transports was reported to Washington by Lafayette, who believed that they were headed for

10 Wickwire and Wickwire, *Cornwallis and the War of Independence*, pp.350-351.
11 Chadwick (ed.), *Graves Papers*, pp.101-102.
12 Wickwire and Wickwire, *Cornwallis and the War of Independence*, p.352

Baltimore. He put his army in motion northwards, but while en route received word that the transports had now entered the York River, and turned back accordingly. He saw at once that this might yield an opportunity, noting that 'should a fleet come in at this moment, our affairs would take a very happy turn'.[13]

The possibility that was so obvious to Lafayette was equally apparent to Cornwallis, Clinton and Graves, or should have been. A curious fatalism seems to have overtaken the British leaders at what was clearly a critical moment in the war. Clinton had begun the month of August still convinced that the united forces of Washington and Rochambeau were preparing for an attack on New York. When, on 19 August, Washington's army began its move southward in response to the information received from de Grasse, Clinton was soon informed. As the days went by, and it became clear that the movement was not directed towards New York at all, Clinton took no action. To the suggestion by one of his staff that he should take steps to follow the Franco-American army as it marched southwards, Clinton replied that he would not 'for fear that the enemy might burn New York in his absence'. Nor did he judge it appropriate to go to meet Cornwallis and consider with him in a face-to-face discussion the situation which they faced. Clinton disliked disagreeable meetings:

> In the summer of 1781 he should have gone to the Chesapeake, as he should have gone to Rhode Island the summer before, to feel out the situation for himself; but again he fell back on letters. Even if he had been a forthright and pellucid correspondent, he would have had trouble in concerting plans in that way; and he was far from pellucid.[14]

The burgeoning threat from the French fleet had been apparent in New York since the beginning of July, when Graves had reported to Rodney in a letter of 2 July on the intelligence which had been received:

> The importance of that obtained here, which was taken from an intercepted post, will show you the apprehension of a considerable force, expected from the French commander-in-chief in the West Indies, in concert with whom M de Barras seems to act; and will demonstrate how much the fate of this country must depend on the early intelligence, and detachments which may be sent by you hither, upon the first movement of the enemy.[15]

13 Sands, *Yorktown's Captive Fleet*, p.41.
14 William B Willcox, 'Sir Henry Clinton: Paralysis of Command' in Billias (ed.), *George Washington's Generals and Opponents*, p.96.
15 Chadwick (ed.), *Graves Papers*, p.19.

At this time it was already known that Rochambeau's army had marched from Rhode Island to join Washington, which certainly raised the possibility of launching an attack on Barras's squadron in Newport. Now would be the time to do so, before a junction with de Grasse's fleet took place, but instead Graves put to sea on 21 July with the object of intercepting a French supply convoy that was believed to be heading for Boston. The information about this convoy arrived in New York on 19 July in dispatches from London. Dated 22 May, they spoke of 'large supplies of money, clothing and military stores, which young Laurens was preparing to send for the use of the rebel army in America'.[16] The convoy was expected to leave France before the end of June, and was believed to be carrying one of the most important deliveries of supplies which the French had sent, and which was essential to the rebels if they were to carry on the war. The Admiralty directed that a good look out for this convoy should be kept, but left it to the admiral as to the action that should be taken. Graves concluded that he should put to sea with his whole force to look for it. Given the uncertainty about the naval situation, it was a remarkably risky decision. His departure from New York with all of his ships of the line left the city, from a naval standpoint, without defences. If de Grasse had appeared while Graves was absent, 'he had but to enter the bay and New York would have been his, and the main part of the British army in America defenceless'.[17] In making this comment, Rear Admiral Chadwick goes on to observe that if de Grasse had arrived at any time before 30 August, Hood's fleet, on reaching New York, would also have been at his mercy. Washington could not have guessed that Graves would uncover the city in this way, and in any case de Grasse would not have arrived in time, but his instinct that New York should be the primary target was not far wrong.

However, there is another aspect of the matter which may explain why Graves was prepared to take the risk of leaving New York undefended. Apart from the obvious importance which the Admiralty appeared to attach to the interception of the convoy, Graves also had to take into account not only convoys passing between New York and the Chesapeake but also a convoy to Quebec, as he explained in a letter written to Sandwich on 21 August, after he had returned to the city:

> The first moment that the weather admitted of the squadron's putting to sea, I hastened to Boston Bay in hopes to intercept some of the expected supplies from France, though without success. As the convoy to Quebec, expected with so much anxiety, was about to sail in a day or two, and we had troops moving in transports in the Chesapeake, I concluded that the squadron's being at sea would keep the French in suspense and prevent their attempting anything either by detachment or collectively to disturb

---

16 Chadwick (ed.), *Graves Papers*, pp.24.

17 Chadwick (ed.), *Graves Papers*, p.lxi.

our convoys or to intercept the return of the *Royal Oak*, until they knew which way they were gone.[18]

The *Royal Oak*, which was very leaky, was coming back from Halifax after being heaved down.

Graves's mission had occupied four weeks. Its pointlessness appears from the report which he made to the Admiralty on 20 August:

> The intense fog which prevailed without intermission as we approached St George's Bank, deprived us of all possibility of seeing, and soon convinced me how much the squadron wou'd be exposed to accidents, and that the Fog Guns necessary to keep the ships from separation wou'd give notice of our situation. I therefore after having made Cape Ann, determined to withdraw, and we returned to Sandy Hook the 18th of August.[19]

In the Leeward Islands, Rodney was already aware of the threat posed by de Grasse, supposing that the French commander, having sailed from Fort Royal on 5 July, would in due course head for North America. However, it was still Rodney's view that only a part of the French fleet would take this course, but even before he learned of de Grasse's sailing, he had written on 7 July to Arbuthnot that he would send reinforcements. This message did not arrive in New York until after Graves had sailed to look for the French convoy. Rodney's dispatch, aboard the sloop *Swallow*, was sent on to inform Graves of the situation, but on her way she was driven ashore and wrecked on the coast of Long Island by three American privateers. As a result, it was only when Graves returned to New York that he learned that reinforcements would be coming north from the West Indies.

It remained to be seen who would be in command of the fleet that came north. In his letter of 7 July, Rodney had spoken of his sending a squadron to America, which suggested that he would not himself be in command, but he had not altogether abandoned the idea of himself taking the fleet northwards. He had sent Hood with his squadron of seven ships of the line to Antigua to provision while the rest of the fleet did so at Barbados. Rodney's flagship *Sandwich* was found to be in such a poor state that she could not continue in line of battle, and she was sent to Jamaica to refit. She was accompanied by the *Prince William* and *Torbay*, ordered to escort the homeward bound Jamaica convoy, and Rodney shifted his flag to the *Gibraltar*, which had been Lángara's flagship *Fénix*. The *Prince William* and *Torbay* were to detach themselves from the convoy once it was safe and not to enter harbour but to head at once to North America. In the event they did go into port.

18   Barnes and Owen (eds), *Private Papers of John, Earl of Sandwich*, Vol.IV, p.180.
19   Chadwick (ed.), *Graves Papers*, p.32.

On 31 July Rodney finally made up his mind, and sent for Hood, telling him that he was to command the fleet going north. He was to take 14 ships of the line and five frigates, returning to the West Indies in October after the end of the hurricane season. Rodney himself sailed with the homeward bound convoy in the *Gibraltar*, accompanied by the *Triumph*, *Panther* and *Boreas*, all ships in need of repair. The frigate *Pegasus* also sailed with the convoy, in order to give Rodney a last chance to change his mind if a few days at sea so improved his health that he could after all sail in her to take command of the fleet. This was not to be, however, and in the latitude of Bermuda he sent the *Pegasus* off to join Hood, with instructions to place himself under Arbuthnot or whoever was in command on the North American station.[20]

Hood's force had temporarily been reduced by four ships of the line which had been sent under Drake to St Lucia. He now sent orders to the latter to join him at Antigua. On his way there he fell in with the armed brig *Active*, which carried dispatches from Clinton to Rodney. These were dated 28 June, and confirmed that intelligence received at New York indicated that de Grasse was coming north. In Clinton's opinion he would proceed to Newport to join Barras. The commander-in-chief also addressed the situation of Cornwallis and his army, writing that 'since his Lordship's operations in Chesapeake must now cease from the inclemency of the season, I have … recommended it to him to occupy defensive stations in the York and James Rivers until the season for operations in that climate shall return'.[21] Here, no doubt, lay a large part of the reason for Clinton's lack of immediate concern for the safety of Cornwallis, since he appeared to be confident that the climate would inhibit any operations being taken against him. This letter was of course written at a time when Clinton was still convinced that Washington was planning to move against New York.

20   Spinney, *Rodney*, p.378.
21   Pengelly, *Sir Samuel Hood and the Battle of the Chesapeake*, p.106.

20

Convergence

Rochambeau had joined Washington on 6 July, and on 19 July they held a further conference, at Dobbs Ferry, to discuss their next move. It had been Barras's wish that a specific plan be sent to de Grasse, but Washington believed that for the moment there were too many imponderables to be taken into account. He was unsure of how strong a force he could take south, and he did not know how many troops de Grasse would bring with him, or when or where he would arrive. He wrote in his diary:

> Upon the whole, I do not see what more can be done than to prosecute the plan agreed at Wethersfield and to recommend to the Count de Grasse to come immediately to Sandy Hook, and if possible possess the harbour of N. York at the Moment of his arrival, and then, from a full View and Consideration of the Circumstances which exist, form a definitive plan of Campaign upon the surest Grounds.[1]

Writing to de Grasse two days later, Washington reiterated his belief that New York should be the target. However, if the combined allied forces on land and sea were not strong enough for this, he went on: 'The second object … is the relief of Virginia, or such of the southern states as the enemy may be found in, by transporting the principal part of our force suddenly to that quarter; and that we may be ready for such an event, preparations are making to facilitate such a movement'.[2]

In the meantime, Washington had proposed that Barras should put to sea, but the latter objected, insisting that he should not do so until the arrival of de Grasse. In the face of this flat refusal, Washington realised that he had no choice but to accept the position. He was still of a mind to attack New York, and he and Rochambeau conducted a personal reconnaissance, which brought home forcibly to Washington the difficulties of such an operation. His doubts increased with

1   Lewis, *Admiral de Grasse*, p.143.
2   Lewis, *Admiral de Grasse*, p.143.

rumours that part of Cornwallis's force was returning to New York. If it was not going to be possible after all to take the city, then the second option must be considered. He recorded in his diary on 2 August that he had turned his views more seriously than he had previously to an operation in the south.[3] That day he wrote to Philadelphia to enquire about the availability of shipping if it became necessary to transport a large body of troops down Chesapeake Bay.

In Virginia, Lafayette did not know what to make of the British movements. He had a healthy respect for Cornwallis, whom he thought 'much wiser than the other generals with whom I have dealt. He inspires me with a sincere fear, and his name has greatly troubled my sleep'.[4] On 14 August he told Wayne that he had been sure that part of Cornwallis's army was destined to New York, but the move to Yorktown confused him, and he wondered whether this was a feint to lure him further down the peninsula.

For the Americans, however, everything changed when the letter dated 28 July from de Grasse arrived announcing his intention to sail from Cap Français and head for Chesapeake Bay. Sent aboard the frigate *Concorde,* it arrived at Newport on 12 August and, forwarded at once by Barras, reached Washington and Rochambeau two days later. The precise information which it contained, and the clear evidence of de Grasse's determination to see the thing through, was just what Washington and Rochambeau wanted to hear. The allies could now make their plans accordingly. Washington decided that he must leave half his army on the Hudson, under major General William Heath. With the rest, and with Rochambeau's army he would march south to Virginia, concealing his intentions for as long as possible.

Barras, in forwarding the letter from de Grasse, shocked Washington and Rochambeau by then announcing that he was planning an attack on Newfoundland. Both of them regarded this as a distraction from the principal object of the campaign, and Washington wrote to Barras: 'I cannot avoid repeating therefore in earnest terms the request of the Count de Rochambeau that you would form the junction, and as soon as possible, with the Count de Grasse in Chesapeake Bay'.[5] Barras, reading this, yielded, though he wrote to Rochambeau to point out the dangers to his squadron; de Grasse, he said, knew better than anyone what force he would bring and what force Rodney would take to oppose him:

> However, as the opinion of yourself and Washington is opposed to mine, I have decided to go to Chesapeake with my fleet, and bring your artillery and some transports. I must repeat, however, that this is dangerous, and I presume that de Grasse understands its disadvantages, as he has given

---

3   Lewis, *Admiral de Grasse*, p.144.
4   Philbrick, *In the Hurricane's Eye*, p.138.
5   Lewis, *Admiral de Grasse*, pp.146-147.

me freedom not to join him at Chesapeake if I do not think it fit to do so. Graves' fleet, whatever it may be, will certainly not stop me.[6]

It was important that Barras should go; apart from a substantial increase to de Grasse's fleet, the artillery would be essential for siege operations.

In his diary for 14 August, Washington recorded his final abandonment of his plan to attack New York, not without a certain regret:

> Matters having now come to a crisis and a decisive plan to be deter-mined on, I was obliged from the shortness of de Grasse's promised stay on this Coast, the apparent disinclination in their Naval Officers to force the harbour of New York and the feeble compliance of the States to my requisitions for Men hitherto, and little prospect of greater exertion in the future, to give up all idea of attacking New York; and instead thereof to remove the French Troops and a detachment from the American army to the Head of Elk to be transported to Va. for the purpose of cooperating with the forces from the West Indies against the Troops in that State.[7]

Washington could see at once that there was not a moment to lose, and next day issued his general orders for the march southward. For as long as he could, he intended to maintain perfect secrecy, and no announcement was made to the army as to its destination. Lafayette was ordered to prevent any move by Cornwallis into North Carolina; he was to establish communication with de Grasse the moment the French fleet arrived, and discuss with him joint action until Washington and Rochambeau appeared on the scene. To de Grasse, Washington sent a letter to tell him that he would reach Head of Elk by 8 September, and to ask him to send frigates and transports there; it would be essential that the movement down the bay be protected against interference by ships of the British squadron based in the Chesapeake. In his letter, Washington suggested that de Grasse should establish a base for the fleet at Portsmouth, and went on to consider what might be done if the British got away and withdrew to Charleston or New York.[8]

The combined army which set off on the march south consisted of 2,000 American and 5,000 French troops. It made good time; Washington himself reached Philadelphia by 31 August, and the army entered the city two days later. Washington, with no further news of de Grasse, was becoming extremely anxious. To take advantage of the arrival of the French fleet, it had been necessary to move at once, but it was a considerable gamble. If de Grasse was seriously delayed, or was defeated by the British fleet, the situation for the allied army could become

6   Tilley, *The British Navy and the American Revolution*, p.119.
7   Lewis, *Admiral de Grasse*, p.145.
8   Knox, *The Naval Genius of George Washington*, p.93.

critical. In the meantime, though, Washington's efforts to prevent the British from knowing his intentions had been largely successful; it was not until 2 September that Clinton became aware of the situation, and that it was not New York that was in danger. That day he wrote to Cornwallis: 'By intelligence which I have this day received, it would seem that Mr Washington is moving an army to the southward with an appearance of haste, and gives out that he expects the cooperation of a considerable French armament'.[9] The warning of Cornwallis's peril came much too late; by then he was already entirely conscious of the danger that threatened his army.

In Philadelphia, Washington was still in ignorance of the movements of the French fleet. He had, though, received news of the arrival of a substantial British fleet at New York, and was gravely anxious for the safety of Barras, who had sailed from Newport for the Chesapeake on 24 August, by which time it had been supposed that de Grasse would have arrived. In the letters which Washington wrote to Lafayette and to Greene he expressed his concern: 'Nothing has since been heard of either of the fleets; from the circumstances related, you will readily conceive that the present time is as interesting and anxious moment as I have ever experienced. We will hope, however, for the most propitious issue of our united exertions'.[10]

It was still to be several days before Washington's anxiety was stilled; but south of Chester on 5 September he received letters with the longed-for news that de Grasse had arrived at the Chesapeake with 28 ships of the line and 3,000 troops. The news soon spread through the city. The excitement there was vividly expressed by a British historian:

> The whole city was in a transport of hope, exultation, and patriotic fervour and the army traversed the streets amidst a tempest of cheering and a rain of flowers from the open windows. The white and blue uniforms of the regiment of Bourbonnais and the regiment of Deux Ponts, and the rose coloured facing of the regiment of Soissonais, brought home to the spectators visible and flattering evidence that the richest monarch of Continental Europe had cast in his fortunes with theirs; and they were still more profoundly stirred when the ragged battalions of their own countrymen went past with swinging strides, and weatherbeaten, resolute visages.[11]

There was, though, still a long way to go before victory was won.

9   Philbrick, *In the Hurricane's Eye*, p.169.
10 Lewis, *Admiral de Grasse*, p.148.
11 George O. Trevelyan, *George the Third and Charles Fox: The Concluding Part of the American Revolution*, (London: Longmans Green, 1914), p.243.

De Grasse, when taking the fleet to pick up the *Aigrette* off Matanzas, had displayed considerable boldness when choosing the Old Channel along the Cuban coast and then tacking northwards through the channel between the Bahamas and Florida. On his way to Cuba he had been joined by two ships of the line which had been left behind, and this had brought his fleet up to 28 ships of the line, which were organised in three squadrons commanded by Monteil, de Grasse himself, and Bougainville. With him sailed a convoy of 15 transports with the arms and equipment for the 3,300 troops under the command of the Marquis de Saint Simon.

The constant and rapid current that flows northward through the Bahamas Channel would, it has been calculated, 'carry a ship even against contrary winds from 30 to 45 leagues in 24 hours'.[12] By 22 August the fleet was through the channel, and picked up the Gulf Stream which hastened its progress though carrying it further out into the Atlantic. Several prizes were taken en route, one of them carrying Lord Rawdon, returning to England after giving up the command in the south due to his ill-health. On 30 August the fleet reached the entrance to Chesapeake Bay, where the British sloop *Loyalist* was taken; the frigate *Guadeloupe* escaped to the safety of the batteries at Yorktown. The fleet anchored in the roadstead of Lynnhaven Bay, in three lines. De Grasse sent two frigates to cruise outside the entrance to the bay. Three ships of the line, *Vaillant*, *Triton* and *Glorieux*, moved up the bay to block any sortie that might be attempted by the small British squadron at Yorktown. De Grasse also sent the 50-gun *Experiment* and the frigates *Andromaque* and *Diligente* to the James River to ensure that Cornwallis did not attempt to escape into North Carolina.

De Grasse wasted no time in putting ashore Saint-Simon's troops, which moved off to join Lafayette's army. He was seriously tempted to launch an assault on Cornwallis without delay, but on 2 September he received Washington's letter of 17 August setting out his plans, and he thought better of it. He was pleased to learn that Barras had sailed from Newport and was on his way south to join the fleet.

Rodney, while he was still dithering about whether to take command himself of the fleet to be sent north, had written his orders to Hood on 24 July. At this point, although he had not finally made up his mind, he was assuming that Hood would probably be in command. After having taken the steps necessary to ensure the safety of the convoy for Jamaica, Hood was to make his way to North America with the remainder of the ships of the line, together with four frigates. He was to go first to Chesapeake Bay, then to the Delaware, and so on to Sandy Hook. He was to return to the Leeward Islands after the first full moon in October.[13] In these orders Rodney gave no indication of the size of the French fleet to be expected, though presumably there was some discussion of this between the two men. It is noteworthy that references in the correspondence to de Grasse's fleet appearing on

---

12 Lewis, *Admiral de Grasse*, p.141.
13 Chadwick (ed.), *Graves Papers*, pp.47-49.

the coast of North America frequently mention 'a detachment' or 'part' of it, since at all times there was a continuing assumption on the part of such as Rodney and Hood that it would not be the whole of the French fleet that would be encountered there.

Some idea of the collective view of the British as to the number of French ships of the line that would be met on the coast of North America can be seen from a letter which Hood's secretary, Joseph Hunt, wrote to Middleton on 29 August, the day after arriving in New York. In this letter he appears confident that the British would reach the Chesapeake first:

> And therefore, our previous arrival on the coast will operate greatly in our favour, as it will not only effectually enable the commander-in-chief to counteract the motions of the enemy, but will also allow of their adopting such measures as will be most efficacious towards preventing a junction of their squadrons, which cannot fail to lessen the French interest in the Colonies, and will, in its consequences, prove a decisive blow to the American cause, which, from all accounts, is in a tottering state and verging towards its decline.[14]

In any case, he thought that the British fleet would have the numerical advantage, imagining that the French would not detach more than 12 ships of the line which was the number which they had coppered, so it was probable that the British would be in superior force.

There had been a number of significant reductions made in the fleet that was to go north. The *Prince William* and *Torbay* would be escorting the convoy to Jamaica, and the *Sandwich* was to accompany them. Rodney was taking three more with him back to England, so it was with only 14 ships of the line that Hood sailed from Antigua on 10 August.

It was an uneventful voyage. Hood later recorded that he did look into the Chesapeake, making Cape Henry on 25 August. On that date of course there were no French ships to be seen. However, it is by no means certain that Hood did actually look into the Chesapeake. Graves later insisted that he had not done so, and a recent analysis of the ships' logs of Hood's fleet by Michael Crawford appears conclusively to demonstrate that this was correct. Graves later asserted that rather than being off the Chesapeake on 25 August, Hood was off the southern part of Virginia somewhere about Curratuck on that day and that 'he never saw the capes of the Chesapeake, nor any land until he made the Neversink'.[15] This does cast an uncomfortable light on Hood's reliability and the extent to which statements

---

14 Laughton (ed.), *Letters and Papers of Charles Lord Barham*, Vol.I, p.123.
15 Michael J. Crawford, 'New Light on the Battle of the Virginia Capes: Graves vs Hood', *The Mariner's Mirror* (August 2017), p.338.

made by him concerning his own conduct can be unequivocally accepted. It is odd that he should have found it necessary to be untruthful; presumably the reason is that having been given a specific order, he was reluctant to admit that he had not carried it out, in a letter in which, as always, he was putting the best face he could on his own conduct. He might, of course, instead have said that in the interest of speed he was obliged to proceed direct to New York. In any event, it made no difference; when Hood passed by on his way north de Grasse was still five days away from the Chesapeake.

Before Hood departed from Antigua, the brig *Active* was sent off on 6 August to New York with the information that the fleet was preparing to come north. There was no information to hand about the strength or movements of the French fleet, but the news of its sailing, if it had reached its destination, would at least have put Graves on notice of Hood's coming to join him. As it was, however, the message did not reach New York, the *Active* being taken by the Americans as she sailed northwards. On 13 August Rodney, heading home in the *Gibraltar*, got round to sending to New York news of intelligence which had been received concerning de Grasse:

> I left Sir Samuel Hood preparing to sail with all possible dispatch with 12 sail of the line, four frigates and a fire ship, for the Capes of Virginia, where I am persuaded the French intend making their grand effort. Permit me therefore to recommend it to you to collect all the force you can, and form a junction with Sir Samuel there.[16]

The intelligence on which this was based had been in Rodney's hands since the night of 31 July, the day before he sailed for England. It came via Saint Thomas, and stated that 30 pilots for the Chesapeake and Delaware had arrived, which gave as clear an indication as it could that the French fleet that was expected from Martinique would proceed immediately to America.[17]

Rodney, whose letter was addressed to Arbuthnot or whoever was in command at New York, sent it off by the frigate *Pegasus* which took 26 days to arrive there, on 8 September. By then, of course, events had moved on; but if the information had been passed on at once, Graves could have acted on the suggestion that he should sail to meet Hood off the Chesapeake, though it still might have been difficult to get there before de Grasse.

Hood arrived off Sandy Hook at daylight on 28 August, which was a day on which Graves had arranged to meet Clinton at the general's headquarters at Denis's Ferry on Long Island. It was just as he was about to leave his flagship that he became aware of a substantial number of ships in the offing, and he left

16   Chadwick (ed.), *Graves Papers*, pp.59-60.
17   Chadwick (ed.), *Graves Papers*, p.50.

instructions that the channel into the harbour be buoyed to assist their entrance. Before Graves reached Clinton the *Nymphe*, which had been sent on ahead by Hood on 25 August with a letter announcing his imminent arrival, reached the harbour. Graves at once wrote to Hood, telling him the situation so far as he knew it; there was no news of de Grasse, and Barras was still at Newport. He was sending pilots to bring Hood's fleet over the bar. Finally, he warned that his squadron was 'slender and not yet ready to move, as I should not hesitate upon your coming over the bar; as we are circumstanced it is a clear point'. He added that he was meeting Clinton for a consultation.[18]

This letter, Hood later recorded, made him 'very uneasy' about the delay that would result from his fleet moving into the harbour, over the notoriously difficult bar. In the letter which much later in the year Hood wrote to Middleton recounting the events which followed his arrival at New York, he described his reaction to the letter from Graves:

> Though I was at a great distance I immediately took to my boat and got to Denis's in the afternoon, where I found the general and admiral talking upon a plan of destroying the French squadron in the Chesapeake. They expressed great surprise at seeing me. I told Mr Graves the motive of taking so long a row arose from the letter I had received from him that morning, as I could not bring myself to think it right that the squadron under my command should go within the Hook; 'for whether you attend the army to Rhode Island, or seek the enemy at sea, you have no time to lose; every moment is precious'. My arguments prevailed, and he promised to be over the bar next day.[19]

The discussion between Graves and Clinton which Hood interrupted was of course about an operation against the French squadron at Rhode Island, not the Chesapeake; as it happened, that same evening news came that Barras had sailed from Newport, so the planned attack would have come to nothing.

Tilley suggests that Hood was on that day behaving in 'an astonishing manner,' in refusing to enter the harbour and in having his bargemen row him 10 miles to meet Graves and Clinton. Hood knew no more about de Grasse than they did, but his instinct, strongly expressed, was to go and look for him. The risk to Cornwallis, with a French fleet of unknown strength heading north, and which might form a junction with Barras, must have been plain to Clinton and Graves, yet they were displaying no urgency. In brusquely pressing for action in the way he did, Hood was clearly justified, as subsequent events were to prove.[20]

18   Laughton (ed.), *Letters and Papers of Charles Lord Barham*, Vol.I, pp.121-122.
19   Laughton (ed.), *Letters and Papers of Charles Lord Barham*, Vol.I, p.130.
20   Tilley, *The British Navy and the American Revolution*, p.250.

Graves was marginally senior to Hood, and would be in command of the fleet when it sailed. He yielded to Hood's urging of the need for haste, and agreed to get his ships to sea as soon as possible. However, they could not be got over the bar until 31 August, due to contrary winds. He had only five ships of the line and the *Adamant*, 50, fit to go to sea, so the fleet when it set off southward consisted of 19 ships of the line, not all of which were in a good condition; some of Hood's ships were in a very poor state, in particular the *Terrible*. The fleet was organised in three squadrons; Hood was in the van, with six ships of the line, flying his flag in the *Barfleur*, 98; Graves was in the centre with seven ships of the line, his flagship being the *London*, 98; and Drake commanded the rear squadron of the six ships of the line, his flag being aboard the *Princessa*, 70. The immediate objective was, if possible, to meet the French before the junction of Barras and de Grasse.

21

The Battle of the Chesapeake

The Fighting Instructions and the associated signal books in force in 1781 were about to be subjected to a severe test. Rear Admiral Chadwick, in his introduction to the *Graves Papers*, observed that they 'had long obtained and in the main long continued in the letter, were hidebound and forbade anything like originality'.[1] The difficulties of using signal flags in action have already been referred to, but some progress was being made. In 1777 Howe had issued a printed signal book to take the place of the signals provided in the Fighting Instructions. In 1780 Kempenfelt, serving in the Channel Fleet, produced a new set of Fighting Instructions and Signal Book. When Arbuthnot came out to take command of the North American station in 1779, he had brought with him his own set of Fighting Instructions and Additional Instructions. In the West Indies, Rodney had complained bitterly of those of his captains who followed to the letter the 'old' Fighting Instructions, and made alterations of his own to the existing Additional Instructions. Rodney had no regular signal book, but relied entirely on the instruction books, as had been the traditional practice.[2]

In 1781 Arbuthnot issued a further set of 'Additional Instructions for the North American Station,' and these were in force at the Battle of Cape Henry, and continued in force when Graves succeeded to the command. Julian Corbett carefully analysed these, which he considered 'show a strong trace of Channel Fleet influence … possibly that of Graves, who, with Affleck under him, had recently come out with reinforcements, after serving a campaign with Kempenfelt'.[3] At this remove, it is hard to understand why, in view of the importance attached to faithful compliance with the Fighting Instructions and associated signals, the Admiralty permitted local commanders so much discretion; it was clearly a recipe for potential confusion.

---

1   Chadwick (ed.), *Graves Papers*, p.xxxiii.
2   Julian S. Corbett, (ed.), *Signals and Instructions 1776-1794* (London: Navy Records Society, 1908), p.267.
3   Corbett, (ed.), *Signals and Instructions*, p.53.

As a result of the violent controversy that followed the battle of Chesapeake Bay, historians have speculated about the extent to which Graves, Hood and Drake may have discussed differences between the Fighting Instructions, Additional Instructions and Arbuthnot's signal book as used by Graves on the one hand, and those with which the captains of ships from the West Indies were familiar while under Rodney's command on the other. If not, the question then is whether the lack of such discussion contributed to the outcome of the battle. The editors of the Sandwich's papers thought that there might not have been such a discussion:

> Considering the larger cares in the Admiral's mind, it seems possible that this matter went overlooked. At the same time, the difference in methods between the two squadrons, besides Graves's limited acquaintance with his junior flag officers and most of his captains, seems to give reason enough for his cautious approach towards the French fleet.[4]

There appears to be no firm evidence of the issue of the prevailing signals and instructions to all of the captains of the West Indies ships. There is, however, no real reason to suppose that they were not issued, even though time was short; it was not until the morning of 5 September, for instance, that the chest of repeating flags was issued to Graves's own repeating frigate, the *Nymphe*. Peter Padfield, following Brian Tunstall, presumes that a set of signals and instructions was generally issued, 'although the total lack of comment on the point afterwards suggests he made no particular explanations of the many differences between these and the conventional Admiralty instructions and additional instructions' which the captains would have used under Rodney.[5] Certainly there was little or no time for Graves and the captains from the West Indies to get to know each other, and no opportunity to conduct any exercises on the hurried passage southwards.

Due to the number of occasions during this war when the acts or omissions of subordinates led to vigorous controversy, the system of signalling, and the Fighting Instructions under which the British fleet fought, have been the subject of close enquiry by historians. Rear Admiral Chadwick notes that 'a great deal which is more or less nonsense has been written about breaking the line'. He quotes Corbett's conclusion on the point that by the end of 1781 there was a signal for breaking the line on every principal station 'except that which Rodney commanded', and adds that 'one of its chief exponents, in theory at least, was the Admiral who lost the battle against de Grasse off the Capes of the Chesapeake'.[6]

4   Barnes and Owen (eds), *Private Papers of John, Earl of Sandwich*, Vol.IV, p.143.
5   Peter Padfield, *Maritime Supremacy and the Opening of the Western Mind* (London: John Murray, 1999), p.262; Brian Tunstall (ed. Nicholas Tracy), *Naval Warfare in the Age of Sail* (London: Conway Maritime Press, 1990), p.265.
6   Chadwick (ed.), *Graves Papers*, p.xxxvii; Corbett, (ed.), *Signals and Instructions*, p.57.

As the fleet sailed south, Graves had no news about de Grasse. The frigates which he had posted off the Delaware had nothing to report. The winds were favourable, and a speedier passage might have been possible, but for the problems arising from the condition of some of Hood's ships. On the third day out from New York, the *Terrible* made the distress signal. All the way from Antigua en route to New York five pumps had been constantly at work, and these had been barely able to keep the water level in her hold from rising. In addition to the *Terrible*, the *Ajax* was, 'but little better; the *Montagu*, 74, a leaky thing; some of the rest had masts sprung, and several more were very short of water and bread'.[7] Graves was extremely displeased about this, since Hood had assured him that his ships were fit for sea for a month. The *Europe*, one of Graves's own ships, was not in a good condition either, and Graves had instructed her captain that if she could not keep her position in the line of battle, she was to fall out and be replaced by the *Adamant*, 50. As the fleet neared the Chesapeake, Graves sent the frigates *Solebay* and *Richmond* ahead to look into the mouth of the bay and see what was there.

During the night of 4/5 September there were high winds and heavy seas, but conditions gradually eased and at daybreak there was a fresh north-north-easterly breeze. By 9:30 a.m. the *Solebay* signalled the presence of a fleet bearing south-west. The immediate assumption aboard the *London* was that this must be Barras's squadron, newly arrived from Rhode Island, but as the distance shortened it became increasingly clear that the French were in much greater numbers, which could only mean that de Grasse had arrived. At 10:05 a.m. Graves hoisted the signal for the fleet to clear for action and headed for the entrance to the bay, across which in Lynnhaven Roads the lines of French ships could be seen lying at anchor. The British fleet was probably making about four knots at this time.

De Grasse learned of the approach of the British fleet when the frigate *Aigrette*, scouting off the entrance to Chesapeake Bay, signalled that she had sighted a number of ships. Like Graves, de Grasse had been expecting Barras to appear on the scene, and his first assumption was also that these ships must be the squadron from Rhode Island. As further signals came from the *Aigrette*, each steadily increasing the number of ships that were in sight, it became evident that it was the British fleet. The final number reported by the frigate as she sailed back into the bay as fast as she could was 27, an accurate estimate: Graves had, in addition to his 19 ships of the line, the 50-gun ship *Adamant,* six frigates and the fire ship *Salamander.*

De Grasse decided at once to go out and fight. It was a decision which Chadwick considers to have been unnecessary; in his view, the position of the French fleet was one which it should not have left. Strategically, the objective which brought de Grasse north had been achieved. He was in such strength that the British could not force their way into Chesapeake Bay, and it would thus be impossible for

---

7   Harold Larrabee, *Decision at the Chesapeake* (London: Kimber, 1965), p.157.

Cornwallis to be relieved.[8] De Grasse, however, chose to come out and fight partly because if he had remained immobile within the bay, it would have meant Barras arriving to encounter a far superior fleet which would, in all probability, have been able to destroy his squadron.

De Grasse's position, however, was not good. The opening to Chesapeake Bay, between Cape Charles to the north and Cape Henry to the south, is some 10 miles across, but the main channel, about three miles wide, lies between Cape Henry and a shoal known as the Middle Ground. It was in this channel, in three lines, that the French fleet lay at anchor, and it was from this channel that the French must, with difficulty, emerge to fight the oncoming British. Since he was expecting, sooner rather than later, the British to appear, de Grasse was incautious in mooring his fleet in such a position. His situation was made significantly worse by the fact that on the morning of 5 September some 90 officers and 1,800 men were absent from their ships, engaged further up the bay in various tasks, but principally in getting Saint-Simon's troops into position. Although signals of recall were hoisted, in most instances they were too far off to be able to re-join the fleet.

When the British were reported, the wind was unfavourable, blowing from the north north-east; worse, the tide was still running strongly into the bay, and it would be noon before the ebb tide made it possible for the leading ships to get out to sea. At 11:30 a.m. de Grasse signalled for all ships of the fleet to slip their anchors and get under way on the port tack. The situation of some of the French captains was extremely difficult. Bougainville's flagship, the *Auguste*, was moored to windward of most of the fleet, and was hampered by a shoal. He had rigged a stern cable that could be used to swing the head of the ship around in order to miss the shoal as she moved out. When the signal came to make sail, the *Auguste* was one of the first ships to get under way, and for a time at least was at the head of the French fleet as it emerged. Another ship, the *Citoyen*, which had intended to leave as instructed on the port tack, was warned by the captain of the *Aigrette* that if she did so she would be in danger of running aground on Cape Henry; her captain shifted to the starboard tack, and she did not go on to the port tack until about 1:15 p.m., clearing Cape Henry half an hour later.[9]

A number of other French ships were also obliged to change tack. The *Souverain* at one point found herself in only four fathoms of water. Other ships also encountered traffic problems. In the confusion, the *Languedoc*, carrying the flag of Monteil, was at one point ahead of the *Ville de Paris*; de Grasse, realising that this meant that there was no flag officer in the rear of the fleet, ordered Monteil to take station in command of the rear division, although apparently it was 3:30 p.m. before he was able to do so. There was no time to get the fleet into the predetermined order of sailing, and when de Grasse hoisted the signal to form line of

---

8   Chadwick (ed.), *Graves Papers*, p.lxxiv.
9   Chadwick (ed.), *Graves Papers*, pp.228-229.

battle, it was for the ships to take their place according to their speed (*rang de vitesse*). The *Ville de Paris* herself had cleared Cape Henry by about 1:45 p.m.

At about 11:00 a.m. Graves made the signal for the British fleet to form line of battle at two cables' length. By noon he had reached a point 'four or five leagues' from Cape Henry, according to the *London's* log;[10] if it was four leagues, or 12 miles, it would mean that the fleet had covered only six miles since the *Solebay* had first reported the enemy, but no great reliance can be placed on either estimate of distance. At 12:45 p.m. Graves reduced the sailing distance between ships to one cable's length.

As the British fleet moved ponderously towards Chesapeake Bay, the line was led by Hood's squadron, the *Alfred* leading and the *Barfleur* fourth in line. The lead ship of the centre squadron was the *America*, with Graves in the *London* fourth in line. Finally came Drake; his leading ship was the unfortunate *Terrible*, and his flag was aboard the *Princessa*, third in his line. The weather now became squally, and at 1:08 p.m. Graves ordered reefs to be taken in the topsails. The reliability of the logs of the *London* and the *Barfleur* is dubious. At 1:35 p.m., for instance, the *London* signalled for the leading ship, the *Alfred*, to 'lead more large' which, with the wind as it was, meant to steer to port; but the *Barfleur's* log recorded it as a signal 'to alter the course to starboard'.[11]

Graves later explained to Sandwich what his intentions were at this time: 'My aim was to get close, to form parallel, extend with them, and attack altogether; to this end I kept on until the van drew so near a shoal called the Middle Ground as to be in danger'.[12] In order to take up the parallel position at which he aimed, he had made a signal for the line ahead to be on an east-west line. As the fleet approached the Middle Ground, at 2:04 p.m. he made the preparatory signal for the fleet to wear. He was close enough now to de Grasse to see that the French had 24 ships of the line, with two frigates, bearing south and heading eastwards out to sea in line ahead on the port tack. At 2:11 p.m. he made the signal to wear together, which meant that Drake's squadron was now in the van, with *Shrewsbury* the lead ship. The weather was by now becoming squally.

One of Graves's main concerns was that de Grasse, with a numerical superiority of five ships, might use this to double the rear of the British fleet, and to avoid this he must extend the British line until its rear was opposite the French rear. The effect of this was that each British ship would not have a single identifiable opponent in the French line, and he brought to, according to the *London's* log, 'in order to let the centre of the enemy's ships come abreast of us.[13] In his report to Sandwich, Graves described this somewhat differently:

10   Chadwick (ed.), *Graves Papers*, p.165
11   Chadwick (ed.), *Graves Papers*, p.203.
12   Barnes and Owen (eds), *Private Papers of John, Earl of Sandwich*, Vol.IV, pp.181-182.
13   Chadwick (ed.), *Graves Papers*, pp.180-181.

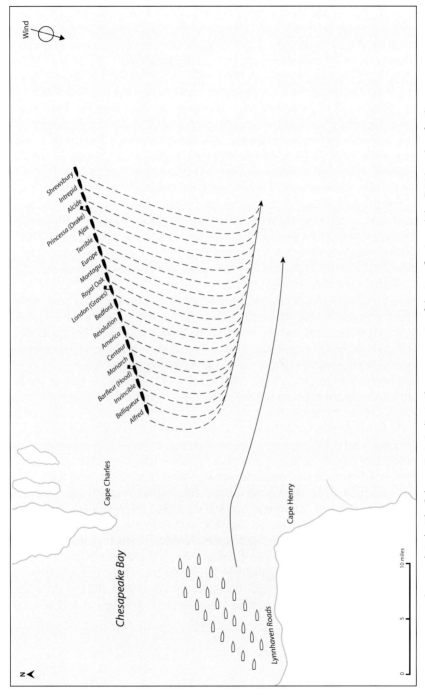

Approach to battle. Schematic to indicate the movements of the two fleets and the British order of sailing.

I therefore wore the fleet altogether and came to the same tack with the enemy, and lay with my main topsail to the mast dressing the line and pressing toward the enemy until I thought the enemy's van was so much advanced as to offer the moment for a successful attack.

Hopeful that there might be some opportunity to employ the fire ship *Salamander*, Graves gave her the order at 2:40 p.m. to prime; but there seems to have been no chance to launch her at the enemy. Meanwhile at 2:30 p.m. he signalled to the *Shrewsbury* to lead more to starboard, towards the French line. This, however, created a problem of understanding. The signal he had made, which derived from Arbuthnot's Additional Instructions, read: 'If at any time I would have the leading ship in the line alter course to starboard I will hoist a flag half red, half white at the main topmast head'. Drake and his captains took this to be an order to alter course in succession, turning at the point of the *Shrewsbury's* turn, with the result that the British line was approaching the French at an oblique angle instead of maintaining a parallel course. Graves now hoisted signals between 2:52 and 3:00 p.m. to the *Royal Oak, Terrible, Princessa* and *Alcide* to get into line, in an effort to correct the effect of the misunderstanding of the signal to the *Shrewsbury*, which, to emphasise the point, he repeated at 3:17 p.m.[14] He was also concerned that Hood's squadron was not keeping up, and he signalled for the ships astern of the flagship to make more sail. At this time the French van under Bougainville was somewhat ahead of the centre and rear; a French officer described it as 'entirely separated from the rest of our fleet; a disagreeable position'.[15]

There had now been reached the critical point of the manoeuvring of the fleets before the action commenced. At 3:34 p.m. Graves made the signal for the ships in the van to keep more to starboard, which did not significantly change the situation. He followed this up with a signal for line ahead at one cable's length, the *London's* log noting 'the enemy's ships advancing very slow'.[16] His fleet was not in the position in relation to the enemy that Graves wished, but the time had come to launch his attack, and he immediately signalled 'for each ship to steer for and engage his opponent in the enemy's line'. This signal, taken from Arbuthnot's signal book, was made with a white pendant at the fore topmast over a red flag. The *London's* log records that, suiting her action to the signal, she 'fill'd. the main topsail and bore down on the Enemy'. The signal was repeated at 4:03 p.m.; and then, at 4:11p.m. 'haul'd down the Sigl. For the Line ahead that it might not interfere with the Sigl. to Engage close'. Evidently concerned that his ships were bunching up, Graves again hoisted the signal for line ahead, the log recording as the reason 'the ships not being sufficiently extended'. This was at 4:22 p.m.; then

14   Padfield, *Maritime Supremacy*, p.265.
15   Shea, *Operations of the French Fleet*, p.70.
16   Chadwick (ed.), *Graves Papers*, pp.180-181.

The Comte de Bougainville. Hand-coloured engraved plate by and after Boilly; the tropical background references his earlier career as an explorer and circumnavigator.
(Anne S.K. Brown Collection)

five minutes later down came the signal for line ahead and the signal for close action was again made.[17]

At this crucial point the log of the *Barfleur* departs significantly from that of the *London*:

> 54 Minutes past 3. the Admiral made the Sigl for the line ahead one Cables length a Sunder. At 4 the Admiral made a Sigl. with a blue and yellow checquered flag with a white pendant over it. At 11 minutes after 4 the Admiral fir'd a gun to enforce the last main signal. 1/4 past 4. We repeated the Sigl. At 17 past 4. We repeated the signal to engage the enemy … 20 Minutes past 4 hauled down the white pendant and kept the blue and yellow checquered flag flying under the red flag – 25. Minutes past 5 hauled down the signal for the line. At the same time the signal for Closer Action was flying.[18]

As Padfield points out, this confirms that the red flag calling for close action was seen aboard the *Barfleur*. The problem was that, in the belief that the signal for line ahead was still flying, 'Hood and the captains who had been drilled by Rodney to unquestioning obedience and allowed no latitude whatever for initiative were unable to resolve the apparent contradiction'.[19] It was in order to address that problem, of course, that Graves hauled down, twice, the signal for line ahead.

Firing began at 4:15 p.m., and the ships of Drake's squadron were soon heavily engaged. As the first broadsides were exchanged, Captain Robinson of the *Shrewsbury* lost a leg, and his first lieutenant was killed; and aboard the *Réfléchi*, the fourth ship in the French line, *Capitaine de Vaisseau* de Boades was killed, causing the ship to bear away followed by the *Caton*. The four leading French ships were for a while under fire not only from Drake's division but the leading ships of the British centre as well. The French ships had the advantage of firing from their windward ports, so that as they heeled slightly away from the wind they were clear of the water; the British, on the other hand, heeling slightly towards the enemy, were somewhat hampered both in range and accuracy.[20]

The ferocity of the engagement at the head of the line is to be seen from the account of a young Marine officer aboard the 64-gun *Intrepid*:

> We, the second ship in our van, engaged two hours and 10 minutes, during which time we had three ships firing at us, and we blazed away at them above 80 barrels of powder… The van ship, the *Shrewsbury* was

17 Chadwick (ed.), *Graves Papers*, pp.182-183; Padfield, *Maritime Supremacy*, p.265.
18 Chadwick (ed.), *Graves Papers*, p.204.
19 Padfield, *Maritime Supremacy*, p.266.
20 Pengelly, *Sir Samuel Hood and the Battle of the Chesapeake*, p.142.

disabled a good deal and we took the fire of her ship from her and obliged her to bear out of the line, for which the little *Intrepid* had the thanks of the Admiral the saving of a 74-gun ship.[21]

The *Intrepid* was engaged with the first two ships of the French line, the *Pluton* and *Marseillai*s, and in the course of the action suffered 'sixty five shot holes in the starboard side, nineteen between wind and water; the rudder much damaged; two shot through the middle of the bowsprit; three shot in the foremast; two in the main mast; main top mast almost cut into and in great danger of falling; sails and rigging very much cut; all the boats damaged'.[22]

The *Shrewsbury,* which had been rescued by the prompt action of Captain Molloy of the *Intrepid*, had, before she turned away, suffered even more severely. Her 'foremast was shot through in three different places… Three shot through the head of the main mast… mizzenmast almost cut off in two places… five shot underwater, one of these gone thro' … two 18-pdrs disabled and the carriage of another'. Overall, with her masts, yards and sails so shattered, she was unable to keep the line.[23] These two ships suffered the heaviest British casualties during the battle, *Shrewsbury* having 66 killed and wounded and *Intrepid* 56.

The rest of Drake's ships also suffered considerably. The *Alcide*, third in the line, lost 20 men killed and wounded; her mainmast and mizzentopmast were both shot through, and she was hit several times below the waterline. Following her, the *Princessa* had extensive damage to her masts and rigging, and she was also hit several times below the waterline; she suffered a total of 17 casualties. The *Ajax* lost her foretopgallantmast, and her mizzentopmast was shot through, and her rigging much cut up. She had 23 men killed and wounded. Finally, the hapless *Terrible* had two large shot through her foremast and two buried in it, and several shot between wind and water. Her pumps were blown and were barely kept together, and she was now making two feet two inches of water in 25 minutes. She had lost 25 men.[24]

During this engagement between the respective van squadrons, the French had unmistakeably had the better of it. Nevertheless, they were not unscathed. The *Caton*, which had been following the *Réfléchi* when she turned out of line at the start of the action, was badly damaged, suffering 54 hits. So was the *Diadême*, which was heavily engaged with the *Princessa* at close range; Drake's flagship, according to one French observer 'set fire to her at every shot, the wadding entering her side'. The *Diadême*, he wrote, 'was utterly unable to keep up the battle, having only four 36-pounders and nine 18-pounders fit for use… At this juncture M de Chabert,

---

21   Quoted in Alan G. Jamieson, 'Two Scottish Marines in the American War,' *The Mariners Mirror* (February 1984), p.27.

22   Chadwick (ed.), *Graves Papers*, p.70.

23   Chadwick (ed.), *Graves Papers*, pp.69-70.

24   Chadwick (ed.), *Graves Papers*, pp.71-72.

commanding the *Saint Esprit*, which had for a long time been engaged with the British admiral, and who was himself wounded, seeing the imminent danger of the *Diadême*, hoisted sail and was soon in her wake, opening a terrible fire.[25]

Bougainville, in the *Auguste*, also became closely engaged with the *Princessa*, and at one point was close to boarding her. Drake succeeded in avoiding this, and Bougainville turned his attention to the *Terrible*, and subjected her to a fearful pounding. He noted in his journal that the *Auguste* had fired 684 shot during the course of the action; his ship suffered a total of 68 men killed wounded. De Grasse, between whom and Bougainville there had existed a distinct coolness, was enormously impressed, singling his second-in-command out for particular commendation when later describing the battle to Washington and Rochambeau.

Having displayed the signal for close action, the *London* headed for the French line. She was, however, almost at once hampered by the *Montagu*:

> In bearing down, when the signal was made for that purpose, the *London* by taking the lead had advanced further toward the enemy than some of the ships which were stationed immediately ahead of her in the line of battle; and when luffing up, to bring her broadside to bear, they having done the same thing, her second ahead (the *Montagu*) was nearly brought on the weather beam. The other ships ahead of her likewise crowded together.[26]

When the centre division opened fire it was at very long range. The master's log of the *Princessa* noted at 4:17 p.m. that 'some of the leading ships in the centre division began to engage, but at too great a distance' and at 4:28 p.m. noted that 'being abreast of our opponent (the fourth ship in the line) began to engage at two cables' length distance'. The master's log of the *Royal Oak*, second ahead in the centre, refers to the incident in which the *Montagu*, her next ahead, hampered the *London*, about 50 minutes after the action began: 'Hove all aback for the *Montagu* to preserve her station in the line, as she dropped abreast of us to windward; immediately the Admiral made our signal to keep the station on the line'. The *Montagu* was apparently the first to open fire followed by the *Royal Oak*.[27]

At the range at which the *London* first opened fire, her shot was indeed falling short of the French line, but the range gradually closed, and the leading ships of the centre division soon began to suffer considerable damage. The leading ship, the *Europe*, had received four shot in her main mast, with the main yard damaged and twelve shot between wind and water as well as a great number in her upper works.

25   Shea, *Operations of the French Fleet*, p.71.
26   Robert Beatson, *Naval and Military Memoirs of Great Britain from 1727 to 1783* (London: J Strachan, 1804), Vol.V, p.273
27   Barnes and Owen (eds), *Private Papers of John, Earl of Sandwich*, Vol.IV, p.190.

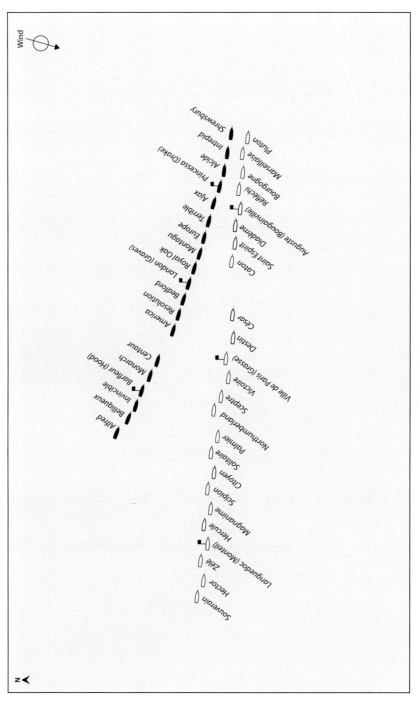

The two fleets engage.

The opposing fleets at the Battle of the Chesapeake. The *Pluton*, left, engages the *Shrewsbury* at the head of their respective lines of battle. (US Navy Naval History and Heritage Command)

It was reported that she was making water. Her total casualties were 27 men killed and wounded. The *Montagu* had been more seriously damaged, her 'hull much shattered by shot – shot through the main piece of the rudder, which has split it – the fore topgallantmast shot through; five shot in the mainmast, one of which is gone through – the main yard shot half off – main top mast shot through seven feet above the cap'.

Four of her guns had been dismounted and her rigging and sails had been very much cut. The total casualties amounted to 30 men killed and wounded.[28]

Next in line, the *Royal Oak*, suffered less severely, although having taken 17 hits, and she had proportionately fewer casualties amounting to nine men. The *London*, however, had been hit repeatedly with a number of shot in her side, several of which were under water, and three of her guns were dismounted. She lost 22 men, killed and wounded. Following her the *Bedford* had taken 14 shots in her side, several of which were under water, and damage to both her mainmast and foremast. She lost 22 men. Next came the *Resolution* which suffered damage to her main mast and bowsprit, her total casualties amounting to 19. Last of the centre division, the *America* was undamaged and suffered no casualties. The same was true of the six ships of Hood's division, although both the *Centaur* and *Monarch* sustained hits to their mainmasts.

The Comte d'Ethy, captain of the *Citoyen*, 74, part of the French rear, recorded his impressions of the fighting, particularly with regard to Hood's division:

> The vans were fighting at very close range … but the enemy, instead of fully engaging themselves, hauled their wind at the moment that they fired their broadsides. Their admiral himself, for fear of approaching to close, laid everything against his mast at 4:30 p,m. The action commenced at the centre of the fleet from the van and to the rear of Admiral de Grasse. The enemy, although master of the wind, only engaged from far off and simply in order to be able to say that they had fought. In that part of the line it was not at all the way it was in the van of the two fleets, where one could see only fire and smoke billowing on both sides.[29]

These statistics demonstrate clearly the limited extent to which the rearmost ships became involved in the battle. Their engagement with the French rear, such as it was, was at long range. Hood did not feel able to bear down towards the enemy until 5:25 p.m., the time at which, according to the log of the *Barfleur*, the signal for the line was hauled down. At this point he was three quarters of a mile downwind of the centre division. As Hood's division altered course to close, however, the enemy rear itself bore away to leeward, and barely came within range at all.

---

28   See Chadwick (ed.), *Graves Papers*, pp.73-74 for the various log entries quoted.
29   Chadwick (ed.), *Graves Papers*, p.232.

During the fierce engagement between the two van divisions de Grasse became concerned about the punishment being taken by his ships, and he ordered Bougainville to bear away to leeward. This was not, however, practicable, because the two lines were fighting at close range, and if the French ships had turned away, presenting their stern, they would have been raked by the British. When the French van did finally begin to open the range, it might have appeared, excusably, to British eyes, that this amounted to a retreat, but in fact de Grasse was merely endeavouring to turn his fleet into one continuous line without gaps between divisions. According to one French account:

> With much eagerness he [de Grasse] desired a general engagement, he signalled to the Van to go more freely in order to invite Admiral Graves to follow, but as the English fleet was already severely punished, the latter determined to keep the advantage of the wind and fight at a greater distance in order to avoid the fire of the last French ships which were approaching.[30]

As the range opened, firing became less general, and at about 6:30 p.m. finally ceased, Graves having at 6:23 p.m. made the signal for line ahead, hauling down the red flag. It was his firm intention to renew the action on the following day, and he sent a message to Drake to this effect adding that the line of battle should be kept. The *Solebay* was sent to the rear, and the *Fortunée* to the van with orders for the night sailing, which Graves intended should enable him to maintain his position relative to the French fleet.

The captain of the *Citoyen* continued his somewhat derisive comments about the ineffectual performance of Hood's division as the battle came to its end:

> By 5:15 p.m the wind was very light and variable from east to east north-east. Our rear squadron found itself close hauled by the dropping away of the light breeze. At 5:45 p.m the three decked ship [the *Barfleur*] commanding the enemy rear came up, as well as the two ships ahead of her, opposite the *Palmier* and *Solitaire*. Some moments after their arrival, they hove to and experimented to see whether their cannonballs would reach our ships. The enemy admiral [Hood] began by firing several shots and the other ships, which had also hauled their wind, followed suit. The ships of the enemy rearguard always held the windward position; their fire became general up as far as my ship, but it did not last long, the enemy remaining hove to … I had much the better of the exchange with the three decker, for it appeared to me that nearly all her cannonballs fell into the

---

30   Quoted in Pengelly, *Sir Samuel Hood and the Battle of the Chesapeake*, pp.147-148.

sea before they reached us, while the few that we fired were not wasted, or if so, it was because they overshot the enemy.[31]

Although Graves had intended to remain in close touch with a view to renewing the battle on the following morning, this soon began to appear too sanguine. When the *Fortunée* returned to the flagship at about 10:00 p.m., she brought alarming news of the extent of the damage suffered by Drake's division, and in particular the *Shrewsbury, Intrepid* and *Princessa*. Graves was already aware of the leaky state of the *Terrible* and *Ajax*, and at about 9:00 p.m. the *Montagu* had notified him that she was in danger of losing her masts and could not keep her place in the line. It began to look to Graves as though a resumption of the engagement in the morning might well not be feasible, since the French had the appearance of not having suffered nearly so much damage as the British had sustained. During the night, as he pondered his situation, the wind was light and variable from northeast by east to east north-east. The two fleets, visible to each other from their signal lanterns, remained about three miles apart. A French account noted:

> The fleet passed the night in the presence of the enemy in line of battle, the fires in all the vessels lighted. These signs of victory were not belied in the morning, for we perceived by the sailing of the English that they had suffered greatly.[32]

At dawn on 6 September the weather was moderate and clear, and in both fleets emergency repairs were carried out to masts and rigging. At 5:45 a.m. Graves made the signal for the fleet to form line ahead, at half a cable's length. During the morning, as the work of repair continued, Drake shifted his flag to the *Alcide* while the *Princessa* replaced her topmast. Graves felt uncertain as to what should be his next move. Lacking, perhaps, in self-confidence, he sent a message to Hood, 'desiring his opinion whether the action should be renewed'. Hood's response was, entirely characteristically, cold and unhelpful: 'I daresay Mr Graves will do what is right; I can send no opinion, but whenever he, Mr Graves, wishes to see me, I will wait upon him with great pleasure'.[33]

Both Graves and Hood had already spent part of the morning at their desks. Graves was concerned to leave his captains in no doubt as to the meaning of the signals which he had been displaying during the battle. Given the controversy that was about to break over his head, his memorandum is, as Corbett noted, of no small interest:

31 Chadwick (ed.), *Graves Papers*, p.232.
32 Shea, *Operations of the French Fleet*, p.157.
33 Chadwick (ed.), *Graves Papers*, p.91.

It practically amounts to his reading Hood a lecture on the theory of the line, and reproving him for adhering to its letter instead of acting boldly in its manifest spirit. The signal for the line, he says, is not to be understood as rendering the signal for battle ineffectual 'by too strict adherence to the former'. It is merely to be regarded as 'the line of extension,' to develop the full fire face of the fleet, and captains are 'desired… to keep as near to the enemy as possible whilst the signal for close action continues out'. Had Nelson written these remarks we should know them like household words, but Graves is a dog that won himself a bad name. He concluded with an injunction that captains were to see they kept a line parallel with the enemy without regard to any particular point or bearing, and the same day he issued a new signal with that signification.[34]

This, of course, was locking the stable door after the horse had bolted. Hood, always ready to take offence, was duly offended; he wrote indignantly on his copy of Graves's memorandum:

It is the first time I ever heard it suggested that too strict an adherence could be paid to the line of battle; and if I understand the meaning of the British fleet being to be formed parallel to that of the enemy, it is, that if the enemy's fleet is disorderly and irregularly formed, the British fleet is, in compliment to it, to form irregularly and disorderly also. Now, the direct contrary is my opinion … According to Mr Graves's memo, any captain may break the line with impunity when he pleases.[35]

That of course, was not what Graves's memorandum said, but Hood was no doubt extremely cross when he read it.

Hood, meanwhile, had taken up his pen to launch a pre-emptive strike on the subject of the blame to be attached to the outcome of the previous day's battle, and composed a paper setting out his opinion in no uncertain terms. This he entitled 'Sentiments Upon the Truly Unfortunate Day,' and the frame of mind in which he approached the fleet's present situation can be judged from his opening paragraph: 'Yesterday the British fleet had a rich and most plentiful harvest of glory in view, but the means to gather it were omitted in more Instances than one'.[36] Further reference to this remarkable document will be made in the concluding chapter.

As night fell on 6 September, Graves summoned Hood and Drake to a conference aboard his flagship. By this time the opposing forces had moved to a position some 20 miles or so south west of Cape Henry. Their stately manoeuvring had

34   Corbett, (ed.), *Signals and Instructions*, p.55.
35   Laughton (ed.), *Letters and Papers of Charles Lord Barham*, Vol.I, p.12
36   Chadwick (ed.), *Graves Papers*, p.89.

steadily improved de Grasse's position relative to the wind. In the light airs de Grasse had by 4:00 p.m. got into the windward position, and Graves was becoming concerned, as he subsequently reported:

> In the present state of the fleet, and being five sail of the line less in number than the enemy, and they having advanced in the wind very much upon us during the day, I determined to tack after eight, to prevent being drawn too far from the Chesapeake, and to stand to the northward.[37]

Graves did not leave an account of the meeting with Hood and Drake, but the former did, although he appears to have conflated his recollection of this meeting and a subsequent meeting held two days later, since he refers to intelligence having been received from the two frigates which Graves sent into the Chesapeake, which could not have been received before 8 September.[38] Hood mentioned also that on 6 September Graves referred to a letter which he had received from Clinton to be passed to Cornwallis, and this could only relate to the later meeting. In fact the *Medea* had been sent into the Chesapeake on the morning of 6 September, but it was not until that evening that she met the *Iris*. However, Hood did tell Jackson, in a letter of 16 September in which he enclosed a copy of his 'Sentiments,' that he had mentioned them to Graves at the meeting, which could not have made for a comfortable discussion. An account of the meeting was published in the following year by the *Political and Military Journal*, although the source for its contents was not revealed:

> Admiral Graves asked Admiral Hood why he did not bear down and engage? The answer was: 'You had up the signal for the line'. Admiral Graves then turned to Admiral Drake, and asked him how he came to bear down? He replied: 'On account of the signal for action'. Admiral Graves then said: 'What say you to this, Admiral Hood?' Sir Samuel answered: 'The signal for the line was enough for me'.[39]

On the French side, from where it could be seen that the British were engaged in carrying out considerable repairs, it appeared to Bougainville it was unlikely that the British would renew the action that day. The French had suffered much less damage to their ships, though their total casualties – 209 killed and wounded – were not greatly different from the British total of 336. One ship, the *Diadême*, had been particularly badly damaged; the *Pluton*, which had been leading the line, had lost a topmast and was replaced in that position by the *Souverain*. All the while the

---

37   Hannay (ed.), *Letters Written by Sir Samuel Hood*, p.42.
38   Larrabee, *Decision at the Chesapeake*, p.181.
39   Larrabee, *Decision at the Chesapeake*, p.181.

British were in the windward position de Grasse was content to watch and wait for a favourable opportunity.

During the following day the fleets remained in sight of each other, in variable winds and squally showers. The distance between them varied from six to 12 miles. Although de Grasse tacked towards the British fleet, it kept well away. During the day, the *Medea*, having left the *Iris* at Cape Henry, went into the Chesapeake to reconnoitre, and occupied herself cutting away the buoys that had been left behind by the French when they slipped their anchors. That night her captain reported to Graves on the ships moored in Chesapeake Bay, which included at least three ships of the line.[40]

De Grasse hoped that he might find an opportunity to launch an attack, next day writing to Bougainville:

> If the wind continues and the English do not escape us tonight, we shall meet them at close range tomorrow morning, and I hope the day will be a happier one, which will permit us to go back and take those Johnnies in the Chesapeake. What a joy it will be to have the ships of de Barras united with us! What a body blow that will be, and decisive, too, instead of this uncertain state of affairs where the forces are only equal and poorly manned. I have great hope based upon the damage to the enemy which I can see.[41]

For all the enthusiasm which he expressed for a renewal of the engagement, de Grasse's movements were extremely cautious, rather tending to justify his description as 'a bold strategist but a timid tactician'. On 8 September the British again gained the windward position, at which time the French fleet was in chequerboard formation, close hauled on the port tack; it immediately tacked and formed line ahead, The British fleet was not, however, in a well-formed line, and was on the opposite tack; Graves abandoned the weather gauge, and edged away.

During the day the *Terrible* made the signal for distress. On the following day her condition worsened, and in a letter to Graves which her captain sent over, he reported that she would, but for the pumps, be taking on water at the rate of six feet an hour, and he was 'apprehensive the ship cannot be saved, our Foremast is much wounded'.[42] Her condition continued to deteriorate, and next day she began throwing over the lower deck guns. By 11 September her captain was reporting that this had not made any difference, and at a council of war aboard the *London* that day Graves, Hood and Drake resolved 'to take out her people and sink her'. That evening she was set on fire and burned. Her poor condition was due to the electrolytic effect of her coppering on the iron bolts that held the hull together,

40 Chadwick (ed.), *Graves Papers*, pp.82-83.
41 Larrabee, *Decision at the Chesapeake*, p.183.
42 Chadwick (ed.), *Graves Papers*, p.81.

a problem that afflicted ships that had been coppered in the early stages of the programme before a solution was found. Lord Robert Manners, captain of the *Resolution* at the Chesapeake, wrote:

> We felt severely the danger of keeping coppered line of battle ships long out without looking at their bottoms, as the *Terrible*, one of the finest seventy-fours we had, by her exceeding bad state even before she left the West Indies, and by the firing of her own guns, and the enemy's shot in the action, was found in so desperate a state that she was ordered to be scuttled and set on fire.[43]

Graves was meeting regularly with his two flag officers during this period. It must have been on 8 September that he spoke of the intelligence from the *Medea*, and said that he had sent the *Richmond* and *Iris* back to the Chesapeake with the letter from Clinton and for further reconnaissance. This was a decision which Hood criticised, as he later reported in his letter to Jackson of 16 September: 'The *Richmond* and *Iris* were detached upon that service, I fear to be cut off, and think the whole squadron should have gone; they might then not only most effectually have succoured Lord Cornwallis, but have destroyed the enemy's ships there'.[44]

On 9 September de Grasse had made up his mind that after all there was not going to be any further engagement, and that he should return to the Chesapeake. That evening he gave orders accordingly. Bougainville, writing in his journal, thought that this decision was long overdue: 'I was very much afraid that the British might try to get to the Chesapeake under press of sail ahead of us. It is what we ought to have been doing since the battle'.[45]

The disappearance of the French, when dawn broke on 10 September, prompted a letter from Hood to Graves:

> By the press of sail de Grasse carried yesterday (and he must even have done the same the preceding night, by being where [he] was at daylight), I am inclined to think his aim is the Chesapeake, in order to be strengthened by his ships there, either by adding them to his present force, or by exchanging his disabled ships for them. Admitting that to be his plan, will he not cut off the frigates you have sent to reconnoitre, as well as the ships you expect from New York? And if he should enter the bay, which is by no means improbable, will he not succeed in giving most effective succour to the rebels?[46]

43   Quoted in Rodger, *Command of the Ocean*, p.375.
44   Hannay (ed.), *Letters Written by Sir Samuel Hood*, p.29.
45   Larrabee, *Decision at the Chesapeake*, p.185.
46   Chadwick (ed.), *Graves Papers*, p.92.

In his letter to Jackson, Hood described how he had come to write to Graves. Alarmed by the disappearance of the French, he said, he debated with himself as to whether he should write to Graves, 'as it is rather an awkward and unpleasant business to send advice to a senior officer'. However, he found the courage to do so, and this led to a further meeting aboard the *London* with Graves and Drake, as Hood described:

> I found, to my very great astonishment, Mr Graves as ignorant as myself where the French fleet was, and that no frigates were particularly ordered (for we had several with us) to watch and bring an account of the enemy's motions. The question was put to me, what was most proper to be done? To which I replied that I thought the letter I had taken the liberty to send had fully and clearly explained what my sentiments were.[47]

If pressed to say more, he added, it could only be to get into the Chesapeake to succour Cornwallis, but he was afraid that the opportunity of doing so had passed by. Hood was a master of putting the words and actions of others in the worst possible light. His prediction about the fate of the *Richmond* and the *Iris* came true next day, when they were both captured by the *Aigrette* and *Diligente* as they attempted to escape the bay to re-join the fleet.

Graves waited, for no obvious reason, until 12 September to send in the *Medea* to ascertain the position in the Chesapeake, and on the morning of the following day her captain, Henry Duncan, reported that the French fleet was now at anchor off the Horseshoe Shoal, in the Chesapeake. Advising Hood of this, Graves rather feebly asked his opinion of what he should now do with the fleet and how to dispose of the *Princessa*. Hood's reply was predictable; he was concerned to hear that the French fleet was in the Chesapeake, though it was no more than he expected; he 'would be very glad to send an opinion, but he really knows not what to say in the truly lamentable state we have brought ourselves'.[48]

Graves's response was to call another council of war for later that day. This minuted that, after receiving the *Medea*'s report:

> Upon this state of the position of the enemy, the present condition of the British fleet, the season of the year so near the Equinox, and the impracticability of giving any effectual succour to General Cornwallis in the Chesapeake; it was resolved that the British squadron ...should proceed with all possible dispatch to New York, and there use every possible means for putting the squadron in the best state for service.[49]

47 Chadwick (ed.), *Graves Papers*, pp.88-89.
48 Chadwick (ed.), *Graves Papers*, pp.93-94.
49 Hannay (ed.), *Letters Written by Sir Samuel Hood*, pp.35-36.

It was a tame end to the proceedings of the British fleet, but in the circumstances there was really no alternative, not least because on entering the Chesapeake de Grasse had found the squadron of Barras at anchor, bringing the total of ships of the line potentially available to 36 (although Duncan had made no mention of this).

22

Aftermath

While on his way back to New York Graves composed his official report of the battle to the Admiralty, which he sent to Philip Stephens on 14 September. With his report he enclosed a number of papers to explain the movements of the fleet, the events of 5 September and the current condition of his ships, but he made no comment on the failure of Hood's division to support the rest of the fleet.[1] At the same time he wrote his private letter to Sandwich, previously quoted, in which he explained his tactical intentions in conducting the battle, aiming 'to get close, to form parallel, extend with them and attack all together'. His constant attention, he said, 'was to press the enemy close; the signal for close action was made at the time when the enemy's centre and rear were too far behind to support their van'. He went on to explain that he had taken in the signal for the line before the firing began:

> Unfortunately the signal for the line was thought to be kept up until half after five, when the rear division bore down; but the fair occasion was gone … The French line was 24 heavy ships, ours 19; yet I think had our efforts been made together, some of their van, four or five sail, must have been cut to pieces. The signal was not understood. I do not mean to blame anyone, my Lord. I hope we all did our best.[2]

It was a fair, even generous, account of the battle.

The fleet returned to New York on 20 September. Graves's immediate concern was the need for repairs to so many of the ships of the fleet, for which the resources of the dockyard at New York were known to be inadequate. Clinton had been aware since 17 September of the outcome of the battle on the 5th, and, as soon as Graves arrived, wrote to him asking for a meeting to discuss the strategy to be adopted for the relief of Cornwallis. Clinton had by no means given himself up to despair; he

1   Chadwick (ed.), *Graves Papers*, pp.61-84.
2   Barnes and Owen (eds), *Private Papers of John, Earl of Sandwich*, Vol.IV, p.182.

knew that Digby was en route from England with at least three ships of the line, and that two more were expected from Jamaica, while the total of 24 with which de Grasse had faced Graves was supposed to have included Barras's squadron. With the *Prudent,* 64, which had replaced the *Terrible*, and the *Robust*, 74 which it was hoped would soon be repaired, a total of 25 ships of the line should be available to contest the control of the Chesapeake.

Even before he received news of the battle, Clinton had been turning his mind to the question of what means to adopt for the relief. By 6 September he was aware of the size of the enemy forces converging on Yorktown. He wrote to Cornwallis on that day to promise that a relief expedition would indeed be sent. It was an upbeat letter, referring to the imminent arrival of Digby with reinforcements. Clinton continued:

> I think the best way to relieve you is to join you as soon as possible, with all the force that can be spared from hence, which is about 4,000 men. They are already embarked, and will proceed the instant that I receive information from the Admiral that we may, and that from other intelligence the Commodore and I shall judge sufficient to move upon.[3]

Cornwallis received this letter on 14 September. It led him to abandon the attempt to break out of Yorktown which he had been planning. He had intended to launch his army down the long straight road to Williamsburg in a night advance, having chosen this simpler plan than a more complex scheme which involved sending a sizeable part of his force in small boats up the York River to attack Lafayette's rear, while the rest of the army attacked his front. To attack Lafayette would have been a bold move, but it could only have succeeded if it was launched before the troops of Washington and Rochambeau arrived on the scene – in other words, before 26 September. Even so, he would have been outnumbered by Lafayette and Saint-Simon. As it was, Cornwallis concluded that the wiser course was to await relief; when it came, the whole British force might then be strong enough to strike a decisive blow at Washington. By 17 September he had made up his mind, and wrote to Clinton: 'If I had no hopes of relief I would rather risk an action then defend my half finished works. But as you say Admiral Digby is hourly expected, and promise every exertion to assist me, I do not think myself justifiable in putting the fate of the war on so desperate an attempt'.[4] In thus abandoning his only narrow window of opportunity Cornwallis gave up the last chance of being the master of his fate.

While aware of the substantial odds that Cornwallis would have faced once Washington and Rochambeau had arrived, Clinton was nonetheless surprised and displeased that the earl had not launched an attack on Saint-Simon's force once it

---

3   Wickwire and Wickwire, *Cornwallis and the War of Independence*, p.362.
4   Wickwire and Wickwire, *Cornwallis and the War of Independence*, p.364.

had been landed; but this was hardly reasonable, since Lafayette had been on hand to join the battle, and it would have meant abandoning the works at Yorktown.

Back in New York, Clinton had warned Germain in a letter of 12 September that if the French retained command of the sea for only a few weeks 'we shall certainly be beat in detail,' and that if Graves could not defeat de Grasse he would despair of being able to relieve Cornwallis.[5] He convened a meeting of his senior officers on 13 September with Commodore Edmund Affleck, the senior naval officer, at which the latter suggested that 5,000 troops, escorted only by the *Robust*, should be sent to the Chesapeake, the navy forcing a way through to effect a landing on York Island. Since de Grasse would be in the way unless Graves had destroyed his fleet, and since the force would lack supplies, this suggestion was rejected out of hand.[6] An alternative plan to land in New Jersey and march on Philadelphia was considered, before Major General James Robertson, whom Clinton disliked, suggested that no action be taken before Digby arrived. No decision was reached, and Clinton asked Robertson to review the position and give his opinion.

Next day Robertson put his suggestions to Clinton. All were based on his belief that if Yorktown fell, and with it Cornwallis's army, the war was as good as lost. Action was essential, wrote Robertson, since 'all the ills that may be foreseen are at most probabilities; possibly they may not happen. But the destruction of the whole is certain if the Army in Virginia is destroyed'.[7] In spite of this clear recognition of the desperate situation of Cornwallis's army, there still pervaded these discussions an extraordinary lack of urgency, perhaps due to what might be hoped from Digby's arrival, and perhaps because it was calculated that Cornwallis could hold out until the end of October. At all events, a further meeting took place on 14 September. It should be remembered that at this time the outcome of the battle of 5 September was not known. Clinton read out the correspondence that had passed, and reported Graves's pessimism about 'anything getting into the York River'.[8] Predictably enough the meeting temporised, unanimous in agreeing to wait for favourable news from Graves or until Digby arrived.

On his return to New York Graves was concerned to make clear to Clinton the condition of his fleet, writing on 21 September that he was willing 'to undertake any service in conjunction with the army that shall be thought advisable,' but adding:

> At the same time I should be greatly wanting were I not to apprise your Excellency that the injuries received by the fleet in the action, added to the complaints of several very crazy ships, makes it quite uncertain how soon

---

5   Syrett, *American Waters*, p.205.
6   Syrett, *American Waters*, p.205.
7   Syrett, *American Waters*, p.205.
8   Syrett, *American Waters*, p.206.

the fleet can be got to sea. One ship we have been obliged to abandon, and another is in a very doubtful state.[9]

The letter from Cornwallis announcing his decision not to attempt to break out arrived on 23 September. It sharpened the general awareness of the need for urgency that had hitherto been lacking by concluding: 'This place is in no state of defence. If you cannot relieve me very soon, you must be prepared to hear the Worst'.[10] Clinton at once convened another council of war, attended by his four most senior officers, which agreed that there must be a landing of troops near Yorktown, and this very soon. Next day, the army officers met again, this time with Graves and his senior colleagues. Graves reported the outcome of the meeting to Philip Stephens:

> It was concluded upon, that the Ships of war Shou'd take on board what provisions they could for the army, embark the General Sir Henry Clinton and six thousand troops if possible, and so soon as it cou'd be got ready, to make an attempt to force its way, and that three fire ships shou'd be added to the one already here which are now preparing with every possible exertion, and it was hoped the whole might be ready in 10 days.[11]

Cornwallis's letter had also brought the disquieting news that the French fleet now had 36 ships of the line. Even though this cast grave doubts on the prospects of the relief expedition, Clinton, at least outwardly, remained optimistic.

While the council of war was in session, the arrival of the squadron bringing Digby was signalled. His flag was in the *Prince George*, 98, and with him came the *Canada*, 74 (commanded by Cornwallis's brother William), the *Lion*, 64, and a frigate. The wind prevented their entering harbour; next morning Hood hurried out by boat to pay his respects to the King's son, Prince William, who was serving aboard as a midshipman. Meanwhile the council of war had concluded by agreeing the text of a letter to be sent to Cornwallis. The cheerful confidence of the letter reflected the optimism of the commander-in-chief rather than the more realistic attitude of the admirals:

> At a meeting of the flag and general officers held this day, in consequence of your Lordship's letter of the 16th and 17th instant, it was unanimously determined that above five thousand men should be embarked on board the King's ships, and the joint exertions of the fleet and army shall be

9   Larrabee, *Decision at the Chesapeake*, pp.195-196.
10 Syrett, *American Waters*, p.208.
11 Chadwick (ed.), *Graves Papers*, p.97.

made in a few days to relieve you. There is every reason to hope that we shall start from hence about the 5th of October.[12]

Those present may well have sincerely believed that a departure on 5 October was possible, but the work of repairing the fleet was by no means proceeding at a satisfactory pace. Graves had warned Stephens of this in his account of the discussion at the council of war: 'The whole fleet are as busy as they can be but I am very apprehensive that so much as is wanted to the fleet, such a poverty of every kind of stores and provisions, and so much to do for the army afterwards, will consume more time than was foreseen'.[13]

By now it was necessary for Graves to discuss with Digby the ticklish question of the latter's assumption of command according to his orders. Perhaps as an act of courtesy towards the admiral who had hitherto borne the burden of the campaign against de Grasse, and perhaps with a consideration that the expedition would in all probability not end well, Digby deferred taking over the command for the time being. Whatever Graves may have thought about this, he realised that it was only temporary, and that he must in due course make his way to Jamaica to take up the position of second-in-command there to Sir Peter Parker in accordance with the Admiralty's orders. He wrote to Stephens plaintively to complain that such a posting implied 'such a disapprobation of my conduct as will certainly discredit me in the opinion of mankind' and to express the hope that their Lordships would not suffer him to remain long in so painful a situation.[14]

The work of repair went on as quickly as possible. Graves may well have had serious doubts about the wisdom of the planned operation, but did not express them. Affleck was certainly pessimistic; he had observed of an earlier proposal that he would only carry it out with written statements from the senior officers involved approving such a plan. Hood, though, seems to have been more bullish, and chafed at the continued delay, observing to Jackson that every moment was precious. It must have been evident to all that this was so, since apart from the risks of the planned operation, the danger to Cornwallis from the Franco-American army that would shortly surround him increased by the day. And the risks were considerable. With the three ships that Digby had brought, there were, until the two Jamaica ships arrived, only 23 with which to attack 36 ships of the line. Even if Clinton's force was successfully put ashore, there was a serious danger that it and Graves's fleet might be trapped in the Chesapeake by the superior numbers which they faced.

While the expedition was being prepared, Cornwallis's situation in the Chesapeake had been steadily deteriorating. Washington and Rochambeau, riding

12   Larrabee, *Decision at the Chesapeake*, p.194.
13   Chadwick (ed.), *Graves Papers*, pp.97-98.
14   Chadwick (ed.), *Graves Papers*, p.111.

some days ahead of their marching armies, entered Williamsburg on the evening of 14 September, and later that night learned the news of the victory of the French fleet on 5 September. Washington hastened to send a letter of congratulation to de Grasse on recent events, which with the decided superiority of the French fleet, 'gives us the happiest presages of the most complete success in our combined operations in this bay'.[15] De Grasse, however, conscious of the fact that he had a deadline to meet in getting back to the West Indies, was discontented with the slow progress of the army of Washington and Rochambeau in closing on Cornwallis, reminding them that 'the season is approaching, when, against my will, I shall be obliged to forsake the Allies for whom I have done my very best and more than could be expected '.[16] Washington and Rochambeau, with a number of their senior colleagues, had an opportunity to discuss the situation with de Grasse when, on 17 September, they paid a visit to his flagship. It was a joyous occasion, and at a lavish dinner many enthusiastic toasts were drunk. More importantly, de Grasse was able to give reassuring answers to a number of questions which Washington put to him. Although his instructions had been to leave on 15 October, he would stay until 1 November. Saint-Simon's troops would stay as long as he did. He would reconnoitre before deciding whether to send ships upriver beyond Yorktown; he would land 1,800- 2,000 seamen to serve ashore in the siege operations, and would supply both guns and ammunition. He was not, however, prepared to spare ships to blockade the British forces at Wilmington and Charleston. De Grasse's response was very welcome to Washington, who wrote to him on 20 September to express his 'high satisfaction'.[17]

At Yorktown, Cornwallis was heavily engaged in the task of strengthening his defences. His outer line was based on a number of natural features which gave it some support. To the west of Yorktown, a ravine ran from the York River, curving around about half of the semicircle of defences, and at the river end there was a strong fortification known as the Fusiliers' Redoubt. The outer line continued from the ravine to Wormley Creek, which began half a mile to the east. The position was sited to command each of the four roads which approached Yorktown. There were a number of small redoubts near the head of Wormley Creek, and three redoubts in the sector between that and the ravine. Cornwallis's inner line of defence was based on a series of 10 redoubts. Two, on his right, faced the river road from Williamsburg. Three more were constructed in the back of Yorktown, and three more on his left, facing eastward. In advance of the latter he built two more redoubts, numbers 9 and 10, to strengthen what might, during the siege, become the weakest point of his defences.[18] He had 65 guns in the 14 batteries along his

15   Philbrick, *In the Hurricane's Eye*, p.196.
16   Lewis, *Admiral de Grasse*, p.174.
17   Lewis, *Admiral de Grasse*, p.175.
18   Wickwire and Wickwire, *Cornwallis and the War of Independence*, pp.365-366.

defence line. Along the river frontage, a number of vessels were sunk to prevent any enemy assault along the beaches.

While waiting for the siege to begin, Cornwallis sent out Tarleton to clear away American snipers who were harassing those engaged in building the defence works. At the same time, Commodore Symonds organised the fitting out of four small vessels as fireships; it had been observed from guard boats that the French ships blockading the York River were not keeping a good look out. This force consisted of three ships of the line and a frigate, and it was resolved to launch an attack on them by the fire ships as soon as the wind served. The attack was under the command of Captain Palmer of the *Vulcan*. Lieutenant Bartholomew James, who commanded one of the fireships, wrote in his journal that 'the vessels we had the command of were patched up and very ill fitted out, being all of them schooners and sloops'.[19]

On the evening of 22 September there was a favourable wind, and at midnight the fire ships cut their cables and ran down the river. At 2:00 a.m. the privateer captain of one of the fireships prematurely set fire to his vessel, alerting the French, who cut their cables and fled in disorder. The other fireships pursued them, and were set on fire, the *Vulcan* getting within a ship's length of a 74, but in the event none of them found a target. Symonds reported the attack to Graves, writing that although Captain Palmer 'did not meet with the success that was to be wished, he obliged all the enemy's ships to cut, and two sail of the line were run ashore and on board each other'.[20]

Meanwhile news had been received by Washington of Digby's arrival at New York; the report inaccurately was to the effect that he had brought with him 10 ships of the line. Washington reported this to de Grasse, who was seriously alarmed, and wrote back to say that 'it would be imprudent of me to put myself in a position where I could not engage them in battle should they attempt to come up with relief'. He proposed to leave two vessels at the mouth of the York River, and those blockading the James River, and to sail with the rest of his fleet to meet the enemy in the open sea. He warned Washington that it was possible that in the course of the battle he might be driven to leeward and be unable to return.[21]

This suggestion caused Washington the gravest concern, and he at once dispatched a long letter to de Grasse which he gave to Lafayette to deliver by hand. In this, Washington pointed out that 'the enterprise against York under the protection of your ships, is as certain as any military operation can be rendered by a decisive superiority of strengthened means, that it is in fact reducible to calculation'. The surrender of Cornwallis, he wrote, 'must necessarily go a great way towards

19   Sir J. Laughton (ed.), *Journal of Rear Admiral Bartholomew James* (London: Navy Records Society, 1896), p.116.

20   Sands, *Yorktown's Captive Fleet*, p.64.

21   Knox, *The Naval Genius of George Washington*, pp.105-106.

terminating the war, and securing the invaluable objects of it to the Allies'.[22] Rochambeau supported this with a letter of his own to much the same effect, and Lafayette went off to deliver the letters and add his own persuasion. When he reached the *Ville de Paris*, however, he found that de Grasse, after a council of war of his senior officers, had decided after all to stay put. De Grasse wrote to Washington to tell him of this; the close personal sympathy and understanding between the two of them appears from the conclusion of his letter:

> Your Excellency may be very sure that I have, so to speak, more at heart than yourself that the expedition to York may terminate agreeably to our desires. Pardon me, I beg of you, this slight uneasiness, which has been caused by my anxiety not to tarnish the glory of my master, by forfeiting the esteem of your Excellency, whose friendship and esteem I wish to preserve.[23]

The allied armies began to move into position opposite Yorktown on 28 September, the French on the western side of the defences and the Americans on the east. For Cornwallis, the key decision now was how long he should endeavour to hold his outer line. The longer he did so, the longer he could hope to hold Yorktown while awaiting relief; but a prolonged battle for the outer line would cost heavy casualties, leaving him with fewer troops should that relief arrive and offensive action become possible. It was while he was contemplating this question that on the evening of 29 September the important letter sent from New York after the council of war of 24 September, promising relief, arrived at Cornwallis's headquarters. This decided him, and he wrote at once to Clinton: 'I have this evening received your letter of the 24th which has given me the greatest satisfaction. I shall retire this night within the works, and have no doubt, if relief arrives in any reasonable time, York and Gloucester will both be in possession of his Majesty's troops'.[24] If relief did not arrive, the decision to retreat to the inner line certainly shortened the length of time he could hold out.

Back in New York the atmosphere was extremely tense, and there was widespread concern about the practicability of a rescue attempt in the Chesapeake. A young infantry officer, Frederick McKenzie, kept a diary of events, and recorded comments on the morale of some of the naval officers:

> It appears very doubtful that the Navy will after all attempt … the relief of Lord Cornwallis. The general conversation among them from the captains downwards, is, of the great superiority of the French fleet, the

22   Knox, *The Naval Genius of George Washington*, p.106.
23   Lewis, *Admiral de Grasse*, p.179.
24   Wickwire and Wickwire, *Cornwallis and the War of Independence*, p.370.

impossibility of destroying any of them by fireships, or forcing them in the position they have taken, and the certainty that they will come out immediately on the appearance of the British fleet, and attack it. They talk very freely of the conduct of the Admiral on the 5th of September, and appear more ready to censure the conduct of others then to refit their own ships.[25]

The doubts entertained by the navy soon communicated themselves to Clinton, who began to think that the relief of Cornwallis might have to be attempted by the army alone, by launching an offensive towards Philadelphia. This thought was confirmed by a letter which Graves wrote to him on 6 October asking what the position might be, should it be impossible to relieve Cornwallis, if the fleet with Clinton's troops aboard was ordered to the West Indies. This was an attempt by Graves to weaken Clinton's resolve by floating the possibility that a large part of his army would be carried away to the West Indies, and thereby perhaps persuading the commander-in-chief to call off a profoundly dangerous operation. Clinton, however, was having none of this, replying next day that the objective was the relief of Cornwallis at Yorktown, but if this failed, 'I should hope, sir, the whole fleet would return to this Port. For should any misfortune happen to the Army in Virginia, and a considerable part of this army should be carried to the West Indies, these posts would be exposed to great danger'.[26] Clinton had, before writing this, held a council of war of his senior officers, which resolved that he should attend a meeting with Graves and his flag officers; hearing of this, Graves backed off, and reassured Clinton that his letter had been mere speculation.

However, Graves remained profoundly apprehensive about the proposed expedition which he was beginning to think was impossible to carry out. He had already convened a meeting with the other admirals and Captains Cornwallis and Reynolds for 8 October, when he proposed to raise the question. This came as a great surprise to Hood, as he wrote six days later to Jackson:

> Soon after we were assembled, Mr Graves proposed, and wished to reduce to writing, the following question, 'Whether it was practicable to relieve Lord Cornwallis in the Chesapeake?' This astonished me exceedingly, as it seemed plainly to indicate a design of having difficulties started against attempting what the generals and admirals had *most unanimously* agreed to, and given under their hands on the 24th of last month, and occasioned my replying immediately that it appeared to me a very unnecessary and improper question, as it had already been maturely discussed and

25 Pengelly, *Sir Samuel Hood and the Battle of the Chesapeake*, p.180.
26 Syrett, *American Waters*, pp.213-214.

determined upon to be attempted with all the expedition possible; that my opinion had been very strong and pointed (which I was ready to give in writing with my name to it).[27]

Hood went on to repeat his view that the landing of the army should be attempted 'under every risk' and that if that was effected without much loss, the French fleet should be attacked as soon as a favourable opportunity arose.

Hood may be supposed to have expressed his views with more vigour than tact; he had plainly come to feel contempt for Graves, as he made clear in his letter to Jackson:

I own to you I think very meanly of the present commanding officer. I know he is a <u>cunning</u> man, he may be a good theoretical man, but he is certainly a bad practical one, and most clearly proved himself on the fifth of last month to be unequal to the conducting of a great squadron.[28]

Hood added a postscript: 'I trust you will bear in mind that I write to you most <u>confidentially</u>. *Desperate* cases require *bold* remedies'.

The strength of Hood's opinions was such as to ensure that the meeting was a difficult one for Graves, who seems not to have had much support from the other admirals. He raised the point that if the expedition failed, the fleet would have to return to New York to disembark the army before Hood could take his squadron back to the West Indies. Hood swatted this away imperiously; his reply, as recorded by Graves in a letter that night to Clinton, was that 'where much was at stake, something must be risked, and the West India Islands in that case must take their chance in the general event'.[29] This has the authentic ring of Hood making his point. Confronted by Hood's passionate advocacy of the proposed expedition to the Chesapeake, and his dismissal of the question which Graves wished the meeting to consider, the admiral backed down, and preparations continued.

Hood's enthusiasm for the relief expedition seems to have been based on an optimistic assessment of the situation at Yorktown, about which he wrote to William Cornwallis on 10 October:

The *Charon* is burnt by red hot shot, and the enemy threw shells into Lord Cornwallis's works, but cannot move his Lordship, who is in high spirits, has plenty of provisions, and the only man he has lost of any consequence is the head Commissary. This is all I yet know, which I thought

---

27   Chadwick (ed.), *Graves Papers*, pp.117-118.
28   Chadwick (ed.), *Graves Papers*, p.118.
29   Tilley, *The British Navy and the American Revolution*, p.207.

would be some satisfaction to you. I expect to hear more tomorrow from headquarters.[30]

At New York, planning proceeded on the assumption that de Grasse had only the 24 ships of the line with which he had fought on 5 September, and that this included the eight ships of Barras's squadron. No account was therefore taken of the actual strength of the enemy which, with those eight ships, and the four which de Grasse had sent upriver, amounted to a total of 36 ships of the line. The false assumption engendered unwarranted optimism about the task ahead.

The repairs to the more seriously damaged ships continued but only slowly. One piece of good fortune was the arrival of a French prize on 8 October, captured by the frigate *Carysfort* on her way back to New York. In a letter to Philip Stephens of 16 October Graves told him that the prize carried 'a considerable quantity of masts for large ships' which was just as well, since as he explained there was hardly a spar left in the yard. His letter also carried the news of the belated arrival of the *Torbay* and *Prince William* from Jamaica. However, not all the news was good; the weather was proving a considerable source of delay:

> The 13th inst. in a squall of wind the *Alcide* parted her cable and fell on board the *Shrewsbury* which carried away her fore yard and bowsprit. This ugly accident threw us back just at the time the troops were embarked to fall down with the first division of the men of war from Staten Island to Sandy Hook. Two ships parted their cables at Staten Island, and several drove in the North River.[31]

The pessimism which Graves had shown in convening the discussion on 8 October and which had prompted Hood's savage criticism was deepening. The latest letter from Cornwallis to Clinton, written on 11 October, had arrived in New York, and repeated that only a successful naval action could save his army. As it was, Cornwallis wrote, 'with such works on disadvantageous ground against so powerful attack, we cannot hope to make a very long resistance'.[32] With the delays to the repairs to his 'crazy and shatter'd squadron' and the accidents which had occurred, Graves saw no end to disappointments.

At Yorktown, Cornwallis had been doing his best. He still held Gloucester, on the other side of the river, where a not insubstantial force had built a line of trenches and four redoubts, supported by 19 guns. Washington had been observing the place with a force of militia, which he reinforced at the end of September with some 1,400 troops under the command of the Marquis de Choisy. Cornwallis

---

30   G. Cornwallis-West, *The Life and Letters of Admiral Cornwallis* (London: Holden, 1927), p.107.

31   Chadwick (ed.), *Graves Papers*, p.120.

32   Chadwick (ed.), *Graves Papers*, p.122.

thought that Tarleton's cavalry, which served no useful purpose in the siege lines at Yorktown, might achieve something against Choisy. On 2 October this force was shipped over to Gloucester, and next day advanced to support a foraging expedition. Returning with laden wagons, Tarleton bumped into Choisy's force, and launched a precipitate attack on the French cavalry that was leading it; this got nowhere, and he was obliged to retreat into the British lines. However, when the French horsemen followed up they ran into heavy fire from the British infantry, and fell back in their turn on Choisy's main force. Subsequently, the French invested Gloucester more closely.[33]

By 6 October Washington's artillery had arrived at the siege lines, and he could now embark on the formal siege operations by opening his first parallel. This faced Cornwallis's left, running for about 2,000 yards from the British centre, curving eastwards to the York River, and sited between six and eight hundred yards from the defence line. Within this parallel Washington now installed his artillery in a series of batteries. At 5:00 p.m. on 9 October the bombardment of the defence works began, and soon was inflicting heavy casualties on the defenders. One particular casualty of the bombardment was the destruction of the *Charon*, referred to previously. Moored off Yorktown, she was a target for the allied artillery using red hot shot. Lieutenant James, one of her officers, was on shore in charge of some of the naval guns that had been landed, and watched in dismay as his ship was set on fire:

> The enemy having opened fresh batteries on this day, and also commenced an additional fire on the *Charon* with red hot shot, she was set on fire at 6:30 o'clock in three different places, and in a few minutes in flames from the hold to the mastheads. From our being quartered at the guns in front of the army, that timely assistance could not be given her which was necessary to extinguish the fire, and she broke adrift from her moorings and drove on board a transport to which she also set fire, and they both grounded on the Gloucester side where they burned to the water's edge.[34]

On the night of 11/12 October, the allies began work on the second parallel, which advanced their siege lines to a point some 200 yards from the British works. The key objectives would be Redoubts 9 and 10, in front of which a large breastwork was constructed to serve as a jumping off point for an assault. For the next three days a heavy bombardment of the two redoubts was maintained, inflicting heavy casualties on the defenders. The hopeless position of the remaining vessels in Symonds' squadron led to orders being given that they be scuttled; the post-ship

33   Wickwire and Wickwire, *Cornwallis and the War of Independence*, pp.373-374.
34   Laughton (ed.), *Journal of Rear Admiral Bartholomew James*, p.121.

Fowey was sunk on 13 October, the frigate *Guadeloupe* two days later, and other shipping was also destroyed as the bombardment continued.[35]

In spite of the progress being made with the siege, de Grasse was becoming restless. The abortive fireship attack had made him uneasy, and he had declined to send his ships upriver to attack the British ships that had been moored off Yorktown because of the risks to which they would be exposed. In due course, however, that problem went away when the warships were scuttled. He wrote to Rochambeau defending his decision not to send his ships upriver, and went on, somewhat petulantly: 'I have trusted too much in circumstances, and I have launched myself into an affair that can turn out to my own disadvantage and to the humiliation of the nation'.[36] Repenting of these words, a few days later de Grasse sent Rochambeau a letter remorsefully explaining that he was a Provençal and a sailor, which explained why he was impulsive: 'I admit my guilt and depend upon your friendship'.[37]

In New York, in spite of all the difficulties in preparing the ships for the expedition to the Chesapeake, Clinton and his officers were, like Hood, prepared to risk everything to relieve Cornwallis. The plan was to force an entrance to Chesapeake Bay, and then to land an army of 5,000 men near Yorktown, Gloucester, or Newport News which would then join forces with Cornwallis. His army was supposed to be some 8,000 men strong. In fact, when the siege began, Cornwallis had 5,761 men fit for duty, together with about 800 sailors and marines from the warships at Yorktown. Once the junction was effected, it was thought that the British would face a total of approaching 20,000 men, consisting of Washington's Continentals, Rochambeau's army, and American militia. If the relief army got ashore, it was just possible that they could beat the enemy, in spite of the numerical disparity; but an even greater doubt was the feasibility of forcing an entrance to the Chesapeake in the face of a vastly superior fleet. De Grasse could defeat the British simply by blocking the entrance to Chesapeake Bay. Alternatively, he could let Graves into the bay and then shut the door behind him, taking in that way three prizes instead of one. Syrett concludes that Graves should at least have put his reservations about the expedition on paper, and submitted it to Clinton; in this way at least he would be relieved of any of the collective responsibility for a potential disaster.[38]

The desperate situation of Cornwallis's army was by now entirely clear, and Graves was prepared to take much greater risks in an attempt to relieve him than had been the case previously. On 15 October, in preparation for an operation that would require the absolute commitment of all engaged, he issued a set of additional signals which show how he intended to proceed. The first nine of these

35 Sands, *Yorktown's Captive Fleet*, p.82.
36 Lewis, *Admiral de Grasse*, p.184.
37 Lewis, *Admiral de Grasse*, p.185.
38 Syrett, *American Waters*, p.215.

signals were addressed to the van, centre, and rear respectively, ordering them to attack the enemy's van centre or rear, 'to force through the enemy,' or to retreat. The next five signals conveyed orders for the fleet to go into Hampton Roads, to push up to Yorktown, or to anchor as soon as it got above the enemy's fleet. Graves was plainly ready to fight, notwithstanding the unfavourable odds that he faced. Brian Tunstall observed:

> Thus, on paper, he had done everything possible to provide for fighting his way through to relieve Cornwallis, for avoiding tactical misunderstandings, and for being prepared for the manoeuvre of breaking the enemy line without any qualifying restriction. Could any admiral have done better, at that particular moment, in making his paper preparations?[39]

Morale in the fleet appears not to have improved, as McKenzie noticed in his diary on 16 October:

> If the navy are not a little more active, they will not get a sight of the Capes of Virginia before the end of this month, and then it will be too late. They do not seem to be hearty in the business, or to think that the saving that army is an object of such material consequence. One of the captains has exposed himself so much as to say, that the loss of two line of battleships in effecting the relief of that army, is of much more consequence than the loss of it. Sir Samuel Hood appears to be the only man of that corps who is urgent about the matter, and sees the necessity of doing something immediately. The others think too much of the superiority of the French fleet, and say ours is by no means equal to the undertaking.[40]

Even if the opinion ascribed to the unidentified captain was merely an unsubstantiated rumour, it does seem that the spirit in the fleet did not augur well for the difficult operation ahead.

As it was, the preparations continued. The ships of the line were moving down to the harbour entrance as each got ready, and in 17 October, as soon as the tide served, Graves got under sail with the rest of the squadron, with the exception of the *Shrewsbury*, *Montagu* and *Europe*, and made his way down to Sandy Hook. Next morning the troops came aboard the ships of the line; it had been decided not to embark in transports, which would slow down the fleet as it made its way south to the Chesapeake. Graves recorded 7,149 officers and men having been taken on board. During the afternoon, the ships with a shallower draught went over the bar, and on the morning of 19 October the assembly of the fleet was completed.

---

39   Tunstall (ed. Tracy), *Naval Warfare in the Age of Sail*, p.177.
40   Pengelly, *Sir Samuel Hood and the Battle of the Chesapeake*, p.182.

'Siège d'York-Town'. Hand-coloured engraving by J.M. Fontaine after Couder, depicting Washington and Rochambeau with their respective staffs. (Anne S.K. Brown Collection)

Twenty-five ships of the line, two 50-gun ships and eight frigates set sail for the Chesapeake. In the light of the depressing news from Cornwallis, it remained to be seen if he had been able to hold out long enough for relief to arrive.

At Yorktown the allies were still concentrating their attention on Redoubts 9 and 10, which were subjected to a continuous bombardment. On the night of 14/15 October attacks were launched on both, the French attacking Redoubt No 9 and the Americans Redoubt No 10. In each case the defenders were heavily outnumbered, and in each case the attack was successful, the two redoubts being taken with their garrisons. Washington wasted no time in adjusting his line to add the two redoubts to his siege lines, and Cornwallis wrote a final dispatch to Clinton on the morning of 15 October:

> My situation here becomes very critical; we dare not show a gun to their old batteries, and I expect their new ones will open tomorrow morning. Experience has shown that our fresh earthen works do not resist their powerful artillery, so that we shall soon be exposed to an assault in ruined

works, in a bad position, and with weakened numbers. The safety of the place is therefore so precarious, that I cannot recommend that the fleet and army should run great risk in endeavouring to save us.[41]

In an effort to stave off the final defeat which he knew must be inevitable in a few days, Cornwallis launched a desperate sortie at 4:00 a.m. on 16 October. Lieutenant Colonel Abercrombie was sent forward with 350 men, his mission being to spike the enemy's guns. Abercrombie's men entered the second parallel and turned westward into the French positions, surprising a battery of four guns, which were spiked. They pushed on into the communications trench, and spiked three more guns, in an American battery, before being driven off. The work of spiking the guns had, however, been done too hastily, and in a few hours the batteries were again operational.

Cornwallis now played his last card. He decided during the night of 16/17 October to get his army over the river to Gloucester and there to launch an attack on Choisy's troops investing the place. He still had enough vessels to get his troops across in three waves. It would mean the abandonment of his artillery, his stores, and his sick and wounded, but he reckoned that there was just a chance that the move might succeed. At first all went well; the first wave landed at midnight, and the boats returned to embark the second wave. However, just as they were preparing to cross, the weather turned, and a violent squall made it impossible to proceed. For two hours the storm raged, and by then there was no chance of getting the rest of the army across in time to attack Choisy. He gave orders that the troops that had crossed should return: the divided army would have had no chance of resisting the inevitable assault, which was bound to cost heavy casualties.

As the sun came up, the bombardment resumed. It was soon apparent to Cornwallis that the end had come, and at 10:00 a.m. a drummer mounted the parapet and sounded the parley. Cornwallis sent an officer forward with a letter to Washington proposing a cessation of hostilities for 24 hours, and for two officers from each side to meet to settle the terms of surrender. They met next day, and by early evening the draft of the surrender document was completed, and taken back to Cornwallis and to Washington. On the following day the capitulation took place, and the British garrison of Yorktown marched out and piled their arms. The siege was over; and so, effectively was the last chance for Britain to suppress the American Revolution.

Cornwallis had done all he could. He wrote to Clinton a letter on 20 October explaining his decision to capitulate: 'I thought it would have been wanton and inhuman to the last degree to sacrifice the lives of this small body of gallant soldiers who had ever behaved with so much fidelity and courage, by exposing

41   Chadwick (ed.), *Graves Papers*, p.140.

them to an assault, which from the numbers and precautions of the enemy could not fail to succeed'.[42]

While Cornwallis's troops were marching out to surrender, the relief expedition was sailing southwards. The van division was commanded by Digby, with Graves in the centre, and Hood in the rear. Since the fleet was divided into the three traditional divisions, Drake, with no division to command, was accorded the honour of leading the fleet in the *Princessa*. There was no news of events at Yorktown until on the morning of 24 October a small schooner was encountered, with three men aboard, one of whom had been the pilot of the *Charon*. They had left the Chesapeake on 18 October. From them Graves learned of the negotiations for a capitulation that was intended to take place on the day after they left. Next day the frigate *Nymphe* joined the fleet from New York, bearing the final letter from Cornwallis, and no doubt remained that the fleet was too late to save the army.

Graves continued on to the Chesapeake, to find of course de Grasse with his 36 ships of the line blocking his way. He sent in the *Nymphe* and the 50-gun *Warwick* to reconnoitre closely, but in truth what could be seen from the mastheads of the fleet was quite enough to show him that no useful action was possible. However, before the fleet sailed back to New York, there appears to have been some discussion at a council of war about what should be done. According to an account in the not necessarily reliable *Political and Military Journal*,:

> Sir Samuel Hood was of the opinion, that the fleet should remain and block up de Grasse in the Chesapeake. In this bold advice he was supported by Rear Admiral Drake. But Admirals Graves and Digby, the two superior officers, being of a different opinion, the fleet returned to New York.[43]

Hood did not comment on this meeting in his next letter to George Jackson, also written on 29 October, remarking only that he felt too much, and his mind was 'too greatly depressed with the sense I have of my country's calamities, to dwell longer on the painful subject'. When the fleet got back to New York, and the troops disembarked, he would, he said 'push away to the protection of the West India Islands.[44]

As the fleet headed back northwards, Graves reported sadly to Philip Stephens. After pointing out the huge disparity of force confronting him, he went on:

> I shou'd however have been happy to have tried every possible means to effect a relief cou'd we have arrived in time, that prospect being at an end, no addition of troops intended for Charleston, nor an attempt against

42   Sands, *Yorktown's Captive Fleet*, p.85.
43   Larrabee, *Decision at the Chesapeake*, p.199.
44   Hannay (ed.), *Letters Written by Sir Samuel Hood*, p.39.

Rhode Island thought advisable, under the present situation of things, there appeared nothing so proper as to return with the fleet to New York.[45]

Graves added the hope that the Admiralty would not find that any part of the failure had 'proceeded from the want of attention or exertion on my particular part'. He can have been in no doubt that his management of the fleet during the period of his command would be the subject of close scrutiny by government, press and public. There was, though, nothing more that he could have done. Reviewing the course of events that led to the loss of Yorktown, it is possible to see one point in particular at which the fate of Cornwallis and his army was sealed, and with it the outcome of the war for American independence. This was during his dialogue of the deaf with Clinton in the summer of 1781. Neither man was unaware of the forces that might be concentrated against Cornwallis; neither was unaware of Germain's desire to see effective action taken in Virginia; but above all neither was unaware that the arrival of a superior French fleet was entirely possible, and could and probably would mean disaster. Knowingly to accept the grave risks being incurred in Virginia in pursuit of a really significant objective might have been justifiable; but the British did so to no great purpose at all. As a result, only a convincing victory in the Battle of the Chesapeake could have reversed the situation.

45   Chadwick (ed.), *Graves Papers*, pp.137-139.

23

Les Saintes

Ironically, just as matters were coming to a head on the other side of the Atlantic, the balance of naval advantage at home was beginning to swing Britain's way. Although the Royal Navy's responsibilities in European waters were still enormous, the Franco-Spanish dominance that had inhibited the Admiralty from sufficiently reinforcing the fleets in the West Indies and North America was beginning to decline. The war had become a real test of stamina, and the British rate of shipbuilding had been increasing as the war went on, while on the other hand the French had not been able to keep up.

This had not been immediately apparent, however, during 1781 when the Combined Fleet again posed a serious threat. Darby cruised with the Channel Fleet in June and July in the west of the Channel until he was driven back into Torbay by westerly gales on 7 July, thereafter returning to Spithead. Meanwhile the Combined Fleet had sailed from Cadiz on 23 July to escort a convoy carrying an expedition to take Minorca. Once that convoy was through the Straits of Gibraltar, de Guichen and Córdova turned back and headed northwards to the Channel with 49 ships of the line. The Admiralty disbelieved news of this and sent an order to Darby to put to sea to escort an inbound convoy from Jamaica. This, however, he did not do. On reaching Torbay he had taken up a defensive position, sending off frigates to divert the convoy. When news came that the Combined Fleet had been sighted off the Scilly Isles, the government became alarmed, and it was decided to direct Darby to put to sea immediately to seek the enemy notwithstanding the disparity in numbers. As it turned out, the threat from the Combined Fleet had already evaporated; having split into its component parts, de Guichen and Córdova then returned to Brest and Cadiz respectively.

Before the end of the year a major threat to Jamaica appeared to be developing, with reports that the French were planning a substantial reinforcement of their forces in the West Indies in order to attack the island. At meetings on 20 and 22 October the Cabinet decided on an attempt to intercept the French, and the task was assigned to a squadron under Kempenfelt. He sailed with 12 ships of the line, a 50-gun ship and seven frigates on 2 December. Ten days later he encountered the French convoy for the West Indies escorted by de Guichen, who had with him 19 ships of the line. As Kempenfelt closed, de Guichen was to the leeward of the convoy, and the British squadron was in its midst before the escort could do anything about it. Kempenfelt took 14 prizes. With the odds stacked against him he had done extremely well; although there was some misconceived criticism that he had not done more, it was generally recognised that he had conducted the affair with considerable skill.

At the end of 1781 the political situation of the government had become extremely precarious. The news of the capitulation of Yorktown was followed by widespread criticism of the Admiralty for sending out Kempenfelt with an inadequate force. Nevertheless, in spite of all this, Sandwich was prepared at this point, when reviewing the navy's strategy for 1782, to accept the advice of those professionals closest to him and to adopt a radically different policy. The advice from such as Mulgrave, following the opinions of Kempenfelt and Middleton, was to maintain a western squadron composed of no more than 20 coppered ships of the line; to direct incoming trade around the north of the British Isles; and to employ the forces thus released to achieve a decisive superiority in the West Indies. Nicholas Rodger observes that 'this strategy was as unsound as ever in 1782', but notes that the fact that the admirals were now prepared to take risks with home defence arose from 'a growing sense of their own power, and a growing realisation of the weakness and disunion of the enemy'.[1]

While Sandwich was reconsidering his strategy in the post-Yorktown situation, Germain was doing likewise. He wrote to Clinton to say that Cornwallis's army would not be replaced, but it was hoped that the forces in America would be sufficient to retain possession of the places held on the Atlantic coast. The main aim of retaining them was to serve as rallying points should loyalist movements make headway against Congress, a false hope which Germain shared with the King. Clinton was, he said, to supply arms and ammunition to any body of loyalists which attempted to restore the constitution. Beyond this, Germain hoped that merely by prolonging the war there was a hope that the rebels might just give up. Clinton's removal had, of course, become inevitable; his intended successor was Sir Guy Carleton but in the interim, before the latter could arrive, Robertson was temporarily in command. Germain's subsequent instructions to him were that he should undertake such operations 'as may best tend to defend our present possessions, or distress the rebels in that manner which may most incline them to peace'.[2]

Following the capitulation of Yorktown, both the British and the French fleets made preparations to return to the West Indies. Hood sailed south with his squadron from Sandy Hook on 11 November, taking with him also the *Prince George, Royal Oak, Canada* and *America*; he had strongly pressed Digby to allow him to take all the coppered ships of the line, and Digby agreed to this, save only

1   Rodger, *The Insatiable Earl*, pp.293-294.
2   Ian R. Christie, *The End of North's Ministry 1780-1782* (London: Macmillan, 1958), pp.322-323.

for the *Bedford*, which he retained for the time being to drive off any ships which de Grasse might leave, and to protect supply vessels going down to Charleston. Graves went off to Jamaica in the *London*; he was still deeply resentful of the way in which he supposed himself to have been treated by the Admiralty in being replaced by Digby. Sandwich, in the following year, shortly before leaving the Admiralty, did his best to reassure Graves that the decision as to his posting was not a mark of criticism; he wrote to him on 13 March 1782 to say that, Digby having been appointed, he thought it would have been 'very grating' for Graves to be called home, telling him that it was necessary for his credit that his flag should remain flying in actual service. If he judged wrong, Sandwich wrote, it was an error of judgment, but not of intention.[3]

De Grasse left the Chesapeake on 4 November. Before he sailed, Washington tried to pin him down to an agreement that he return in the following May, with a view to an attack on New York or Charleston, but de Grasse refused to make any such commitment; he did not know what his government was planning for the following year, and besides, as he told Rochambeau, he was in a very poor state of health: 'My sickness grows worse every day, and I do not know how it will end. The longer I live the more I am convinced that a man 60 years old is not fit to direct a fleet such as this'.[4] De Grasse had with him, including Barras's squadron, 34 ships of the line and the *Experiment*, 50. En route to Martinique he detached four ships to Sainte Domingue, with orders to escort a convoy from there to France. The bulk of his fleet anchored in Fort Royal on 25 November, and the rest on the following day. He found that de Bouillé, the governor, was away, and it was several days before he learned that he had taken an expedition to recapture St Eustatius, an operation that was entirely successful.

Hood, who had sailed from New York with 17 ships of the line, lost contact with two which parted during a gale on 17 November, but he arrived in Barbados with the rest on 5 December. During the following weeks he was joined by the stragglers, and a number of other ships which brought his total strength by the end of January to 22 ships of the line, with which to face the 30 in de Grasse's fleet.

De Grasse resolved to make Barbados his first objective. Although his crews had been much reduced by sickness, he sailed on 17 December. Due to contrary winds and very stormy weather, causing damage to several ships, the mission proved abortive, and he put back into Fort Royal after a week. On 28 December he tried again, but was again driven back after a further week of storms. Frustrated, he gave up on the Barbados plan, and on 5 January sailed with 26 ships of the line and transports carrying 6,000 troops under de Bouillé in an effort to capture St Kitts. The fleet arrived on 11 January and disembarked the troops, which swiftly overran the island with the exception of the fortress of Brimstone Hill, into which

3   Barnes and Owen (eds), *Private Papers of John, Earl of Sandwich*, Vol.IV, pp.209-211.
4   Lewis, *Admiral de Grasse*, p.197.

the garrison retreated. The rest of the island, together with the neighbouring island of Nevis, was surrendered to the French, who now proceeded to besiege Brimstone Hill.

The governor of St Kitts had sent off a message to Barbados when the French fleet came in sight, and Hood at once put to sea, pausing on 16 January at Antigua to pick up two ships of the line, which brought him up to his total strength of 22, together with 1,000 troops. Hood, reporting these events, wrote to Stephens at the Admiralty, saying that with this fleet he would 'seek and give battle to the Count de Grasse, be his numbers as they may'.[5] On his way, Hood bemoaned to Middleton his lack of frigates:

> Never was such weather remembered in this country as we have had for several weeks past; every frigate I have sent to sea has returned a mere wreck … When the French fleet were at sea I had not a single frigate; all were shifting their masts and rigging. I was obliged to purchase two or three schooners for dispatch vessels.[6]

While at Antigua, Hood worked on his plan of attack with Drake and Affleck, and they each then met with their captains to explain it. Hood intended to take de Grasse by surprise; mindful of past misunderstandings, he issued an additional instruction with the necessary signals:

1. In attacking the enemy's ships to leeward at anchor, the ship to exchange her fire with the first and second ship of the enemy, stop at the third, and having given her fire to the third ship, to veer short round and fall into the rear, each ship following in succession.
2. To discontinue the same.
3. To anchor in line ahead with springs.[7]

Hood's fleet arrived under cover of darkness on the morning of 24 January, and stood on and off Nevis waiting for daylight. Unluckily, a collision between the *Alfred*, 74, and the frigate *Nymphe* cost him the advantage of surprise, as the day was spent in the *Alfred* undertaking essential repairs. This gave de Grasse time to leave his anchorage in Basseterre Roads. During the day the fleets were in sight of each other, Hood having the advantage of the wind. During the night he decided on a bold move, forming his line of battle at one cable apart. He reported his intention in his dispatch to the Admiralty: 'As I thought I had a fair prospect of gaining

5   Hannay (ed.), *Letters Written by Sir Samuel Hood*, pp.59-62.
6   Laughton (ed.), *Letters and Papers of Charles Lord Barham*, Vol.I, p.137.
7   Corbett, (ed.), *Signals and Instructions*, p.189.

the anchorage he left, and well knowing it was the only chance I had of saving the island if it was to be saved, I pushed for it'.[8]

At 2:00 p.m. on 25 January the French opened fire on the British rear. Hood ordered his leading ships to take up their position in the anchorage, and by 3:30 p.m. they had begun to anchor. There was a dangerous moment when de Grasse sought to drive the *Ville de Paris* through a gap in the British line, but the captains of the three ships ahead of the gap managed to thwart this by backing their sails. As the rear of the British line came up to the turning point, the anchored ships were able to exchange a heavy fire with the French fleet, which then wore round and withdrew. Next day it reappeared, and twice sailed past the anchored British line, again exchanging a heavy fire. Thereafter de Grasse cruised off the island, and Hood landed his troops. They were, however, far outnumbered, and they were soon re-embarked and returned to Antigua. Hood remained in position, hoping that Brimstone Hill could hold out; but on 12 February it surrendered, and on the following night, under cover of darkness, he slipped away to Antigua, arriving on 19 February, and then going on to Barbados where he hoped to find Rodney with reinforcements from England.

Back home, Rodney had been receiving treatment for his illness; he had also soon become heavily enmeshed with the legal and administrative fallout from St Eustatius. However, the government was keen for him to return to sea, and he was awarded the honorific post of Vice Admiral of Great Britain. He was, he said, 'determined to serve again,' and he wrote to Sandwich from Bath on 6 November: 'Nothing shall be wanting in me; I will therefore set out on Saturday or Sunday for London, and if my health can be so far restored so as to do my duty, I will not hesitate one moment'.[9] He was given the *Formidable*, 98, as his flagship, and a squadron was prepared for him to take to the West Indies. Before he sailed, he had to endure an attack in Parliament, led by Edmund Burke; Rodney and Vaughan, both members of the House, defended themselves vigorously, and Burke's motion was defeated. By 17 December Rodney was at Cawsand Bay, awaiting his flagship and other units of his squadron. He was very dissatisfied with the services of Plymouth dockyard; when he wrote to Sandwich on 6 January to say that the squadron was now finally ready, he added that 'not a single ship would have been now near ready, had not my arrival obliged them to exert themselves in a manner unusual at this port'.[10] Inefficiency of this kind constantly delayed British fleets in putting to sea; Rodney put it down to the effect of party and faction which created slackness, and this caused him the utmost disgust.

After an abortive attempt to get away on 8 January, prevented by adverse winds, Rodney finally cleared from Torbay on 14 January with 12 ships of the line, dropping

8   James, *British Navy in Adversity*, p.323.
9   Barnes and Owen (eds), *Private Papers of John, Earl of Sandwich*, Vol.IV, p.226.
10   Barnes and Owen (eds), *Private Papers of John, Earl of Sandwich*, Vol.IV, p.230.

anchor at Barbados on the evening of 19 February. With the news of the critical situation at St Kitts, he wasted no time in putting to sea again after watering his fleet; he met Hood's fleet on 25 February, and after hearing of the fall of Brimstone Hill, took the combined fleet back to Gros Islet Bay. De Grasse, meanwhile, at Fort Royal, was preparing his next strike, which the British suspected would be aimed at Jamaica.

This was indeed the case, but the operation was not altogether straightforward, since de Grasse had to proceed first to Cap Français with his supply vessels, and escort at the same time a merchant fleet that would there join the next convoy to Europe. He sailed from Fort Royal on 8 April with 33 ships of the line, one being left behind awaiting completion of repairs. Ahead of the fleet were 150 sail, said to be the richest convoy ever to leave Martinique.[11] De Grasse chose a route which kept close to friendly ports in which the convoy might seek refuge if threatened by the British fleet.

During March the chief preoccupation of the British fleet had been with the French reinforcement expected at Fort Royal. Hood and Rodney disagreed as to the measures to be taken to intercept it; the former argued that the fleet should be divided to cover each of the approaches to Martinique, but Rodney refused to consider this. From 20-27 March the fleet patrolled an 80 mile stretch of sea from Dominica, but saw nothing; the French force, consisting of three ships of the line and three frigates, escorting transports with 6,000 troops, had slipped past and reached Fort Royal in safety.

Relations between Hood and Rodney were often strained, but on 3 April the commander-in-chief paid a visit to his captious subordinate, who wrote that day to Middleton to say that Sir George had been with him for more than two hours: 'I never found him more rational, and he gave me very great pleasure by his manner of receiving what I said respecting the future operations of the fleet'.[12] Since Hood was always certain that he was right, the meeting understandably pleased him. Sadly, however, his distrust of Rodney reappeared in the same letter: 'But there is, I am sorry to say it, no great reliance to be placed in a man who is so much governed by whims and caprice, even in matters of the highest importance to the welfare of the State'.

It was not long before the two men were in action again together. As soon as Rodney received news in St Lucia that de Grasse was leaving port, he put to sea in pursuit of him. By noon on 8 April the whole of the British fleet, of 36 ships of the line, was hastening after the French, and by 6:00 p.m. the two fleets were in sight of one another. Next day nine of Hood's ships had become somewhat detached, but de Grasse spurned the chance of falling upon them, contenting himself with a distant cannonade, a decision which was endorsed as prudent by the subsequent

11 Lewis, *Admiral de Grasse*, p.228.
12 Laughton (ed.), *Letters and Papers of Charles Lord Barham*, Vol.I, p.137.

finding of a court martial; he was justified, it was found, in keeping in mind his ulterior purposes. Geoffrey Marcus observed that this was a settled policy: 'It was always, in short, the fixed and firm belief of the French that ulterior objects were of greater consequence than fighting the enemy's fleet'.[13] Hood was critical of the fact that Rodney had allowed his fleet to become separated, observing to Middleton that he had not shown much judgment in this. He was also derisive about what he saw as the failure of de Grasse to take his chance: 'Had de Grasse known his duty he might have cut us up, by pouring a succession of fresh ships upon us as long as he pleased; but being very roughly handled and to windward, he hauled off and our fleet joined in the evening'.[14]

Three days later, Rodney got his chance, when he was able to catch de Grasse near Les Saintes, a group of small islands off the southern tip of Guadeloupe. De Grasse, who had set out with 35 ships of the line, had detached two of these, the 50-gun *Experiment* and 56-gun *Sagittaire*, to escort the convoy into Guadeloupe. In addition, the *Caton* was so damaged on 9 April that he sent her into Guadeloupe for repair; the *Zélé* collided with the *Jason* on the night of 9/10 April, and the latter also was sent in; then at 2:00 a.m. on 12 April the unfortunate *Zélé* again had a traffic accident, colliding this time with the *Ville de Paris*, and a frigate was sent to tow her into port. All this reduced de Grasse from 35 to 30 ships of the line; Rodney still had 36. As Rodney closed in light airs, de Grasse twice had to wear in order to try to catch a decent wind.

The two battle lines were passing each other, exchanging fire, when at 9:15 a.m. the wind changed abruptly, throwing the French line into confusion. A gap appeared in that line just as Rodney's *Formidable* approached; seizing the opportunity, she steered through the gap, followed by the next five ships. Farther down the French line the *Duke* found a gap, and cut through, while to Rodney's rear the *Bedford* broke through at another point. Broken in three places, de Grasse's line could not be reformed. By noon the wind had freshened from the east, and, led by Bougainville, the bulk of the French fleet made off, leaving three crippled ships, the *Glorieux*, *Hector* and *César,* at the mercy of the British. At 1:00 p.m. Rodney again made the signal for close action, but hauled it down at 1:32 p.m., and gave no orders for a general chase. Later in the afternoon the *Ardent* struck to the *Belliqueux*, and at sunset the *Barfleur* and *Russell* caught up with the *Ville de Paris*, which also struck after a fierce cannonade of 10 minutes. At 6:45 p.m. Rodney called off the pursuit.

It was a decision which Hood bitterly criticised. In his letter to Middleton next day, he wrote:

13   G.J. Marcus, *A Naval History of England: The Formative Centuries* (Boston: Little Brown & Co, 1961), p.447.
14   Laughton (ed.), *Letters and Papers of Charles Lord Barham*, Vol.I, p.159.

After the glorious business of yesterday, I was most exceedingly disappointed in and mortified at the commander-in-chief. In the first instance, for not making the signal for a general chase the moment he hauled down that for the line of battle, which was about 1 o'clock; had he done, I am confident we should have had 20 sail of the line before dark; instead of that, he pursued only under his topsails, the greater part of the afternoon, though the flying enemy had all the sails set their shattered state would allow. In the next, that he did not continue to pursue under that easy sail, so as never to have lost sight of the enemy in the night, which would clearly and most undoubtedly have enabled him to have taken almost every ship this day. But why he should bring to because the *Ville de Paris* was taken is not to be comprehended.[15]

He also wrote to Sandwich in very similar terms. When he came on board the *Formidable* on the morning of 13 April, and lamented the failure to pursue, Rodney merely replied: 'Come, we have done very handsomely',[16] after which Hood felt unable to continue the discussion. He told Middleton three days later that his patience was fairly exhausted.

Even Hood, though, acknowledged that the victory had ended all threat to Jamaica. He and Drake cruised off the west of Sainte Domingue for a week, while Rodney took the more seriously damaged ships to Jamaica for repair. French casualties aboard the ships which escaped were enormous, 502 being killed and 1,611 wounded. This was far greater than the British loss, due to the number of troops being carried aboard the ships of the line. In the ships taken, further casualties of several thousand were sustained. The British, in the fighting on 9 and 12 April, lost 272 killed and 853 wounded.[17] De Grasse left his flagship on the day after the battle and boarded the *Formidable*, where he was courteously treated, talking freely with Rodney and others about all that had occurred. Rodney wrote home to his wife: 'Count de Grasse, who is at this moment sitting in my stern gallery, tells me that he thought his fleet superior to mine, and does so still, though I had two more in number, and I am of his opinion, as his was composed all of large ships, and ten of mine only 64s.[18]

In London, meanwhile, the domestic political situation meant that the government's course was almost run, and with it Sandwich's tenure of the Admiralty. He was attacked in the House of Commons on a number of grounds. These included letting de Grasse get away to North America; the failure to prevent the loss of the St Eustatius convoy; the alleged mismanagement of the naval war against the Dutch;

15 Laughton (ed.), *Letters and Papers of Charles Lord Barham*, Vol.I, p.191.
16 Laughton (ed.), *Letters and Papers of Charles Lord Barham*, Vol.I, p.162.
17 Figures from Lewis, *Admiral de Grasse*, p.252.
18 Lewis, *Admiral de Grasse*, pp.252-254.

and the inadequate resources given to Kempenfelt.[19] Within the government there was mounting pressure for Sandwich and Germain to be thrown overboard in order to avert defeat. Germain was finally removed at the end of January, but this came much too late to save the government, which soon lost its majority in the House of Commons. The North ministry resigned on 20 March; it was succeeded by a ministry led by the Marquess of Rockingham. In the new administration Keppel became First Lord of the Admiralty. An immediate victim of the upheaval was Admiral Darby. The new government wished to replace him by Howe as commander-in-chief of the Channel Fleet; Darby was offered the chance to serve as second-in-command, which he not unnaturally declined. In his place, that post went to Barrington.

The news of the battle of Les Saintes, however, did not reach London in time to prevent the new Cabinet from taking the almost inevitable decision to replace Rodney as commander-in-chief in the West Indies, so committed a supporter had he been of the previous administration. It was Keppel's painful duty to write, on 2 May, to give Rodney the news:

> Reasoning upon the subject I am sure you will think unnecessary. It is enough for me to inform you as shortly as I am able that the King's servants have judged it for reasons of state that Admiral Pigot should immediately proceed to the West Indies and there take upon him the chief command of the fleet at present under your direction.[20]

It was a difficult letter to write. By 8:00 a.m. on 18 May, however, Keppel was reading Rodney's dispatch with news of the victory, and a King's Messenger left for Plymouth that morning in an effort to stop Pigot before he sailed. It was too late. He had put to sea that same morning, and on 29 May Keppel was writing again to Rodney to say that no one friend could have rejoiced more than he did at the glorious success and trusting that 'the measures relating to Admiral Pigot's being sent to the command in the West Indies will remain for your quiet reasoning till we meet'.[21] Rumours of his supersession reached Rodney quickly; so did the news of his peerage, which comforted him. He was back in England by September and received a hero's welcome. Behind him in the West Indies there were no further significant engagements, where Hood was soon offering Pigot the benefit of his advice. Before the autumn came, Vaudreuil took a dozen French ships of the line to North America, and the British followed, but there was no contact.

19 Christie, *The End of North's Ministry*, p.311.
20 Spinney, *Rodney*, p.408.
21 Spinney, *Rodney*, pp.409-410.

24

The End of the War

Yorktown had not ended the war, though it had effectively determined its outcome. In England, in due course, after several months of intense Parliamentary activity, it had brought down the North ministry. Edmund Burke's famous and scathing polemic after the news of the capitulation had arrived reflected the widely held view that the loss of the American colonies amounted to a catastrophic disaster for Britain. As Germain put it, it was the ruin of the British Empire. In his speech, Burke enquired:

> Are we to be told of the rights for which we went to war? Oh, excellent rights! Oh, valuable rights … that have cost England thirteen provinces, four islands, 100,000 men, and 70 millions of money! Oh, wonderful rights, that have lost to Great Britain her empire on the ocean, her boasted, grand, and substantial superiority which made the world bend before her! Oh, inestimable rights, that have taken from us our rank among nations, our importance abroad, and our happiness at home; and that have taken from us our trade, our manufactures, and our commerce; that have reduced us from the most flourishing empire in the world to one of the most unenviable powers on the face of the globe.[1]

Before leaving office in March, Sandwich had had to face searching enquiries into his management of the affairs of the navy. The capitulation of Yorktown provided a stout stick for the opposition with which to beat the government. The particular targets were, necessarily, Sandwich and Germain. A Parliamentary enquiry into the conduct of the war obliged the First Lord to prepare a comprehensive defence. He was surer of himself than the rest of the ministry, even though some of its members had seen a possible route to salvation by throwing both Germain and Sandwich to the wolves. Germain had been compelled to resign in February; even the King was unable to save him.

---

1   Corwin, *French Policy and the American Alliance*, p.363.

A House of Lords enquiry was instituted on 7 February into the loss of Yorktown. Sandwich defended himself vigorously. The enquiry lasted several days, and on 6 March, the Duke of Chandos moved 'that the immediate cause of the capture of the army under Earl Cornwallis in Virginia appeared to be the want of a sufficient naval force to cover and protect the same'. The motion was, however, lost by 72 votes to 37.[2] Although the motion was lost, its terms in reality neatly encapsulated the whole of the story of the battle of Chesapeake Bay.

In the new government, headed by the Marquis of Rockingham, Keppel became First Lord of the Admiralty, and Howe took over command of the Channel Fleet, which he found to be in poor condition to face continuing and serious threat posed by the Franco-Spanish Combined Fleet. Howe encountered it in July; greatly outnumbered, he skilfully avoided action. In August, the Royal Navy suffered an irreparable loss when the *Royal George*, Kempenfelt's flagship, sank at anchor at Spithead, taking with her the admiral and about 800 others. One of the ablest naval minds of the eighteenth century, Kempenfelt would have had so much more to give to a navy that was woefully short of original thinkers. Later in the year Howe conducted a successful relief of Gibraltar, in the course of which he again encountered the Combined Fleet, with which he fought an indecisive and long-distance engagement.

A French writer observed of this relief of Gibraltar that 'the qualities displayed by Lord Howe during this short campaign rose to the full height of the mission which he had to fulfil. This operation, one of the finest in the War of American Independence, merits praise equal to that of a victory'. He went on to accord generous praise to Howe's captains: 'If it is just to admit that Lord Howe displayed the highest talent, it should be noted that he had in his hands excellent instruments'.[3] This was the last major operation of the war in home waters, and once again there had been no substantial engagement with the Combined Fleet.

In France, Vergennes had recognised that Yorktown would not bring an immediate end to the war. He was realistic enough to appreciate that Britain would not fold abruptly on the basis of the defeat there. When de Grasse had gone off across the Atlantic, it had been his hope that a decisive blow would produce such favourable results for Spain that she could be induced to accept a speedy end to the war. The victory had indeed been decisive, but it was America that was the immediate beneficiary. It had therefore become necessary for the French to plan a fresh campaign, directed at Jamaica, that would provide Spain with a suitable prize. With the Spanish in a cooperative frame of mind, it was Vergennes's immediate task to keep the Americans up to the mark. For them, Yorktown was seen as the decisive victory which would secure their independence, which indeed it was. Nevertheless, the American historian William M. Fowler has described the period

---

2   Barnes and Owen (eds), *Private Papers of John, Earl of Sandwich*, Vol.IV, p.271.
3   E. Chevalier, quoted in Mahan, *Navies in the War of American Independence*, pp.232-233.

after the capitulation as 'the dangerous years,' in the course of which despite that victory it was still possible for its fruits to be lost and for the American Revolution to have failed in its purpose. Following Yorktown, the 13 states, welded together throughout the war by the British military threat, might with its disappearance split apart and go their own way. In addition, there was a risk that, as the war neared its end, differences between the allies might arise as they pursued their disparate objectives. Finally, there was a serious danger that the lack of money with which to pay the troops might lead to the dissolution of America's armies.[4] That none of these things occurred was due above all to the powerful will of George Washington.

In Britain the Rockingham ministry, when it came to power at the end of March 1782, had had to take up the responsibility for the conduct of the war, as well as putting in hand negotiations to bring it to an end. In fact, during the rest of the year, Britain's armed forces, and particularly her navy, did rather well. There were a number of fundamental advantages which she possessed which were steadily tipping the balance in her favour. Professor Baugh put it in this way: 'No amount of French or Spanish money could quickly augment the pools of skilled seamen and shipwrights, or suddenly create well-equipped dockyards and overseas bases and well tested administrative procedures, or secure high-quality naval supplies'.[5]

Although the huge naval expenditure incurred by Britain was sharply increasing during the second half of the war, the nation's system of public credit enabled her to bear the cost of this more readily than France and Spain. Vergennes was very much aware of this, as he wrote in September 1782 to the French ambassador in Madrid:

> England, without doubt, is very fatigued, but we are so ourselves. Our means are exhausted by dint of being diffused and it is not yet determined whether our credit or that of England will survive the other. That nation has, in its constitution and in the establishments which it has permitted her to form, resources which are lacking to us. Let us not lose the occasion if it presents itself of honourably terminating.[6]

One of the difficulties which Vergennes faced was the demanding nature of the terms which King Charles III of Spain wished to see incorporated in the peace settlement, and there was prolonged correspondence and negotiation in an attempt to find a basis that would be generally acceptable. The problems of royal obstinacy with which Vergennes had to deal were however not as great as that which faced the British government. King George did not accept that Yorktown meant the loss

---

4   William M Fowler, Jr, *American Crisis* (New York 2011) pp1-2

5   Baugh, 'Why did Britain lose command of the sea during the war for America?', p.163.

6   Baugh, 'Why did Britain lose command of the sea during the war for America?', p.161.

of America. He had supported Germain through thick and thin as the member of the North ministry who most represented his belief that its loss would deal a fatal blow to Britain's position in the world. Germain's removal did not change the King's mind; nor did the subsequent fall of the North ministry, and rather than submit he began to talk of his possible abdication. Instead of carrying this threat into effect, though, he was obliged to watch impotently as the new administration embarked on the lengthy negotiations that would bring the war to an end. To him, the granting of American independence represented a betrayal by his people, a betrayal which he could never forgive.

The military and naval events of 1782 were not without influence on the peace negotiations, and somewhat strengthened Britain's hand. In particular, the failure of the massive Spanish attack on Gibraltar, and its relief by the Channel Fleet were the most significant. The attempt to recover Gibraltar had been a key Spanish war aim, and it was only with the greatest reluctance that it would be abandoned. The negotiations, conducted separately by Britain with each of the allies, were lengthy and complicated. The allies had by no means a united view as to the essential terms which should be incorporated in the peace settlement. The Americans, with some justice, distrusted the French; the French continued to wrestle with the problem of bringing the Spanish to the table; and the British pursued with some success a negotiating policy aimed at detaching the Americans from the French.

For Britain, one of the key issues was the future of Gibraltar; there was widespread and strong opposition to the return of the fortress to Spain, after all that had been endured in its long defence. Eventually the Spanish gave up their claim to Gibraltar, which greatly facilitated the negotiations. The Spanish did well in their territorial acquisitions when the terms of peace were finally settled, even if less than they had hoped for. They retained Minorca, and West Florida, both captured from the British, and gained East Florida, while returning the Bahamas to Britain. The Dutch regained Ceylon, and kept the Cape of Good Hope, but lost Negapatam to the British. They also conceded the British right to trade in the Spice Islands, a long-running bone of contention.

France might be said essentially to have achieved Vergennes's principal war aim, which was the weakening of Britain by detaching from her the American colonies and the re-establishment of France's position in Europe. Territorially, France did not have much to show for the war; she recovered St Lucia, but of her conquests in the West Indies she retained only Tobago. She recovered the islands of Saint-Pierre and Miquelon off the coast of Newfoundland, and extended her fishing rights there. She also regained her possessions in India.

As for America, she had won the independence for which she had fought for so long. Beyond this there had been three principal issues for her negotiators, led by Benjamin Franklin. These were, first, the acknowledgement of the right of westward expansion to the Mississippi; next, the granting of fishery rights in an area of Newfoundland; and finally, the British claim for compensation for those loyalists whose property had been seized. The first two objectives were attained; as to the loyalists, the negotiators conceded only that Congress should recommend to the individual states that such compensation should be paid.

The process of the peace negotiations had exposed serious differences of opinion within the British Cabinet. Shelburne, and a number of his colleagues, had been prepared to give up Gibraltar if this was necessary to achieve a peace settlement. The King supported him, as he valued the other British possessions more highly than Gibraltar. Keppel was strongly opposed, and was supported by the rest of the Cabinet. He argued that rather than lose Gibraltar, Britain should fight on. It was a view he maintained even after the peace terms had been finally agreed. When Shelburne came to present the final terms to Parliament, he still had plenty to do to win approval. His own strongly held view was that a generous peace with America would lead to a fruitful commercial relationship between the two countries in the future.

Keppel's reaction was to make a last vain protest, arguing that 'the 109 ships of the line in service could fight on against the 123 French and Spaniards, many of which were in a deplorable condition; could win a decisive battle in the West Indies, pull down the naval power of our enemies, and obtain a better peace'. Shelburne countered this with a case based on the opinion of Sir John Jervis, which Mackesy describes as 'perhaps the most unrestrained indictment of the Navy's condition which emerged in the course of the whole war'. Jervis pointed to 'the crazy state of our ships' and roundly castigated the quality of both officers and men, the state of the dockyards, the widespread corruption, and the difficulty of forcing the enemy to fight a decisive battle.[7] His was a picture of the navy which really bore no relation to the fleet with which Rodney and Hood had fought in the West Indies, or to the Channel Fleet which had so recently successfully relieved Gibraltar.

Statistically, Keppel could certainly point to the steadily increasing strength of the Royal Navy. Roger Knight, in his examination of its recovery during the course of the war, has shown the steady rise in the number of new warships launched year by year. During the first four years of the war between 1776 and 1779, a total of 97 new warships were completed, with a total tonnage of 53,589. Of these, nine were ships of the line. In the ensuing four years, between 1780 and 1783, the total number of new ships amounted to 106, with a tonnage of 92,803, an increase of over 70 per cent. Of these, no less than 28 were ships of the line. During this latter period there was also a very considerable increase in the number of ships of the line which underwent major repairs.[8]

Keppel was wrong, of course, in preferring to continue the war rather than accept the peace terms; they were in all the circumstances the best that could reasonably be hoped for, and it was necessary to bring the war to an end, not least on financial grounds. On the other hand, he was probably right in arguing that the navy could

---

7   Mackesy, *War for America*, p.509.
8   Knight, 'The Royal Navy's Recovery', pp.15-16.

have continued successfully to prosecute the war against France and Spain. The strictures about the navy's condition put forward by Jervis were almost certainly overstated. Hood, too, was evidently of the same opinion as Keppel. Writing to Jackson from the West Indies in January 1783, he mused on the rumours of peace:

> It is an event I shall have cause to rejoice at on <u>many accounts</u> with respect to myself, but whether I shall have reason to do so on the score of my own country I very much doubt, being clearly of opinion, <u>all things duly considered</u>, formidable as the combination most undoubtedly is against us, we shall, I fear, never again be in so good a condition for retrieving the nation's splendour as at this present moment. Nothing is wanting, I am very confident, to effect it but perfect unanimity at home, and regard into whose hands the King's fleets and armies are trusted. Without that <u>all</u> is over with us as a great and powerful kingdom.[9]

9   Hannay (ed.), *Letters Written by Sir Samuel Hood*, pp.156-157.

Conclusion

Hood's reputational pre-emptive strike immediately after the Battle of the Chesapeake had been largely successful in deflecting any blame from himself, and shifting responsibility for the outcome to Graves. The latter was in any case on the defensive, though he personally had been careful to say that no one was to blame. Once Hood's letters, to Jackson, Middleton and Sandwich, had reached London, there was bound to be a good deal of reproach attaching to Graves. As historian Ben Wilson put it, by the terms of the letters which he wrote, Hood had effectively controlled the narrative. It is perhaps not surprising that he sought to do so; the cases of Byng, Keppel and Palliser could never be very far from the mind of a British admiral of the eighteenth century, especially one whose squadron had not played a very distinguished part.[1]

Hood was forthright in his criticism. After the flowery opening to his 'Sentiments Upon the Truly Unfortunate Day' previously quoted, he went on to set out a series of complaints about Graves. First, he said, the enemy fleet was not 'closely attacked as it came out of Lynnhaven Bay, which, I think, might have been done with clear advantage'. Next, once the enemy fleet was out, it 'might have been attacked with the whole force of the British fleet,' since it was greatly extended beyond the centre and rear. Finally, once the action had commenced, Graves had not signalled for the van to make more sail to allow the centre to come up more closely in support.[2]

Although many later historians have generally been disposed to accept Hood's view of what had occurred, and the reasons for it, in 1824 Rear Admiral Ekins published a history of naval battles, in which he included the Battle of the Chesapeake. In the course of his account, he observed 'that much difficulty was experienced by Admiral Graves in getting some of his ships to keep their stations, and great dilatoriness on the part of the rear division in obeying his signals and closing with the enemy'. This passage was quoted with disapproval by Captain White in his *Naval Researches*. He protested at 'this grave accusation against Sir Samuel Hood and his gallant division,' and went on to put the case for Hood and his duty to comply with the signal for the line displayed by the flagship. Then,

---

1 Ben Wilson, *Empire of the Deep* (London: Weidenfeld & Nicolson, 2013), p.363.
2 Chadwick (ed.), *Graves Papers*, p.363.

having as he hoped, 'thereby rescued from obloquy' Hood's professional reputation, White went on to deal with the case of Graves. He complained that in most of the accounts published, 'writers have most unblushingly asserted, or obscurely hinted' that the loss of Cornwallis's army was attributable to Graves or the fleet he commanded, 'without being able to advance a single fact in proof of their false assertions'. Although he considered that the mode of conducting the battle was a bad one, 'it was agreeable to the tactics of the day; and Admiral Graves had a very difficult card to play'. He accordingly concluded that the censures heaped on Graves were unjust and unmerited, and were due to circumstances which no amount of skill or foresight on his part could have overcome. White did not consider it necessary to investigate Hood's contention that Graves could and should have launched an immediate attack on the French fleet before it had fully emerged from its anchorage.[3] White's opinion of Hood, though, may not have been entirely dispassionate; he had been a midshipman aboard the *Barfleur* at the Chesapeake.

Rodney, recuperating from his serious illness in England, was one of the earliest critics of Graves and his conduct of the battle. After hearing the news of the Chesapeake, he wrote to Jackson in October 1781, claiming, quite incorrectly, that he had foreseen what would happen and that he had given instructions which had been disregarded. In his letter, he wrote that he would never follow Graves's 'mode of fighting'.[4] Whether this letter, written with an imperfect knowledge of the facts, but which was entirely characteristic of its author, carried any weight with anyone is unclear. When Sandwich wrote to Graves in March 1782, he offered no criticism, remarking that 'in times such as these it is not enough to have drawn or executed instructions properly; blame must be laid somewhere, and it is a mere accident where blame will be laid'.[5]

Among Hood's defenders was Sir John Knox Laughton, who pointed to the relevance of the climate of opinion among naval commanders of the time. He noted that it might subsequently be seen by historians that, since he was obliged to disobey one of the signals flown by the flagship, Hood should have chosen to ignore the signal for the line of battle. However, in the eighteenth century strict obedience to this signal was held to be the most important, and that 'no suspicion that he should have acted otherwise than he did ever crossed Hood's mind'.[6]

However, that statement is not strictly true. John Creswell has drawn attention to one passage in Hood's letter to Sandwich in which, as he says, the admiral overreached himself. Hood wrote:

3   White, *Naval Researches*, p.47.
4   Chadwick (ed.), *Graves Papers*, p.135
5   Barnes and Owen (eds), *Private Papers of John, Earl of Sandwich*, Vol.IV, p.209.
6   Sir John Laughton, *From Howard to Nelson* (London: Lawrence & Bullen, 1899), p.378.

Now had the centre of the British line gone on to the support of the van, and the signal for the line had been hauled down, or had Rear Admiral Graves set the example of close action even with the signal for the line out, the van ships of the enemy must have been cut up; and the rear division of the British fleet would have been opposed to those ships the centre fired at, and at the most <u>proper</u> distance for engaging, or the Rear Admiral commanding it would have had a great deal to answer for.[7]

As Creswell observes, 'in other words if Graves had behaved as Hood thought he should, he would have been prepared to disregard the signal for the line ahead; but as he considered that Graves was engaging at a most improper distance, he thought himself justified in adhering to what he held to be the letter of the law'.[8] This assessment of Hood's actions would seem to be entirely justified, leading Creswell to remark that 'it is difficult not to conclude that on this occasion he allowed his annoyance to get the better of his judgement and his loyalty'.

Convincing support for this criticism of Hood's inaction is to be found in Article 17 of the 'Fighting Instructions and Signals by Day' issued by Rodney as commander-in-chief of the Leeward Islands station, with which Hood had necessarily been familiar. This article exactly addressed the situation in which Graves found himself. It prescribed that if the commander-in-chief wished to alter course to lead down to the enemy, he should 'hoist an Union flag at the main top gallant masthead, and fire a gun. Whereupon every ship in the squadron is to steer for the ship of the enemy which, from the disposition of the squadrons it must be her lot to engage, notwithstanding the signal for the line ahead will be kept flying'.[9] This, perhaps more than anything else, serves completely to demolish Hood's case. Whether or not on 5 September the signal for the line had been hauled down, Hood should have complied with the signal for close action. It is not necessary, therefore, to speculate whether the signal for the line did remain flying, as Hood contended, or was hauled down, as the log of the *London* records.

David Hannay, the editor of Hood's letters, noted that 'the friends of Admiral Graves, acting, we must presume, with his consent, endeavoured to show that he had been badly supported by Hood'. This, however, he says 'found no acceptance in the service,' a proposition that Hannay supports by saying that it was well known that Hood would have been 'most willing' to do so if Graves had not persisted in maintaining the line. He comments that the Fighting Instructions had a tendency to impoverish the intelligence of the admirals that had to apply them: 'Why should Graves, for instance, trouble himself to think when he had a printed book to do his thinking for him?' Although Hannay did not address Hood's other

---

7   Barnes and Owen (eds), *Private Papers of John, Earl of Sandwich*, Vol.IV, p.190.
8   John Creswell, *British Admirals of the Eighteenth Century* (London: Allen & Unwin, 1972), p.161.
9   Corbett, (ed.), *Signals and Instructions*, p.293.

complaints about Graves, he did consider that Graves should, after the battle, have gone into the Chesapeake to seize the anchorage. Hood later showed, by his skilful manoeuvre at St Kitts, how this might have been done. However, this would really have served very little purpose, since the fleet had brought with it neither supplies nor men with which to succour Cornwallis. The manoeuvre would have been no more effective in the Chesapeake in saving the garrison of Yorktown than it was at St Kitts, where Brimstone Hill fell anyway, and would simply have meant that the fleet was bottled up in the Chesapeake by de Gasse's superior fleet.[10]

Rear Admiral Chadwick, who edited the *Graves Papers*, had little sympathy with either Graves or Hood. The former, he considered, did his best, but it was a fatally bad best, while he found it impossible to avoid the impression that Hood did not do his duty; 'whatever the cause, he did not wholeheartedly aid his chief'.[11] Neither, though, was entirely to blame, in the opinion of David Syrett. The fatal weakness of the British strategy was its policy of dispersal, which at the Battle of the Chesapeake left the British fleet in a situation of inferiority that was always going to be difficult to overcome.[12]

The historian who has been much the most critical of Graves is Rear Admiral James. In his view the situation at the start of the battle was, for the British fleet, extremely favourable. He puts it in this way: 'Graves was in a position almost beyond the wildest dreams of a sea commander. His whole fleet was running down before the wind, and his enemy was before him, working slowly out of harbour. He had only to fall on their van with full force and the day was his'.[13] It is an extravagant restatement of Hood's argument, but it may be felt that is not justified by the circumstances. Graves was entitled, even obliged, to act with caution, and although Hood felt able to state flatly that an immediate attack would have been successful, it is far from clear that this was so. According to James, Graves then had a second chance for victory, when the French van was not in supporting distance from its centre and rear. The opportunity, if such it was, was at best a brief one, and apart from anything else it depended entirely on Hood displaying the kind of initiative which he so markedly failed to do throughout the battle. James is obliged to concede that it is 'somewhat surprising' that neither Hood nor his captains did show initiative at the critical time. He concludes his analysis by suggesting that if Graves had seen through the eyes of Hood or Rodney, there might have been a different outcome, 'but Graves was not the man for such critical times'.[14]

Piers Mackesy, the outstanding historian of the war for American independence, dealt with the Battle of the Chesapeake succinctly. He described it as having

10   Hannay (ed.), *Letters Written by Sir Samuel Hood*, pp. xxxviii-xl.
11   Chadwick (ed.), *Graves Papers*, pp.lxii-lxiii.
12   Syrett, *American Waters*, p.219.
13   James, *British Navy in Adversity*, p.290.
14   James, *British Navy in Adversity*, p.300.

'every usual feature: a missed opportunity at the outset, signalling confusion, poor support from the subordinate admirals, the British ships shattered aloft at the end of the action'. Commenting on the ensuing controversy, he writes: 'In the subsequent paper engagements it is Graves who appears to the best advantage,' and quoting the admiral's letter to Sandwich blaming nobody, he remarks that 'this was generosity to which few contemporary admirals could have risen'.[15]

Two American historians have dealt particularly with the Battle of the Chesapeake. Harold A. Larrabee, writing in 1964, considered that Graves's theory of the tactics that should have been and could have been employed 'was probably a good one, and his heart was undoubtedly in the right place on September 5, 1781'. That day, however, he had anything but a clear head.[16] In a comment on Hood's inaction, he quotes the observation of the American Admiral Robison: 'Had Hood been a man of less influence, he – like Palliser and Lestock – would have been court-martialed for not doing his <u>utmost</u> to engage the enemy. In fact, he did nothing'.[17]

Colin Pengelly, in his study of Hood and the Battle of the Chesapeake, might easily have been tempted to come down on the side of his principal subject, but his assessment was entirely fair-minded. Graves had, he thought, done his best, with a 'less than perfect' signal book, and handicapped by lack of familiarity with most of his captains. Hood, on the other hand, had shown a total lack of initiative that was inexplicable in so talented a commander. Pengelly also draws attention to Drake's leading of the van, which was the best performance by any of the British admirals that day.[18]

Two centuries after the battle a brisk engagement was fought between two historians writing in the pages of the *Mariner's Mirror*. In 1980 Kenneth Breen challenged what he saw as the generally accepted view of where the blame for the battle's outcome should lie. He too was struck by the terms of Graves's letter to Sandwich, which he also considered to be unusually magnanimous, while on the other hand taking the view that the account given by Hood, 'was written by a man all too conscious of the ineffective role he had played'.[19]

After outlining the allegations made against Graves, and which largely derived from the pen of Hood, he conducted a comprehensive review of the opinions of prominent naval historians. These, he considered showed just how effective Hood had been 'in imprinting his version of the Chesapeake on the work of succeeding historians'. Many of Hood's criticisms have been dealt with already above, but another of them concerned the decision to refit the *Robust* and *Prudent*, with the

---

15   Mackesy, *War for America*, pp.423-424.

16   Larrabee, *Decision at the Chesapeake*, p.234.

17   Rear Admiral S.S. and Mary Robison, *A History of Naval Tactics from 1530 to 1930* (Annapolis Maryland: Naval Institute Press, 1942), p.140.

18   Pengelly, *Sir Samuel Hood and the Battle of the Chesapeake*, p.186.

19   Kenneth Breen, 'Graves and Hood at the Chesapeake', *The Mariner's Mirror* (February 1980) p.84.

244   CRISIS AT THE CHESAPEAKE

result that they were not available to sail with the fleet. Breen points out that if they had not sailed with Graves in his abortive pursuit of the elusive French convoy, but had remained in port to commence their refit earlier, it was nonetheless improbable that they would have been ready in any case. The inferiority of the British fleet might have been alleviated, however, if Rodney had not sent the *Prince William* and *Torbay* to Jamaica, and if he had not chosen to take the *Gibraltar* to carry him home. Hood and Rodney knew that 30 pilots for the Chesapeake and Delaware had arrived at Cap Français, a clear indication that de Grasse was planning to take his whole fleet north, but they continued to act on the assumption that he would leave part in the Caribbean.

Breen disposed of the suggestion by Gerald Graham that Graves 'hoisted signals which completely confused Hood and his frustrated captains,' pointing out that the whole of the van and the *Montagu* in the centre had come with Hood from the West Indies, but managed to comply with the signals without difficulty.[20] Breen also addressed the allegation that instead of forming line of battle, Graves could and should have launched his fleet in an attack while the French were still emerging from the bay. As to this, he noted that Graves and the captains from the West Indies had not had time to get to know each other, or to undertake practice manoeuvres; to throw caution to the winds, and attack, would certainly not have been reasonable. Furthermore, at that time Graves did not know whether Barras had yet joined de Grasse; he might have been running into a fleet of 36 ships. In any case, at 10:00 a.m. on 5 September the British fleet was still some 18 miles from the mouth of the Chesapeake, the time at which it would probably have been necessary for the order to have been given. Breen's conclusion was that Graves 'should not bear all the blame,' and that he 'had been caught in the pincers of other people's incompetence'.[21]

Breen's article is persuasive; but it did not persuade J.A. Sulivan, who delivered a spirited response in the *Mariner's Mirror* three years later.[22] Remarking that it took longer to refute Breen's wholesale allegations than it did to make them, he based his case on Hood's expert knowledge and vigour which, he argued, were well attested and subsequently proved beyond doubt; he cited, for instance, his frequent but unavailing efforts to persuade Rodney to take different decisions, which if his advice had been accepted would have produced vastly different results. This is much the same argument put forward by Mahan, but Hood's later career is hardly relevant to what he actually did, or did not do, at the Chesapeake. Once Hood had gone north, and was under Graves's command, neither of them was in a position to draw firm conclusions from the confusing intelligence available. While

20 G.S. Graham, *The Royal Navy in the War of American Independence* (Greenwich: National Maritime Museum, 1976), p.18; Breen, 'Graves and Hood at the Chesapeake', p.58.
21 Breen, 'Graves and Hood at the Chesapeake', p.64.
22 J.A. Sulivan, 'Graves and Hood', *The Mariner's Mirror* (May 1983), pp.175-194.

Sulivan does not reproach Graves for sailing to look for the French convoy, he does not commend him either, considering that there was intelligence pointing to de Grasse coming north in July or August.

Sulivan observed, correctly, that the Battle of the Chesapeake was fought with eighteenth century tactics, and that the sacred principle of the line of battle had a firm hold on the minds of admirals and their captains. As to Breen's comments on the extent to which Graves's signals were or were not confusing, Sulivan contended that apart from the fact that the log of Drake's flagship and of his repeating frigate differed from the *London*'s log, 'Drake was in the van of the fleet which was in single line ahead converging with an enemy also in single line ahead, and his leading ships almost close enough to engage before the signals from Graves caused confusion'.[23] He quoted with approval the question raised by Barnes and Owen as to whether copies of the North American signals were supplied to the West Indies ships or discussed between the admirals. In particular he picked up the point that although Graves claimed that at 3:46 p.m. he hoisted the signal 'for each ship to steer for and engage his opponent,' thereafter he referred only to the signal for battle and for close action as if they were the same thing. In his view so much depends on whether the signal for the line flew virtually throughout the battle, as Hood and others maintained, and Sulivan found that the logs of the vital ships in the signalling system all go against Graves.[24]

Sulivan insisted that Hood's comment on the memorandum issued by Graves on the day after the battle, that it was 'the first time he had heard that too strict adherence could be paid to the line of battle,' must be read in the context of his belief that a compact line was essential. He then went on to question whether, starting a mile or so behind the centre division, Hood in fact could have obtained the glorious victory expected of him. As for Breen's charge that Hood attacked Graves in order to distract attention from his own inaction, Sulivan conceded that it cannot be proved or disproved. He did, though, point out that Hood was very often censorious about the performance of his superiors, and his correspondence on this occasion was entirely consistent with his general attitude.

The debate between Breen and Sulivan illustrates the breadth of the controversy arising from the battle. There will always remain many facts in dispute, and it is possible, without seeming to be unduly selective, to come down on one side or the other. Graves can certainly be criticised for an unimaginative approach to the tactics to be employed; on the other hand, shorn of his criticisms of Graves, Hood's defence is not compelling.

The ultimate responsibility for the navy's failure in North America lies at the door of the British Cabinet. It ensured, by putting home defence first, that, at the critical moment, the British fleet on the other side of the Atlantic was facing odds

23   Sulivan, 'Graves and Hood', p.185.
24   Sulivan, 'Graves and Hood', p.187.

which inevitably meant that it was almost powerless in the face of de Grasse's superior force. The Battle of Chesapeake Bay was, like most sea battles of its time, an unsatisfactory and indecisive affair; but only an improbably decisive victory could have postponed the loss of America.

Kempenfelt explained the correct strategy as he saw it in a paper which he wrote at the start of 1782. It was a policy that was altogether too bold for the British Cabinet (though it would have appealed to the King):

> If your fleet is so divided as to be in all places inferior to the enemy, they will then in all places have the probability of succeeding in their attempts. If a squadron of sufficient force cannot be found to face the enemy at home, it would be more eligible to let the numbers of that squadron be yet less, that thereby you may be enabled to gain a superiority elsewhere … It may be (or might have been) in our power to send such a force of ships to the West Indies as would frustrate their designs there, but at home I imagine, with our utmost exertions, we must remain inferior by sea, and trust our defence from a descent to our land forces.[25]

This was a view strongly shared by Middleton, who entirely adopted Kempenfelt's prescription that the Western Squadron should be composed solely of two decked ships able to serve as a fast-moving flying squadron operating in the Channel, while the more powerful but slower sailing three-deckers were sent to the West Indies. He had previously recommended that not only should all the available three-deckers go there, but also that the total force there 'must positively exceed that of the enemy by at least four or five sail of the line including 50-gun ships'. He went on to denounce the policy that hitherto had been followed in respect of the Western Squadron:

> The practice that has been pursued for these two summers past of supporting this squadron at the expense of every other important one is so contrary to good policy, that I hope it has not escaped the eyes of his Majesty's ministers. The idea of collecting a force to contend with the enemy in this quarter must be destructive in its consequence if any longer adhered to, and, after every effort, prove insufficient in the end.[26]

David Syrett, as previously noted, takes a diametrically opposite point of view; the Channel Fleet was, he argued, too weak to check French and Spanish naval power in the eastern Atlantic (which is certainly true) because of the government's

25   Barnes and Owen (eds), *Private Papers of John, Earl of Sandwich*, Vol.IV, pp.80-82.
26   Laughton (ed.), *Letters and Papers of Charles Lord Barham*, Vol.II, pp.37-41.

strategy of attempting to maintain naval superiority in North America.[27] Yet this is to ignore the reality so clearly expressed by Kempenfelt. If Britain was to retain the imperial possessions under threat from the enemy, risks must be run, and the greater risk was leaving the fleet in the West Indies in North America too weak successfully to maintain the British command of the sea there, if the French and Spanish challenged it.

Once France and then Spain had entered the war, there was always going to be a shortage of ships of the line for the Admiralty to deploy, which compelled the Cabinet constantly to prioritise its decisions. On 1 September 1781 the Admiralty calculated that out of a total of 87 ships of the line in commission there were 33 in England and 20 in the Leeward Islands.

Nine months later, when there were 96 in commission, there were 34 in England and no less than 42 in the Leeward Islands. The decisions taken in 1781 meant that Graves would fight with an inferior force; if the distribution of ships of the line called for by Middleton and Kempenfelt a few months later had been applied, Graves might have had a marginal superiority and might have won the battle.

It is, though, an open question whether the British government was right in putting home defence first. Paul M. Kennedy is firmly of the view that it was: 'However useful America may have been as an overseas possession, it was clearly in the British Isles and its people that the centre of the Empire's wealth, strength and naval power lay'.[28] The defence of the British Isles must, he contended, be the government's priority.

Richard Middleton, in an article published in the *Mariner's Mirror* of 2014, examined the reasons for the imbalance in numbers between the British and French fleets in North America in the autumn of 1781. He noted the various decisions, by Rodney in particular, which reduced the number of ships of the line with which Hood sailed north. His conclusion is that none of the respective actions of Rodney, Hood, Graves and Parker were primarily responsible for the inferiority on 5 September: 'In reality, more ships alone could have rectified the situation. For this deficiency Lord Sandwich and the ministry in London must primarily answer'.[29] He went on to deal with the shortage of ships of the line and the reasons for this. The traditional view that Sandwich had neglected the fleet before and after the start of the American Revolution is, he argued, unjustified. Having, with the considerable force of Sir Charles Middleton's persuasion behind him, obtained substantial increases in the budget for new construction and repairs, Sandwich could point to the fact that by the time he left office there were 36 ships of the line under construction compared with the peak of 17 in the Seven Years War.

27   Syrett, 'Home Waters or America?', pp.365-377.
28   Paul M. Kennedy, *The Rise and Fall of British Naval Mastery* (London: Macmillan, 1983), p.116.
29   Richard Middleton, 'Naval Resources and the British Defeat at Yorktown, 1781,' *The Mariner's Mirror* (February 1980), p.40.

The later careers of the principal commanders at the Chesapeake were very different. De Grasse went on to face the ignominy of capture aboard his flagship at the battle of Les Saintes, and was subsequently treated as a scapegoat by the French establishment. Hood subsequently enjoyed a glittering career as one of the Royal Navy's most successful commanders, before, in 1794, being obliged to haul down his flag as commander-in-chief in the Mediterranean after a characteristic but injudicious dispute with the Admiralty. Graves, whose professional reputation in the Navy survived the criticism he faced for the Battle of the Chesapeake, served as Howe's second-in-command at the battle of the Glorious First of June, where he was severely wounded, after which he retired with an Irish peerage.

As to the responsibility for the outcome of the Battle of the Chesapeake, there is of course no fresh evidence. There is, though, a great deal of fresh argument. Picking a way through this, it would seem that the proper conclusion is that Graves has been unjustly treated by historians. Faced with an extremely difficult battle to fight, he was naturally and justifiably cautious. If a bolder course might just have won a victory, it is more likely that it would have resulted in a severe defeat. Hood, on the other hand, has got away with less discredit than he deserved, and there is no doubt that his failure to support Graves crucially impaired what chance the British fleet had of achieving anything on 5 September. As it was the battle paved the way for the war's decisive moment, when Cornwallis surrendered at Yorktown. This was a disaster for which neither Graves, nor Hood, nor any other single individual was solely to blame; but it led inexorably to Britain's final defeat in the war for America.

Appendix

The Fleets at the Battle of the Chesapeake, 5 September 1781

British Fleet (Rear Admiral Thomas Graves)

Van (Hood)	Centre (Graves)	Rear (Drake)	Ships not in line
Alfred, 74	*America*, 64	*Terrible*, 74	*Adamant*, 50
Belliqueux, 64	*Resolution*, 74	*Ajax*, 74	*Fortunée*, 38
Invincible, 74	*Bedford*, 74	*Princessa*, 70 (flag)	*Santa Monica*, 36
Barfleur, 98 (flag)	*London*, 98 (flag)	*Alcide*, 74	*Nymphe*, 36
Monarch, 74	*Royal Oak*, 74	*Intrepid*, 64	*Richmond*, 32
Centaur, 74	*Montagu*, 74	*Shrewsbury*, 74	*Solebay*, 28
	Europe, 64		*Sibyl*, 28
			Salamander, Fireship

British order of sailing given as during approach to battle; after the line had worn around, *Shrewsbury* became the lead ship and *Alfred* was at the tail end of the line.

French Fleet (*Lieutenant Général* Comte de Grasse)

Van (Bougainville)	Centre (de Grasse)	Rear (de Monteil)	Ships not in line
Pluton, 74	*César*, 74	*Citoyen*, 74	*Andromaque*, 32
Marseillaise, 74	*Destin*, 74	*Scipion*, 74	*Railleuse*, 32
Bourgogne, 74	*Ville de Paris*, 104 (flag)	*Magnanime*, 74	*Surveillante*, 32
Réfléchi, 64	*Victoire*, 74	*Hercule*, 74	*Concorde*, 32
Auguste, 80 (flag)	*Sceptre*, 80	*Languedoc*, 80 (flag)	*Gentille*, 32
Diadéme, 74	*Northumberland*, 74	*Zélé*, 74	*Aigrette*, 32
Saint Esprit, 80	*Palmier*, 74	*Hector*, 74	*Diligente*, 26
Caton, 64	*Solitaire*, 64	*Souverain*, 74	

French order of sailing given for the line once properly formed for battle.

Bibliography

Alden, J.R., *The American Revolution* (New York: Harper & Row, 1954).

Allen, Gardner W, *A Naval History of the American Revolution* (New York: Houghton Mifflin, 1913).

Andreopoulos, George J. and Selesky, Harold F., *The Aftermath of Defeat* (New Haven: Yale University Press, 1994).

Barnes, G.R. and Owen, J.H. (eds), *The Private Papers of John, Earl of Sandwich* (London: Navy Records Society, 1936).

Beatson, Robert, *Naval and Military Memoirs of Great Britain from 1727 to 1783* (London: J Strachan, 1804).

Billias, George A. (ed.), *George Washington's Generals and Opponents* (New York: William Morrow & Co, 1969).

Black, J.R. & Woodfine, P. (eds). *The British Navy and the Use of Naval Power in the Eighteenth Century* (Leicester: Leicester University Press, 1988).

Bonner-Smith, D. (ed.), *The Barrington Papers* (London: Navy Records Society, 1941).

Breen, Kenneth, 'Graves and Hood at the Chesapeake', *The Mariner's Mirror* (February 1980), pp.53-65.

Buel, R., *In Irons: British Naval Supremacy and the American Revolutionary Economy* (London: Yale University Press, 1998).

Cavaliero R., *Admiral Satan: The Life and Campaigns of Suffren* (London: I.B. Tauris, 1994).

Chadwick, Rear Admiral French Ensor (ed.), *The Graves Papers* (New York: Naval History Society, 1916).

Chernow, R., *Washington: A Life* (London: Penguin Press, 2010).

Chevalier, E., *Histoire de la Marine Francaise* (Paris: Hachette et Cie, 1902).

Christie, Ian R., *The End of North's Ministry 1780-1782* (London: Macmillan, 1958).

Clowes, W. Laird, *The Royal Navy: A History* (London: Sampson Low Marston & Co, 1898).

Cock, Randolph, '"Avarice and Rapacity" and "Treasonable Correspondence" in "an Emporium for All the World": The British Capture of St Eustatius, 1781', *The Mariner's Mirror* (August 2018), pp.265-278.

Corbett, Julian S. (ed.), *Signals and Instructions 1776-1794* (London: Navy Records Society, 1908).

Corbett, Julian S. (ed.), *Fighting Instructions 1530-1860* (London: Navy Records Society, 1905).

Cornwallis-West, G., *The Life and Letters of Admiral Cornwallis* (London: Holden, 1927).

Corwin, Edward S., *French Policy and the American Alliance* (Princeton New Jersey: Princeton University Press, 1916).

Crawford, Michael J., 'New Light on the Battle of the Virginia Capes: Graves vs Hood', *Mariner's Mirror* (August 2017), pp.337-340.

Creswell, John, *British Admirals of the Eighteenth Century* (London: Allen & Unwin, 1972).

Donne, W. Bodham (ed.), *The Correspondence of King George the Third with Lord North from 1768 to 1783* (London: J. Murray, 1867).

Dull, Jonathan, *The French Navy and American Independence* (Princeton New Jersey: Princeton University Press, 1975).

Dull, Jonathan, *The French Navy and the Seven Years War* (London: University of Nebraska Press, 2005).

Ferreiro, Larrie de, 'The Race to the Chesapeake between des Touches and Arbuthnot', *Mariner's Mirror* (November 2018), pp.477-481.

Flexner, J.T., *Washington: The Indispensable Man* (London: Little Brown, 1976).

Fowler, William M., Jr, *American Crisis* (New York: Walker & Co, 2011).

Furneaux, R., *Saratoga: The Decisive Battle* (London: Allen & Unwin, 1971).

Gardiner, Leslie, *The British Admiralty* (London: Blackwood, 1968).

Graham, J.S., *The Royal Navy in the War of American Independence* (Greenwich: National Maritime Museum, 1976).

Grainger, J.D., *The Battle of Yorktown, 1781: A Reassessment* (Woodbridge: Boydell Press, 2005).

Gruber, I.D., *The Howe Brothers and the American Revolution* (New York: Atheneum, 1972).

Hamilton, C.I., *The Making of the Modern Admiralty* (Cambridge: Cambridge University Press, 2011).

Hamilton, Sir R. Vesey and Laughton, Sir J., *Recollections of James Anthony Gardner* (London: Navy Records Society, 1906).

Hamilton, Sir R. Vesey (ed.), *Letters and Papers of Sir T. Byam Martin* (London: Navy Records Society 1903).

Hannay, David (ed.), *Letters Written by Sir Samuel Hood* (London: Navy Records Society, 1895).

Hodges, H.W. (ed.), *Select Naval Documents* (Cambridge: Cambridge University Press, 1922).

Holmes, M.R.J., *Augustus Hervey* (Bishop Auckland: The Pentland Press, 1996).

Hood, Dorothy, *The Admirals Hood* (London: Hutchinson, c.1940).

James, Rear Admiral W.M., *The British Navy in Adversity* (London: Longmans Green, 1938).

Jamieson, Alan G., 'Two Scottish Marines in the American War', *The Mariner's Mirror* (February 1984), pp.21-30.

Jenkins, E.H., *A History of the French Navy* (London: Macdonald & Janes, 1973).

Kennedy, Paul M., *The Rise and Fall of British Naval Mastery* (London: Macmillan, 1983).

Knight, R.J.B. (ed.), *Portsmouth Dockyard Papers, 1774-1783: The American War* (Portsmouth: City of Portsmouth, 1987).

Knox, Dudley W., *The Naval Genius of George Washington* (Boston: Houghton Mifflin, 1932).

Larrabee, Harold, *Decision at the Chesapeake* (London: Kimber, 1965).

Laughton, Sir John (ed.), *Journal of Rear Admiral Bartholomew James* (London: Navy Records Society, 1896).

Laughton, Sir John (ed.), *Letters and Papers of Charles Lord Barham* (London: Navy Records Society, 1908).

Laughton, Sir John, *From Howard to Nelson* (London: Lawrence & Bullen, 1899).

Lavery, B. (ed.), *Shipboard Life and Organisation, 1731-1815* (Aldershot: Navy Records Society, 1998).

Lewis, Charles Lee, *Admiral de Grasse and American Independence* (Annapolis Maryland: Naval Institute Press, 1945).

Mackesy, Piers, *The War for America* (London: Longmans Green, 1964).

Mahan, Captain A.T., *Major Operations of the Navies in the American War of Independence* (London: Sampson Low Marston & Co, 1913).

Marcus, G.J., *A Naval History of England: The Formative Centuries* (Boston: Little Brown & Co, 1961).

Martelli, George, *Jemmy Twitcher* (London: Jonathan Cape, 1962).

McIntyre, Captain D., *Admiral Rodney* (London: Peter Davies, 1962).

Middlekauff, R., *Glorious Cause: The American Revolution, 1763-1789* (New York: Oxford University Press USA, 2005).

Middleton, Richard, 'Naval Resources and the British Defeat at Yorktown 1781', *The Mariner's Mirror* (February 2014), pp.29-43.

Miller, N., *Sea of Glory: A Naval History of the American Revolution* (Charleston: David Mackay, 1974).

Naval Historical Centre, *Naval Documents of the American Revolution* (Washington DC: Department of the Navy, 1964).

O'Shaughnessy, Andrew, *The Men who Lost America* (London: Oneworld Publications. 2013).

Padfield, Peter, *Maritime Supremacy and the Opening of the Western Mind* (London: John Murray, 1999).

Parkinson, C. Northcote, *Edward Pellew, Viscount Exmouth* (London: Methuen, 1934).

Patterson, A. Temple, *The Other Armada* (Manchester: Manchester University Press, 1960).

Peckham, Howard H., *The War for Independence: A Military History* (Chicago: University of Chicago Press, 1958).

Pengelly, Colin, *Sir Samuel Hood and the Battle of the Chesapeake* (Gainesville Florida: University Press of Florida, 2009).

Perrin, W.G. (ed.), *Naval Miscellany* (London: Navy Records Society, 1928).

Philbrick, Nathaniel, *In the Hurricane's Eye* (New York: Random House, 2018).

Randall, W S, *Benedict Arnold: Patriot and Traitor* (New York: Morrow, 1990).

Richmond, Admiral Sir Herbert, *Statesmen and Sea Power* (Oxford: Clarendon Press, 1946).

Richmond, Admiral Sir Herbert, *The Navy in India 1763-1783* (London: Ernest Benn, 1930).

Robison, Rear Admiral S.S. and Mary, *A History of Naval Tactics from 1530-1930* (Annapolis Maryland: Naval Institute Press, 1942).

Rodger, N.A.M., *The Command of the Ocean* (London: Allen Lane, 2004).

Rodger, N.A.M., *The Insatiable Earl* (New York: W.W. Norton & Co, 1993).

Rodger, N.A.M., *The Wooden World: An Anatomy of the Georgian Navy* (London: Collins, 1986).

Sands, John O., *Yorktown's Captive Fleet* (Newport News: University of Virginia Press, 1983).

Shea, J.G. (ed.), *The Operations of the French Fleet under the Count de Grasse in 1781-1782* (New York: Da Capo Press, 1864).

Sherrard, O.A., *A Life of Lord St Vincent* (London: Allen & Unwin, 1933).

Spinney, David, *Rodney* (London: Allen & Unwin 1969).

Stout, Neil R., *The Royal Navy in America, 1760-1775. A Study of Enforcement of British Colonial Policy in the Era of the American Revolution* (Annapolis, Maryland: Naval institute Press, 1973).

Sulivan, J.A., 'Graves and Hood', *The Mariner's Mirror* (May 1983), pp.175-194.

Syrett, David, *Admiral Lord Howe* (Stroud: Spellmount, 2006).

Syrett, David, 'D'Estaing's Decision to Steer for Antigua 28 November 1778', *The Mariner's Mirror* (May 1975), pp.155-162.

Syrett, David, 'The Organisation of British Trade Convoys During the American War, 1775-1783', *The Mariner's Mirror* (February 1976), pp.169-181.

Syrett, David (ed.), *The Rodney Papers* (Aldershot: Navy Records Society, 2007).

Syrett, David, *The Royal Navy in American Waters 1775-1783* (Aldershot: Scolar Press, 1989).

Syrett, David, *The Royal Navy in European Waters during the American Revolutionary War* (Columbia South Carolina: University of South Carolina, 1998).

Talbott, John E., *The Pen and Ink Sailor* (London: Frank Cass, 1998).

Tilley, John A, *The British Navy and the American Revolution* (Columbia South Carolina: University of South Carolina Press, 1987).

Toll, I.W., *Six Frigates* (London: W.W. Norton & Co. 2006).

Tracy, N., *Navies, Deterrence and American Independence* (Vancouver: University of British Columbia Press, 1988).

Trevelyan, George O., *George the Third and Charles Fox: The Concluding Part of the American Revolution* (London: Longmans Green, 1914).

Trew, Peter, *Rodney and the Breaking of the Line* (Barnsley: Pen & Sword, 2006).

Tunstall, Brian (ed. Nicholas Tracy), *Naval Warfare in the Age of Sail* (London: Conway Maritime Press, 1990).

Valentine, Alan, *Lord George Germain* (Oxford: Clarendon Press, 1962).

White, Captain Thomas, *Naval Researches; or, a candid inquiry into the conduct of Admirals Byron, Graves, Hood, and Rodney* (London: Whittaker Treacher & Arnold, 1830).

Wickwire, Franklin and Mary, *Cornwallis and the War of Independence* (London: Faber & Faber, 1971).

Willis, S., *The Struggle for Sea Power* (London: Atlantic Books, 2015).

Wilson, Ben, *Empire of the Deep* (London: Weidenfeld & Nicolson, 2013).

General Index

Index of Ships

From Reason to Revolution – Warfare 1721-1815

http://www.helion.co.uk/series/from-reason-to-revolution-1721-1815.php

The 'From Reason to Revolution' series covers the period of military history 1721–1815, an era in which fortress-based strategy and linear battles gave way to the nation-in-arms and the beginnings of total war.

This era saw the evolution and growth of light troops of all arms, and of increasingly flexible command systems to cope with the growing armies fielded by nations able to mobilise far greater proportions of their manpower than ever before. Many of these developments were fired by the great political upheavals of the era, with revolutions in America and France bringing about social change which in turn fed back into the military sphere as whole nations readied themselves for war. Only in the closing years of the period, as the reactionary powers began to regain the upper hand, did a military synthesis of the best of the old and the new become possible.

The series will examine the military and naval history of the period in a greater degree of detail than has hitherto been attempted, and has a very wide brief, with the intention of covering all aspects from the battles, campaigns, logistics, and tactics, to the personalities, armies, uniforms, and equipment.

Submissions

The publishers would be pleased to receive submissions for this series. Please contact series editor Andrew Bamford via email (andrewbamford@helion.co.uk), or in writing to Helion & Company Limited, Unit 8 Amherst Business Centre, Budbrooke Road, Warwick, CV34 5WE

Titles

No 1 *Lobositz to Leuthen: Horace St Paul and the Campaigns of the Austrian Army in the Seven Years War 1756-57* (Neil Cogswell)

No 2 *Glories to Useless Heroism: The Seven Years War in North America from the French journals of Comte Maurés de Malartic, 1755-1760* (William Raffle (ed.))

No 3 *Reminiscences 1808-1815 Under Wellington: The Peninsular and Waterloo Memoirs of William Hay* (Andrew Bamford (ed.))

No 4 *Far Distant Ships: The Royal Navy and the Blockade of Brest 1793-1815* (Quintin Barry)

No 5 *Godoy's Army: Spanish Regiments and Uniforms from the Estado Militar of 1800* (Charles Esdaile and Alan Perry)

No 6 *On Gladsmuir Shall the Battle Be! The Battle of Prestonpans 1745* (Arran Johnston)

No 7 *The French Army of the Orient 1798-1801: Napoleon's Beloved 'Egyptians'* (Yves Martin)

No 8 *The Autobiography, or Narrative of a Soldier: The Peninsular War Memoirs of William Brown of the 45th Foot* (Steve Brown (ed.))

No 9 *Recollections from the Ranks: Three Russian Soldiers' Autobiographies from the Napoleonic Wars* (Darrin Boland)

No 10 *By Fire and Bayonet: Grey's West Indies Campaign of 1794* (Steve Brown)

No 11 *Olmütz to Torgau: Horace St Paul and the Campaigns of the Austrian Army in the Seven Years War 1758-60* (Neil Cogswell)

No 12 *Murat's Army: The Army of the Kingdom of Naples 1806-1815* (Digby Smith)

No 13 *The Veteran or 40 Years' Service in the British Army: The Scurrilous Recollections of Paymaster John Harley 47th Foot – 1798-1838* (Gareth Glover (ed.))